AF529484

Education for WOMEN

Education for WOMEN

by

Neclam Yadav

Reference Press

4831/24,Ansari Road
Darya Ganj
New Delhi - 110 002
Phone: 23260807
Fax: 23274173
E-mail: essess@del3.vsnl.net.in

© Publisher

First Published 2003

ISBN: 81-88583-18-9

Price Rs.800/-

All rights reserved. No part of this publication may be reproduced, stored in a retrieval system or trransmitted in any form or by any means, electronic, mechanical, photocopying, recording or otherwise without the prior written permission of the copyright holder

Published by
Reference Press
4831/24,Ansari Road
Darya Ganj
New Delhi - 110 002
Phone: 23260807
Fax: 23274173
E-mail: essess@del3.vsnl.net.in

Printed in India by:
Print Line, Delhi

Contents

PART — THREE : PERSPECTIVE

PART — FOUR : PROSPECTS

PART — FIVE : PROTECTIVE COVER

PART — SIX : ISLAMIC VIEWPOINT

Preface

Education is key to success. The same is true for women, but unfortunately, they are a neglected lot in our social fabric. But, it cannot be denied that they have a defined and definite role to play in society, in general and family, in particular. Over the years, the researchers have been engaged in studying and analysing matters, related to the better half of the human beings. Hence, many a book on the issues, concerning women and their problems including education. Still, no one can deny, there is a dearth of comprehensive and exhaustive books on the subject. That was the feeling, which made this author begin a painstaking research, spread over several years, eventually to result in a humble work, which is here.

Perhaps, it wouldn't be fair to say that no body thinks of the plight of illiterate women. Movements for the women education are about two hundred year old now, and there has been an awakening, regarding their problems and the injustice caused to them, for ten decades, in our country. All governments, the colonial one earlier and our own elected one, after independence, have devoted enough attention to women's education, resulting into numerous reforming steps and framing of policies. However, the practical output has not been satisfactory, at all. Hence, a genuine concern about the group of the unlettered, women among the academics and educationists.

Certainly, it would be an honour for the undersigned, if this endeavour makes a breakthrough, by causing the people ponder over the issues, related to women education and feel concerned really, about their problems.

— Author

PART — ONE

General

ONE

Introduction

Regarding education, in India, nineteenth century may be noted for the most abominable conditions for women as well as the initiation of their emancipation. At the beginning of the century, the women were humiliated and tortured, kept illiterate, tradition bound and in complete subjugation to the men's will. As time passed, people began to rebel against this state of affairs.

The impact of western culture created a desire among many Indians to examine their beliefs and ideals. The scientific approach of the west initiated a search of Indian scriptures and mythologies for the causes of maladies that existed in society. A critical outlook among educated Indians aided the reinterpretation of religious texts and rational approaches replaced emotional reaction. These approaches led to the conclusion that blind faith, inability to discern right from wrong, and propagation of erroneous interpretations by decadent priestly class and immoral feudal lords had all been responsible for the existing web of subordination around women.

Reformers began their work in the direction of women's emancipation in the late nineteenth century, This work was continued in the twentieth century. In spite of great zeal and enthusiasm, the reformers achieved little success in breaking the strong notions of women's inferior status. However, the process of awakening to reality was initiated and India passed to an era in which myth around women began to be seriously questioned in terms of realities of human existence. Women started regaining their freedom of will and intellect. Still with the majority of women a major problem remained. They had for long believed that they were emotionally, morally, biologically and intellectually inferior to men and so were unable to contemplate their equal status with men. They failed to realise their full potential and high abilities. To alter this situation it was required that not only women, but the whole society should undergo a transition in its outlook towards them.

Let us now examine the movement for the emancipation of women, which was initiated in the nineteenth century.

It was largely through the efforts of Raja Ram Mohun Roy (1774-1833) that in 1829 Lord Bentinck decreed for the abolition of the sati system. He worked towards widow remarriages, inter-caste and inter-racial marriages, abolition of child marriages and polygamy. He founded a new religious order called the Brahmo Samaj. This reformed order became well known for the privileges it gave to women.

Keshab Chandra Sen (1838-1884) became Roy's spiritual successor and worked tirelessly for women's education. The Civil Marriage Act III of 1872 raised the minimum age for marriage to fourteen, gave permission for widow remarriage and inter-caste marriage and penalised polygamy. This reform was applicable only to members of the Brahmo Samaj and was brought about by Sen's courage and perseverance.

Many other prominent Indians were motivated by the example set by Keshab Chandra Sen. They led a vigorous struggle against child marriage and advocated widow remarriages. Ganga Ram at Lahore, along with others, started campaigns for women's emancipation. Mahadev Govinda Ranade (1842-1901) led a movement in Poona. He was a great patriot and social reformer who worked against existing Hindu customs, which made the life of the Indian women one of sorrow and hardship. It is notable that his reforms started with his own wife whom he taught himself.

In the north, Swami Dayanand Saraswati (1827-1883) founded a religious order named Arya Samaj. The basic tenet of this order advocated equality of opportunity for all irrespective of caste, colour, or sex. In a very active manner, this society worked for women's education. Dayanand broadened the scope of women's education by emphasising education for self rather than linking it to their efficiency in familial roles. The curriculum for education devised by Dayanand was similar for both boys and girls. Hence Dayanand emerged as the first reformer who advocated and evolved a comprehensive scheme of education for raising women's status not only at the level of family and society but for her own development as an individual.

Another prominent person of the nineteenth century, Ishwar Chandra Vidyasagar (1820-1891) helped the British Government to establish the first girl's school in Calcutta in 1849. He was further responsible for the establishment of forty girls' schools in Bengal between 1855-1858. The Government Act of 1856, which legalised widow remarriage for Hindu women, was passed largely because of his efforts.

A brilliant national leader Gopala Krishna Gokhale (1866-1915) worked relentlessly towards raising the status of women in Indian society. He founded "Servants of India Society" in 1905 and established as its main objective the education of women. Two religious leaders who helped in bringing about the renaissance in the Hindu religion were Rama Krishna Paramahansa (1833-1866) and Swami Vivekananda (1862-1902).

Pandita Ramabai (1858-1922) was the most prominent of women of the nineteenth century who fought the battle for her own and her sisters' emancipation. Her book *The High Class Hindu Woman* was published in 1888 and highlighted the burdensome life of the caste Hindu women. She made a fervent appeal to the American (men and women) to render help for the enlightenment of Indian women and society. The last words of her book state:

> "In the name of humanity, in the name of your sacred responsibilities as workers in the cause of humanity, summon you, true women and men of America, to bestow your help quickly, regardless of nation, caste or creed."

American admirers sent Ramabai Rs.6000 to aid a widows' home, Sharda Sadan (home of learning), which she opened.

Another woman closely associated with education for women was Ramabai Ranade (1865-1922) who was the wife of Justice Ranade. She established an educational institution called Seva Sadan. Anandibai Joshi (1865-1887) was the first Hindu woman to take a Degree of Doctor of Medicine in America. Because she died very young, she could not provide a much-needed influence on education in medicine for Indian women. However, her life and work inspired women of late nineteenth and early twentieth centuries. Francina Sorabji (1833-1907) with her daughters, particularly her fifth daughter Cornelia planned and organised the establishment of schools for girls in the Western region of India. Cornelia was awarded a Law Degree from England.

Mohan Das Karamchand Gandhi, a great politician and advocate of the righteous path, raised his voice against injustices to women of India in the 1920's. He took up many causes, including widow remarriage, and drew many women into his fight for freedom. His writings, speeches and private advocacy of the women's cause were attended to with great respect. In an article in a publication called *Young India* on November 18, 1926 he made it clear that if a man could remarry after the death of his spouse, a woman should also have this right: "What is considered desirable for man should be equally so for woman, and therefore, a widow should have the discretion as widowers about remarriage". In the same article he made the following comments:

> "I look to every youth in India to resolve not to marry a girl under sixteen. Let us tear down Purdah with one mighty effort. All that I have said about the wife applies equally to the husband. She is a co-sharer with him of equal-rights and of equal duties."

Gandhi's approach towards women was idealistic. Though he was aware of their woes, he didn't think they had the same failings as men. He believed that their potential goodness incapacitated by years of bondage would, once freed, alleviate all the ills of society. He wrote that woman is sacrifice personified. His ideal of love was feminine as he identified that the greatest asset of a female was the ability to give motherly love. He saw the family as the nucleus of all Social Life and believed that women best functioned at home rather than in the work force. He saw the ideal of women with strong characters tending their families with peace and harmony and leading the world in this direction. He addressed a meeting of mill workers in 1920 at Ahmedabad:

> "It is not for women to work in factories. They have plenty of work in their own homes. They should attend to the bringing up of their children. If women go to work, our social life will be ruined and moral standards will decline".

Although Gandhi's efforts favoured the traditional role for women, he believed they deserved equal recognition for a job well done, just as men received. Gandhi's struggle for women's rights was that of dignity and humanity, rather than one of role differentiations. Certainly, in the tradition bound society into which his ideas were received they were quite revolutionary. His zeal led people to a realisation of injustices to women and prepared men to be more realistic in their attitudes towards women.

However, Gandhi still maintained the goddess image on a pedestal while exploding the myths about the witch like nature of women. He believed in the basic goodness of human nature and propagated the ideal of complete man and complete woman, both able to offer unconditional love while working for a common goal.

Gandhi's influence helped women assert their will. It was due to his leadership that women were given rights equal to men in India's Constitution. The history of the women's participation in the freedom struggle in response to Gandhi's call is one of the most fascinating stories of the rise of the Indian female, The Indian women of the late nineteenth century and early twentieth century who had led a life of drudgery behind purdah finally emerged free of the web that had held them captive for centuries.

Great reformers like Gandhi drew attention to the goodness inherent in women and made an appeal for an understanding of their human need. Men became aware of the love and affection which women were capable of bestowing. Many women realised that they were not inferior beings and were proud of the key role they played in the survival of human race. An important Muslim reformer of the early twentieth century, Sir Sayyid Ahmad Khan, began a movement for the education of Muslims under the western influence. However, he excluded women from his scheme and firmly opposed their education. In contrast Molvi Nazir Ahmad and Hali were in favour of education of women. Perhaps, because of the influence of his mother on his early life Sir Sayyid saw no need for women's education other than home learning. He opposed starting schools for girls but emphasised the education of Muslim boys at Aligarh. On the other hand, Hali had his women characters reflect on the backward condition of Muslim community, the stagnation of vernacular learning, and the need for girls to be educated in order to fulfil their household and family duties. He did not go to extremes; however, the reforms he advocated were justified in terms of women's traditional role. In a magnificent poem called *Homage to Silence* Hali versified the role of women and their right to education.

Among the foreign women who came to India to serve the cause of women's emancipation, the names of Margaret Noble, later known as Sister Nivedita, Annie Besant and Margaret Cousins stand out. These women of Irish origin and former participants in Irish Home Rule agitation took up the cause of the downtrodden and underprivileged in India.

In 1917 the question of women's franchise was mooted. A deputation of women headed by Sarojini Naidu as spokesperson presented a memorandum to the British Secretary of State in 1919. The deputation demanded women's suffrage as well as increased educational and health facilities. The decision about the franchise was left to the Indian legislatures. With little opposition from these legislatures, thanks to the influence of the reformers, by 1929 women were enfranchised equally with men.

Although women were granted political rights equal to men, much reformative work was still needed to be done, as purdah and child marriages continued to be the dominant traditions. The laws of inheritance and divorce to assert their will legally restricted women. Illiteracy was predominant and so also the dowry customs. Women's organisations raised these issues for review. Enlightened Congress leaders like Nehru, Patel and Rajendra Prasad gave their full support for removing social and legal inequalities, which had been put upon women. Some of the women leaders who deserve acknowledgement for their efforts in achieving higher status for women in Indian society are chronologically: Annie Besant, Sarojini Naidu, Muthulakshmi Reddi and Raj Kumari Amrit Kaur.

Some interesting events occurred in 1929 when Gandhiji started Satyagraha, a freedom movement into which many women entered whole-heartedly. Mahatma's Dandi march which was in defiance to the salt law, had the full support of women. Within the next three years of this march, over five thousand women served terms of severe imprisonment suffered from lathi blows, cruelty, loss of livelihood and ill health. They picketed wine shops and shops that sold foreign clothes. They faced trials in law courts, suffered atrocities in prisons and were defamed for denouncing purdah and other evil social customs by the orthodox community leaders. Society came to realise, to some extent, the capacities of women as wilful responsible persons. Men and women began developing mutual respect. The prominent women of this period were neither an enigma nor a myth but were real people fighting for their independence. Sarojini Naidu, Kamla Nehru, Rukmani

Lakhshmipathi, Hansa Mehta, Nellie Sen Gupta, Satyavati Devi, Miraben (Ms Slade), Durgabai and Kuttimala Amma all contributed richly to the destruction of the many strands of the web, which had dictated that women were either goddesses or witches. The above mentioned women were compassionate people who worked very hard for the good of all and for the betterment of their country.

In the general elections of February 1939, nearly five million women voters participated enthusiastically in electioneering. The majority of their votes were cast for Congress. It became clear that women could responsibly vote and the doubts of the orthodox men that the enfranchisement of women would bring their country to doom were quickly dispelled. The women who contested on the Congress ticket were extraordinarily successful. In ,one constituency, a woman elementary school teacher defeated the Vice-Chancellor of the University of her Province. In another, the wife of a doctor overthrew the President of a District Board who had represented the constituency in Parliament for twelve years. In thirty-nine years, India underwent such sweeping changes that by 1939, the political, educational and social position for women had risen so high that eight women were members of provincial and state legislatures. India ranked third among the nations of the world in regards to the political influence and position secured by its women. The United States and Russia were first and second respectively.

Viney Kirpal in her introduction to the edited book, *The Girl Child in 20th Century Indian Literature* writes about the depiction of the girl child in the literature of pre-independence period that "as in ancient literature, girl children are not presented as girl children. Their chronological age might place them as children but they appear in those works as 'miniature women-child brides, child wives, child widows'. The girls may be young in age but the responsibilities they are depicted to be taking up are those of grown up women." She further reports that "the period of adolescence and the transition to womanhood is like a blank page in these texts"

After Independence in 1947 most of the evils in Indian society were vigorously brought to the focus of attention of the nation. The principle of equality among the sexes was effectively put into law. Those ideas were constitutionally accepted by the Indian people who had been prevalent in the advanced nations for a long time. When the Constitution of India was framed in November 1949. Its Preamble stated that equality among the sexes was a fundamental right. Many other laws were enacted, intense efforts were made to remove the long-standing legal disabilities around women. It is worth noting that equal voting rights for women were given the very day the Indian Constitution was adopted.

Presently, the government offers incentives to women to enable them to obtain an education that will remove sex discriminations. No woman can now be refused employment because of sex. At present quite a number of women hold jobs in top administrative and managerial services. Almost all the services are open to women who are involved in serious competition with men for the topmost positions in foreign services, police and engineering. They have also found employment in areas such as nuclear engineering, flying and paratroops.

The Hindu Marriage Act of 1955 gave women the legal right to divorce. The daughter who was completely excluded from the inheritance of property among Hindus after the Vedic period now has this right which was granted by The Hindu Succession Act of 1956. In 1961 the Dowry Prohibition Act was passed. The Government began the family planning incentive programme as a social welfare measure to release women from unlimited child bearing responsibilities.

In spite of these measures to ensure equality, most women of India are sill tradition bound. Cormack, Rama Mehta, Promilla Kapur, Goldstein and others who have studied the thinking and the outlook of modern Indian women through questionnaire and Interview techniques found that the women, even the highly educated ones, are still completely rooted in their families. The unmarried still depend on their fathers for advice and guidance as well as for the choice of their husbands. The married depend on their husbands for advice about their careers, life-styles and future life plans. These women have identities, which have meaning only in terms of men in their lives. Independence as is found in Western women is lacking in most of Indian women who are willing to sacrifice their independence and identity for the family and for their men who get precedence over their own selves. Since society as a whole accepts this orientation, those who challenge this notion have a difficult time. Divorce is still a hated word in most of the Indian families. Nearly ninety per cent of all marriages among the middle classes are the arranged marriages. The choice of marriage partners depends on the parents.

The education of women is now considered as an essential feature of our national life. The point worth consideration is that: "should education strive to change this situation or strengthen these practices?" Many scholars are of the opinion that the stability of the Indian society is due to the prevalent practices while the exponents of the Women's Liberation Movement are very much against the undermining of women's position in any respect. They want them to be assertive and the determiners of their own destiny. And for that the only right part is the path of education.

TWO

In Proper Perspective

In India, education is the most important instrument for human resource development. Education of women, therefore occupies top Priority amongst various measures taken to improve the status of women in India. In recent years, the focus of planning has shifted from equipping women for their traditional roles of house-wives and mothers to recognizing their worth as producers, making a major contribution to family and national income. Efforts have been made over the past three decades of planned development to enrol more girls in schools and encourage them to stay in schools, to contribute their education as long as possible, and to provide non-formal educational opportunities for women. The fulfilment of the Constitutional directives in respect of providing free and compulsory education up to the age of 14 years has been included as one of the components of the 'Minimum Needs Programme' and given overriding priority.

Education in India is constrained by the socio-economic conditions of the people, their attitudes, values and culture. During the pre-British era, education was linked to the socio-religious, institutions, reinforcing the patriarchal social structure. During the British period, education became a tool of colonial power, enabling a small minority to have access to education, and all the benefits it entailed. The social reformers of the nineteenth century raised the demand for women's transformation but to make them more capable of fulfilling their traditional roles. Since Independence, the policy makers have argued for universal education and for making education as a tool for bringing about social equality.

In spite of concerted efforts to improve the enrolment of girls and provide adult education for women, their educational status is still far from satisfactory. Female enrolment in educational institutions is low as compared with males and drop-out rates are higher. There are also regional and inter-group disparities.

The factors which do not permit the closing of the existing gap between the education of men and women are many. While undertaking a review of the educational system at the time of formulation of the National Policy on Education 1986, if was noted that the system is caught in a state of ambivalence, aiming at creating an equal society, while at the same time not disturbing the class, caste and gender relationships. Issues in women's education are, therefore, not issues only of educational sector, but they extend to issues of environment, employment production processes. Indeed, the entire gamut of social and, economic policy has a bearing on women's education. The need for educating girls is not considered worthwhile. In urban areas, by and large, there is a greater acceptance of its need than in rural areas. Some other factors responsible for low enrolment are:

(i) The requirement for older girls to stay at home to take care of siblings when mothers are away at work;

(ii) Need for girls to work in order to help in augmenting the family income;

(iii) Early marriage of girls;

(iv) Social customs that hinder female mobility after puberty;

(v) Lack of relevance of school curriculum; and

(vi) Lack of facilities in the form of school buildings, hostels and women teachers, etc.

The Strategy

Women's education has assumed special significance in the context of the country's planned development.' This is because women constitute nearly half the nation's population representing a valuable human resource and play an important role in the development of the community and the national economy. Education enables women to acquire basic skills and abilities, and fosters a value system which is conducive to raising their status in society. Recognizing this fact, great emphasis has been laid on women's education in the five-year plans. The First Five-Year Plan advocated the need for adopting special measures for solving the problems of women's education. It held that women "must have the same opportunities as men for taking all kinds of work and this presupposes that they get equal facilities so that their entry into the professions and public services is in no way prejudiced". It further added that "at the secondary and even at the university stage it should have a vocational or occupational basis, as far as possible, so that those who complete such stages may be in a position, if necessary, to immediately take up some vocation or other". Accordingly the educational facilities for girls continued to expand in the subsequent plans. The major schemes undertaken encompassed elementary education, secondary education, university education, postgraduate education and research, technical education, scholarships, social/adult education and physical education. The Second Plan continued the emphasis on overall, expansion of educational facilities. The Report of the National C committee on Women's Education (1959) made a strong impact on the Third Five-Year Plan. It launched important schemes like condensed school courses for adult women, Bal Sevika training and child care programmes. Subsequent plans supported these measures and also continued incentives such as free text-books and scholarships for girls. This trend continued in the Fourth and Fifth Five-Year Plans.

Although there was a large-scale expansion of facilities for education up to the Fourth Plan, vast disparities existed in the relative utilization of available facilities by boys and girls at various stages of education. Hence, the major thrust in the Fifth Plan was to offer equality of opportunities as part of the overall plan of ensuring social justice and improving the quality of education imparted. To promote enrolment and retention in schools in backward areas and among underprivileged sections of the population, in addition to the incentives like free distribution of textbooks, mid-day meals, etc., girls were to be given uniform and attendance scholarships. In spite of these schemes, it was noticed that insufficient numbers of women teachers resulted in low enrolment of girls. To remove this bottleneck, scholarships were given to local girls to complete their education and training leading to a teaching career. Besides, condensed and correspondence courses were organized for the less educated women. Emphasis as also laid on the need for orientation of the curriculum to meet the special needs of girls.

A landmark in the Sixth Plan was the inclusion of women's education as one of the major programmes under Women and Development which was an outcome of the publication of the report of the Committee on the Status of Women in India. The programmes for universalization of elementary education were specially directed towards higher enrolment and retention of girls in schools. It was envisaged to promote Balwadi-cum-creches attached to the schools to enable girls responsible for sibling care at home to attend schools. Women teachers, where necessary, were to be appointed in rural areas to encourage girls education. Science teaching in girl schools and colleges had to be strengthened to achieve greater participation of women in science and technology. Streamlining the admission policies to promote greater enrolment of women in engineering, electronics, agriculture, veterinary fishery and forestry courses was stressed. For boosting the education of women belonging to backward classes, the number of girls' hostels were to be increased. Instead of adding more separate women's polytechnics, which were developed as multipurpose institutions for imparting training in arts, crafts, etc. coeducational institutions were encouraged as far as possible. The adult education programme too received a fillip.

The Seventh Plan envisages restructuring of the educational programmes and modification of school curricula to eliminate gender bias. Enrolment of girls in elementary, secondary and higher education courses, formal as well as non-formal, has been accorded high priority. At the elementary stage, education has been made free for girls. Sustained efforts are to be made through various schemes and measures to reach 100 per cent coverage in elementary education. Financial assistance schemes to voluntary agencies to run early childhood education (pre-school centres) as adjuncts of primary/middle schools are to be expanded, particularly to help evolve innovative models suited to specific learner groups or areas. Efforts are to be made to enrol and retain girls in schools, especially in rural areas, and also to enrol children belonging to Scheduled Castes, Scheduled Tribes and other weaker sections. Teacher training programmes are to receive continued priority with a view to increase the availability of trained women teachers, and thereby to enhance girls' enrolment and retention in schools. Incentives by way of distribution of uniforms, free textbooks and attendance scholarships to needy girls are to be continued. Non-formal elementary education is to be expanded to benefit girls in the age group of 6-14 years. Talented girls are to be encouraged to pursue higher education. It is also proposed to expand the 'Open Learning System', including correspondence courses for them. In order to promote technical and vocational education for girls, more women's polytechnics are to be set up and programmes for vocationalization of education are to be expanded.

To expedite education among the girls of the Scheduled Castes and Scheduled Tribes, additional facilities will continue to be provided under the "Development of Backward Classes" sector. Girls above the matriculation stage will get higher scholarships/stipends than male students. Financial assistance is envisaged for construction of hostel buildings for girls at the district level and for purchase of equipment, furniture utensils, books and periodicals in these hostels.

Under the National Sports Policy, participation of women and girls in sports and games is to be encouraged. Stress is to be laid on the identification of sports talent among women, and provision made for sports scholarships, coaching and nourishment support for promising girls with a view to improve the standards of their performance in competitive games. Besides, the schemes for encouraging traditional folk, tribal and hill arts and cultural activities are to be expanded and strengthened.

Situational Analysis

Notwithstanding the planned objectives and endeavours, actual progress in upgrading the educational status of women has been slow. The literacy level among women has risen from 7.9 per cent in 1951 to 24.3 per cent in 1981 (excluding Assam). Among males, the corresponding rise was from 24.9 to 46.3 per cent. Thus the gap in percentage literacy points between male and female literacy increased from 17 in 1951 to 22 in 1981. In absolute terms too, the number of illiterate women has increased during the period, from 158.7 million to 241.7 million (excluding Assam). Women comprised 57 per cent of the illiterate population in 1981, and girls formed 70 per cent of non-enrolled children in the school age group.

There are disturbing regional variations in the levels of literacy in the country. The literacy rate for women varies from 65.7 per cent in Kerala, as per 1981 census, to 11.4 per cent for Rajasthan. The gap between male and female literacy, rates in percentage points is only 9.5 in Kerala, but 24.9 in Rajasthan. States like Madhya Pradesh, Uttar Pradesh and Bihar are also lagging behind in girls education. Certain ecological constraints like difficult terrain, variety of dialects as in Arunachal Pradesh, migratory habits due to unfavourable weather as in parts of Jammu & Kashmir, etc. have also been instrumental in perpetuating low levels of literacy in such areas for the population as a whole and particularly for women.

Elementary Education

High Priority has been accorded to elementary education in

the National Development Plans to fulfil the requirements under Article 45 of the Constitution for universal, free and compulsory elementary education for children upto the age of 14 years.

By the end of the Sixth Plan, it was apparent that in order to achieve universal elementary education, an additional enrolment of 255.3 lakh is required of which the girls constitute 140.7 lakh, i.e., a little more than 55 per cent. Besides, there is a sharp fall in the number enrolled at the middle level, viz., from nearly 332 lakh to 91 lakh indicating a large dropout rate, wastage and stagnation. The enrolment ratio falls from 76.7 to 36.3. The retention of girls in schools from classes I to VIH, therefore is a task requiring urgent attention.

Among Scheduled Tribes particularly, the enrolment of girls is far below that of boys. At the primary stage, the enrolment of Scheduled Tribes boys is almost double the enrolment of girls, and the difference increases at higher stage. Girls belonging to Scheduled Castes communities are also lagging behind boys. The ratio of Scheduled Castes boys to girls in the elementary classes is 2:1. In the VI to VIII classes, 61.9 per cent of girls in the general Population are enrolled, whereas among Scheduled Castes this proportion is only '20.9' per cent; The reasons for Scheduled Castes and Scheduled tribes girls lagging behind boys. The ratio of Scheduled Castes boys to girls in the elementary classes is 2:1. In the VI to VIII classes, 61.9 per cent of girls in the general population are enrolled, whereas among Scheduled Castes this proportion is only 29.9 per cent. The reasons for Scheduled and Scheduled tribes girls lagging behind the boys are mainly rooted in socio-economic conditions and environmental constraints such as inaccessibility of schools in tribal areas. Irrelevance of formal education curriculum to the immediate environment is also responsible for low initial enrolment and subsequent drop-out rates. Among the urban and rural poor, the compulsion on girls to assist in household chores including care of younger siblings, and on children of both sexes to work for their own survival and contribute economically to the household income, forces them to remain outside the education system.

According to the Fourth Educational Survey (1978), in the plains 95 per cent of the rural population have access to a primary school within one kilometer of their habitation (having a population of 360 persons or more). Middle schools are available to 78.8 per cent of rural people within three kilometres from their habitation. But commuting to distant schools does pose a problem for girls. There are very few separate schools for girls. The parents, particularly in rural areas, are reluctant to send their daughters to co-educational schools. Moreover, in most schools, the teachers are male. Despite considerable emphasis in the plans, the proportion of women teachers continues to be low Provision for accommodation for women workers including teachers is far from satisfactory.

A large number of primary and middle schools, in rural areas especially, lack facilities such as a proper building, adequate number of teaching rooms, drinking water and toilets for girls. More than 85 per cent primary and 70 per cent middle schools in rural areas do not have these facilities, according to the Fourth All India Educational Survey (1978). Hostel facilities for girls continue to be meagre.

Secondary Education

There is a progressive rise in the rate of enrolment in secondary education of girls during the various Plan periods as seen below:

The enrolment ratio of girls in the age group 15-18 years for secondary classes is 14.3 per cent as against 29.3 per cent for boys. Secondary education continues to be more or less confined to urban areas, and is affordable and accessible largely to the higher castes and the upper and middle economic strata. Although a large number of secondary schools have come up in rural areas, their enrolment particularly, in respect of girls is low. The main constraints in improving secondary and higher level education among girls have been a lack of availability of trained lady teachers, dearth of separate institutions for girls and lack of hostel facilities.

The 10+2+3 system of education has been introduced with the aim of establishing a uniform pattern of education all over the country in terms of its structure, curriculum and mobility across the States. This system has laid a common foundation for higher education without differentiation between boys and girls. Both girls and boys under the new system Will learn the rudiments of science and mathematics, social sciences and humanities up to matriculation and thus gain a holistic base education which will equip them to play an active and meaningful role in the employment market.

Higher Education

In the higher educational courses, girls constitute 24 to 50 per cent of the students enrolled depending upon the type of courses. The most popular course with girls has been teachers training where they already constitute nearly fifty per cent of those enrolled. The number of girls in science courses had risen to 41 per 100 boys in 1984-85. In engineering and technology courses, however, the enrolment of girls is only 6 for 100 boys. This Proportion has to be enhanced through suitable incentives in the form of scholarships and other facilities for girls studying for these courses.

Girls enrolled for higher education, particularly those in science and technical courses, are mainly from the higher economic strata. There is a need to introduce positive measure to improve the enrolment to girls in higher education courses in rural areas and, among backward groups like SCs and STs.

Non-formal Education

The concept of adult education has found support in several Plan Programmes. However, until the Sixth Plan, no special emphasis was given to women's education. In the Sixth Five-Year Plan, adult education was included as a part of the Minimum Needs Programme and the goal of reaching 100 per cent literacy by 1990 was set under the New Twenty-Point Programme. Adult education centres exclusively for women were set up, which provided education in subjects like health, nutrition and family planning. An effort was made to build up an awareness about these sub among women through discussions, talks and distribution of relevant literature.

Under the Adult Education Programme, apart from increasing adult literacy, the content of education was to be modified to incorporate new value systems regarding the role of women in the family, and community. The Seventh Plan also envisages, among other schemes, the preparation of district level plans with local community participation, both for activating, and implementing the literacy programme, and the creation of special mechanisms to monitor the progress of implementation at the State level. The Integrated Rural Development Programme (IRDP), National Rural Employment Programme (NREP), Training of Rural Youth in Self-employment (TRYSEM), and other such programmes, are also to have a component of functional literacy for women beneficiaries. The programme of Functional Literacy for Adult Women (a component of the ICDS programme) was unfortunately abandoned, though the concept of utilizing Anganwari workers, who belonged to the villages and were in contact with young mothers, could have been an effective mechanism for imparting non-formal education. The scheme has since been revised to focus on issues of immediate relevance to women but has yet to be introduced.

The scheme of 'condensed courses of education and vocational training' for adult women was started in 1958 under the aegis of the Central Social Welfare Board, and was suitably expanded over the years to vocational training in areas with high employment potential. Measures are to be taken to enhance the competence of the teaching staff / training institutions involved in this programme.

The various programmes, however, have not yet been able to make any significant impact on literacy levels of the Indian population, particularly on women. According to a World Bank Report in 2000 A.D., there will be 500 million illiterates in India, constituting 54 per cent of the world's population of illiterates. As per the Seventh Plan, the total number of adult illiterates is about 900 lakhs of whom 580 lakh are women. Although it is encouraging to note that the proportion of women in the adult education centres has gone above 50 per cent (52.34 per cent in 1984-85), women still constitute about 5.7 per cent of the illiterate population. Among these, literacy levels of SC mad ST women are still worse. Even those treated as literates, have very low levels of literacy, scant opportunities for continuing education and use of literacy skills. Therefore they often relapse into illiteracy.

National Policy on education-Initiatives for Women

The National Policy on Education (NPE)-1986 is a landmark in the approach to women's education. It has attempted for the first time to address itself to the basic issues of women's equality. In the section titled "Education for Women's Equality", the policy states:

> Education will be used as an agent of basic change in the status of women. In order to neutralize the accumulated distortions of the past, there will be a well-conceived edge in favour of women. The National Education System will play a positive, interventionist role in the empowerment of women. It will foster the development of new values through redesigned curricula, textbooks, training and orientation of teachers, decision makers and administrators.

It gives overriding priority to the removal of women's inhibiting their access to and retention in elementary education. Emphasis has been laid on women's participation in vocational, technical and professional education at different levels as also to promote women's participation in non-traditional occupations and existing and emergent technologies.

The Programme of Action for Implementation of NPE (POA) spells out the meaning of women's empowerment:

> Women become empowered through collective reflection and decision making. The parameters of empowerment are:
>
> (a) Building a positive self-image and self-confidence.

(b) Developing ability to think critically.

(c) Building up group cohesion and fostering decision making and action.

(d) Ensuring equal participation in the process of bringing About social change.

(e) Encouraging group action in order to bring about change in the society.

(f) Providing the wherewithal for economic independence.

The programme entails the following:

(i) A phased time bound programme of elementary education for girls, particularly up to primary stage by 1990 and up to the elementary stage by 1995.

(ii) A phased time bound programme of adult education for women in the age group 15-35 by 1995.

(iii) Increased women's access to vocational, technical, professional education and existing and emergent technologies; and

(iv) Review and reorganization of educational activities to ensure that they make a substantial contribution towards women's equality, and creation of appropriate cells/units therefore.

A number of measures have been suggested to achieve the state's objectives of the National Policy on Education. The Action Plan enunciates that every educational institution should take up by 1995 active programmes for the development of women. All teachers and non-formal education/adult education instructors should be trained as agents of women's development. Special programmes should be developed by research institutions to promote general awareness and positive self-image amongst women through programmes like discussions, street plays, wall papers, puppet shows, etc. Preference in recruitment of teachers up to school level should be for women.

National Literacy Mission (NLM) which aims at eradication of illiteracy in 15-35 age group by 1995 concretizes what is envisaged in NPE as regards literacy and adult education. The Mission document emphasizes the importance of imbibing the values of national integration, conservation of environment, women's equality, observance of small family norm, etc., and goes on to say that "the focus of NLM would be on rural areas, particularly women and persons belonging to the Scheduled Castes and Scheduled Tribes."

For universalization of elementary and adult education, the present programme of non-formal centres for girls needs to be extended to all educationally backward pockets of the country. Increased assistance should be given to voluntary organizations to run non-formal education centres for girls. In rural areas, special support services should be provided to relieve the girls from sibling care and other household work like fetching water, fuel, etc. Skill development linked to employment opportunities in the villages is required to be given priority so that there is an incentive on the part of the parents to educate girls. It is necessary to develop adult education programmes for women linked with upgradation of their skills and income generating activities. Skill development for girls should be a continuous process of learning and should be supported by programmes administered by others such as Polytechnics, Industrial Training Institutes (ITIs), Women's Centres in Agricultural and Home Science Colleges, etc. Centres should be set up in a phased manner vocational training, provide opportunities for retention skills and application of this learning for improving their living conditions. Their are 104 ITIs functioning exclusively for women and 97 wings in general ITIs reserved for women would need to be revamped during 1988-90 in terms of diversification of trades and courses, keeping in view the job potential and facilities for vocational counselling, imparting information about credit, banking, entrepreneurial development and women's access to technical education, etc.

Women's studies programmes would also have four dimensions, viz., teaching, research, training and extension. Women's issues would be incorporated in courses under various disciplines. Research would be encouraged on identified areas/ subjects. Seminars/workshops would be organized on the need for women's studies, and for dissemination of information and interaction. Educational institutions would be encouraged to take up programmes like adult education, awareness building, legal literacy, information and training support for socio-economic programmes of women's development, instructional programmes through media, etc., which directly benefit the community and bring about the empowerment of women.

All the foregoing endeavours will be planned, coordinated, and evaluated continuously both at the national and state levels. The Women's Cell in the National Council for Educational Research and Training would be revived and strengthened. National, Institute of Educational Planning and Administration and Directorate of, Adult Education would have cells to plan and administer women's training programmes. The Women's cell in the University Grants Commission would, be strengthened to monitor the implementation of various programmes at the higher education level. It is proposed that women cells should be set up in all the States.

The Perspective

The programmes for women's education will have to be implemented as a priority so that women attain a comparable level of education by 2020 A D. The strategy to be adopted for raising literacy levels and education among women has to keep, in view the vast cultural, geographical and ecological variations as also the problems relating to poverty and ignorance. The cultural and geographical variations call for decentralization of educational planning. Within the national perspective planning, implementation and monitoring of educational programmes has to be done at district and block levels, keeping in view the socioeconomic and geographic parameters of the area. The vocational and occupational components have to be designed in accordance with the availability of resources and job opportunities in the regions. Voluntary organizations and women's groups active in the area should be involved in the task.

In view of the social and cultural handicaps that have operated against women's education and taking account of the multiple roles that women are required to play, the need for adopting set of objectives specific to women's education is imperative. The objectives to be achieved by 2000 A.D. in regard to women's education are:

(i) Elimination of illiteracy, universalization of elementary education and minimization of the dropout and stagnation rate in the age group 6-14 years, to negligible proportions.

(ii) Ensuring opportunities to all women for access to appropriate level, nature and quality of education and also the wherewithal for success comparable with men.

(iii) Substantial vocationalization and diversification of secondary education so as to provide a wide scope for employment and economic independence of women.

(iv) Making education an effective means for women's equality by (a) Addressing ourselves to the constraints that prevent from participating in the educational process; (b) Eliminating the existing sexist bias in the system; (c) Making necessary intervention in the content and scope of education to inculcate positive and egalitarian and (d) Ensuring that teachers perceive this as one essential role.

(v) Providing non-formal and part-time courses to women to them to acquire knowledge and skills for their social, cultural and economic advancement.

(vi) Impetus to enrol in various professional degree courses so as to increase their number in medicine, teaching, engineering fields substantially.

(vii) Creating a new system of accountability, particularly of the basic educational services, to the local community, inter alia, by active involvement of women.

In brief, it is reiterated that the goals and strategies spelt out in the National Policy on Education, POA and the National Literacy Mission will ensure a much larger access for women to education.

High priority has to be accorded to creating awareness, through the various communication media, of the need for women's education and their active participation in economic and political development of the nation.

The curricula for school as well as university education have to be reviewed and revised so as to remove sex bias, inculcate among the masses a recognition of equality between men and women, and make women aware of their own potentials as well as provide them necessary opportunities to develop their capabilities in every field. Greater accessibility of educational facilities to girls is to be achieved by reducing the distance of schools from village habitations, and expanding non-formal elementary education, adult education, and the open school system. Appointment of lady teachers in schools would help draw more girls to schools and instil confidence among their parents. Towards this end, provision of quarters for lady teachers would be essential. Efforts should be directed at training local women as teachers. Provision of creche facilities and Balwadis near the elementary and secondary schools for girls would enable the girls to attend schools and ensure care of younger siblings. Incentives like midday meals, better rates of scholarships, freeships, etc., would go a long way in preventing dropout.

Above all, better health facilities, smaller families, and relief from drudgery through improved technology for household chores, are essential prerequisites for better enrolment of girls at school and higher educational institutions. Inputs from other sectors are, therefore, important. Greater coordination of health, employment, welfare and education interventions will have an effect on the status of women and girls.

According to Educational Statistics for 1984-85 published by the Ministry of Human Resource Development, the enrolment of girls at primary level, which covers the age group 6-11 years, is 331.9 lakh. Surveys and field research have pointed out that there is 25 per cent inflation in the enrolment figures, and 22 per cent enrolment is outside the age group. Thus the effective enrolment gets reduced by about 47 per cent. Accordingly, the coverage for 1984-85 for the 6-11 years age group may be estimated as 176 lakh. The population projected for the age group is 422.7 lakh. This means that only 40.7 per cent of the girls in the age group 6-11 are enrolled in schools. On a similar basis, the enrolment of 11-14 years age group gets reduced to 48.1 lakh (from 90.7 lakh) which is only 19.2 per cent of the population of 249.9 lakh estimated for the age group. The population projections for the girls in the age group 6-11 years and 11-14 years for 1989-90 are 462 lakh and 2,67 lakh respectively. In order to have full coverage, the additional enrolment required would be 286 lakh for 6-11 age group and 219 lakh for 11-14 years age group, the total being nearly 5 crore. The task appears to be stupendous. Along with enrolment, there is the problem of very high dropout rates. Stemming from highly inflated enrolment rates and subsequent dropouts in the 6-11 years age group, enrolment of 11-14 years age group girls, even at primary level, may not be possible even by 1995.

In view of the social and cultural handicaps that have operated against women's education, the need for adopting a set of objectives specific to women's education is imperative. These would need to encompass the elimination of illiteracy and measures for retention of girls in schools, substantial vocationalization and diversification to enhance economic opportunities for women, improvement in the quality of education in terms of the values it promotes and inculcates, and finally the provision of access to professional courses for women. Such measures would be necessary as also efforts to remove the inherent prejudices working against women's education.

Recommendations

1. Awareness needs to be generated among the masses

regarding the necessity of educating girls so as to prepare them to effectively contribute to the socio-economic development of the country, to strengthen their role in society and to realize their own capacities. The media and various forms of communication have to be geared to this end.

2. A fruitful rapport has to be established between the community at large and the teachers and other education personnel. As per the Programme of Action under National Policy on Education-1986, every educational institution should actively participate in bringing about such awareness.

3. Involvement of local leaders, voluntary agencies and women's groups is also necessary. Mahila Mandals need to be revitalized and reoriented to provide an effective forum for the purpose. One measure to achieve this could be to assign the responsibility to Mahila Mandals for ensuring that all children in a community attend school. An incentive scheme should be introduced to motivate panchayats to ensure 100 per cent enrolment of girls in their villages.

4. Early childhood care and education introduces children into the school system gradually and smoothly. When children get used to attending schools, it ensures in some measure retention of children, including girls, at elementary stages also. Hence there is needed to have a comprehensive and effective programme of early childhood care and education linked to an integrated package of learning for women. The most comprehensive example of this is the Integrated Child Development Services Programme which needs to be universalized.

5. For improving enrolment and minimizing drop-outs and wastage in case of girl students, it would be helpful if learning is made more attractive by providing adequate teaching materials in schools.

6. The number of teachers should also be increased so that the interaction between the teacher and the taught, which is so essential for good education also increases. This would help in the retention of girls in schools and would be more effective if teachers from the area are employed. In single teacher schools, the teacher must be a woman. In Orissa all jobs of primary teachers have been reserved for women.

7. School curricula should be imaginatively developed to stimulate creativity 'largely through play rather than overburdening children' with formal or rote learning. Regional language should normally be the medium of instruction.

8. School timings should be flexible and fixed to suit local conditions and the needs of the working girls and must be available within the walking distance of the child. A substantial increase is required in the number of schools for girls.

9. In addition to incentives like free textbooks, free supply of uniforms, award of attendance scholarships and mid-day meals, facilities such as proper school building, safe drinking water, and toilet, etc., need to be provided to encourage school enrolment and retention of girls especially girls from educationally deprived social groups and from hilly, tribal, desert and remote areas and urban slums.

10. Local talent must be developed in order to meet the need for recruiting women teachers at the primary and elementary levels especially in rural and tribal areas. In this endeavour national agencies like CAPART and CSWB, voluntary agencies, Mahila Mandals and local self-government agencies can make a significant contribution. They can also play a useful watchdog function to ensure that educational and other programmes are run efficiently and effectively.

11. There should be a reservation of 50 per cent posts for women teachers in elementary schools. Women teachers working in the rural areas should be provided suitable accommodation.

12. Multi-entry system for girls who cannot attend schools continuously should be adopted.

13. Wherever necessary, schools meant exclusively for girls may be set up. The recommended distance of 3 kilometres for locating a middle school is a handicap for many girls. To ensure participation of girls in middle schools, it is necessary to provide hostel facilities.

14. The Savitribai Phule Foster Parent Scheme of Maharashtra could be adopted in other States/Union Territories to help poorer families to at least complete primary school. Under the scheme, well to do persons and organizations are persuaded to adopt one or more out of school girls and contribute in cash or kind or both @ Rs. 25 per month for her education. The money can be spent on uniforms, stationery or anything else, needed by the girls or also partly used to alleviate the economic distress of the parents. The Zila Parishad, Block Education Officer and headmasters play a pivotal role in implementing the scheme, which is purely voluntary and if district level officers are appointed for coordination of programmes for women, they could also actively take it up.

15. Condensed courses of education at elementary and middle school levels for girls must be started in all the rural areas and for weaker sections of the urban community.

16. Many girls in the 11-14 years age group would first have to be brought into the primary stage through non-formal education. By devising alternative education approaches non-formal schooling and through like intelligent use of technology, the pace of middle school education can be

accelerated. If retention up to 73 per cent is achieved up to class V, universal elementary education may be possible in some parts of the country by 2000 A.D. Other backward areas would have to be given much more attention in, professional as well as financial terms to enable them even to universalize primary education for girls by 1995. The National Literacy Mission will need to address these issues on a priority basis.

17. Special efforts are necessary for bringing tribal children particularly, girls into the school system. Tribal dialects, extreme poverty, problems of commuting, rigidity of formal education and its irrelevance to the tribal culture and the tribal's distrust of the ways of the mainstream society, must be borne in mind in formulating strategies.

18. The educational forecasts, may look more achievable if the system is opened up for flexible non-formal education which 'the below average states' should be persuaded to adopt in a large measure. The existing educational infrastructure particularly, in tribal and rural areas should be made effective and responsible.

19. Non-formal education is an alternative to the formal system which has the potentiality of becoming the major programme of education for girls who cannot attend school during normal school hours due to various reasons. The Central Government is already implementing a centrally sponsored scheme under which grants to the extent of 90 per cent are provided towards maintenance of non-formal education centres exclusively for girls in nine educationally backward states. This programme should be strengthened further and extended to other states where education of girls is lagging behind. It should at least cover all the pockets of low enrolments of girls and areas of high dropout rate. Besides literacy, it must also provide relevant information on skill development and inculcation of positive self-image among girls.

20. Secondary education for girls should entail:
    (i) A ten-year course in general education learning and diversified higher secondary education which may be either terminal or lead to further professional preparation; and (ii) Diversified courses after Grade VIII in technical subjects, viz., agricultural technology, health services, food production activities such as dairy and poultry and non-traditional areas need to be untroubled. A legal literacy component is also recommended at this stage.

21. Diversified courses leading to occupational preparation should be of parallel duration to the general secondary courses. In addition, there should be a variety of short and long term, whole time, part-time and apprentice courses. The trend of thinking is now to place emphasis on the last. Keeping in view the rapid modernization and advancement in technology for agriculture, there is an urgent need for skilled artisanship, for promoting productive activities on the one hand, and a variety of learning programmes for adjustment of the rural society to socio-economic change on the other. Efforts should be made to ensure that girls have every opportunity to enter into apprenticeship in areas that are non-conventional, and incentives be provided for the same. Further, at least 30 per cent seats should be reserved for girls in apprenticeship training courses on a non-transferable basis.

22. General and vocational training courses should be combined so that prospects of a career immediately on completion of schooling may attract girls from weaker sections. While designing the vocational courses, available occupational opportunities as well as the need to overcome market stereotypes should be kept in view.

23. Since secondary education has remained almost beyond the reach of weaker sections, liberal incentives and other facilities to release the girls from household chores appear to be essential. It would also help to locate the institutions in the areas of their habitation.

24. Multiple entry system should be introduced in the secondary classes. Part-time education facilities should also be made available.

25. Condensed courses should be organized in cooperation with local vocational training institutions to cover all rural areas and areas inhabited by weaker sections in urban areas. Such courses may be organized for small groups of girls, and combined with job training. Efforts should be made to cover atleast 215 lakh women in the age group 15-30 years under the condensed courses programme wherever possible the condensed courses of the CSWB should be expanded and strengthened. New programmes that are to be initiated must avoid duplication in the areas where the CSWB's programmes exist.

26. Correspondence courses and self-study programmes can be especially useful for girls desirous of continuing education but are unable to do so because of circumstances. Apart from imparting elementary education and knowledge about farming techniques, the curriculum for non-student girls should include courses of training in occupational skills. Similar programmes should also be designed for girls in the urban areas.

27. The open school system should be expanded extending the facility to all the girls in rural and backward areas.

28. Science education for girls has been neglected so far. Secondary schools for girls must be helped to build good science programmes over the Eighth Five-Year Plan. Special scholarships for girls opting for science courses need to be instituted at the secondary and higher education levels.

29. Special scholarship may also be offered to rural women, who opt for teachers' training, especially those who complete the condensed courses at the secondary stage.

30. There is a need to open more colleges and polytechnics for girls, especially in rural areas.

31. Incentives like scholarships, freeships, etc., should be provided to enable girls from rural areas to pursue higher education for girls belonging to weaker sections. In addition to freeships and scholarships hostels should also be provided to meet their requirements for food and lodging.

32. Girls should be encouraged to enter professional courses. Reservation of seats for girls in such courses may be considered to level out the existing bias in access to certain professional streams.

33. Vocational counselling and guidance service be organized exclusively in a more meaningful way to help girls in colleges and universities opt for suitable courses relevant to their talents and interests, and free of traditional bias.

34. Vocational and technical education for women, both formal and non-formal, should be a major feature of the programmes of rural universities. The women's wings of the universities could undertake large-scale extension programmes in order to activate girls and women in the surrounding areas to take advantage of educational and occupational facilities of various types, particularly those leading to meaningful employment, essential for reducing women's marginalization.

35. In order to increase the representation of rural girls in higher education courses, 30 per cent seats, may be reserved for girls to begin with.

36. All agencies, involved with preparation of curricula prescription of textbooks and organization of educational processes will have to evince awareness towards women's issues. University/College Departments of Women's Studies, appropriate voluntary agencies, women's groups,

etc., should be involved in giving a new perspective to the various issues of content and processes of education. Women's universities and women's centres in colleges need to take an active role in women's development and in influencing the attitudes of Future generations.

37. Facilities for part-time self-study and correspondence courses should be provided on a large-scale to enable girls who are not in a position to join higher educational institutions on a regular basis, to continue their studies.

38. In addition to courses leading to degree/diploma, short courses in specific subjects through summer school sessions, and ad hoc programmes like seminars, workshops, etc., should be organized for working women with a view to upgrading their knowledge and skills, not necessarily leading to degrees.

39. Integrated learning programmes for women are recommended which will not only lay emphasis on literacy but on empowering women through awareness building on social issues, bringing about attitudinal change, promoting skill training for employment, providing information on healthcare, nutrition and hygiene as well as on legal rights. Such programmes are beginning and must continue to be designed and structured so as to be relevant for the vast majority of rural women. The revised scheme linked to ICDS known as the 'Women's Integrated Learning for Life', should be introduced as an integral part of the non-formal education system.

40. Entrepreneurship development programmes should be organized separately for education of women in the age group 18-30 years, with a minimum of matriculation level of education. The objective of such training should be to:

(i) Make them aware of the various opportunities for self-employment; (ii)Motivate them to take up self-employment; (iii) Impart needed skills and training; (iv)Promote motivation for achievement among them; and (v)Create access to resources such as capital, credit, etc.

41. A large number of girls cannot participate in whole day education programmes. Provision of non-formal and part-time programmes, with flexible school hours and sensitivity to the agricultural cycle are, of particular importance. In addition to the primary and upper primary stages, distance learning opportunities need to be provided at secondary and higher secondary levels.

42. Adult education will have to be composed of three interrelated stands aimed at:

(i) Continuous flow of new information especially to rural and tribal areas, particularly to inculcate positive attitudes towards women;

(ii) Continuous training of the people in the use of modern tools and methods of production; and

(iii) Acquisition of permanent reading and computation skills.

Following from the above, three types of programmes may be offered to the learner:

(a) Information and literacy.

(b) Information and training in new technology and literacy.

(c) Information and training in new technology with or without literacy. Continuous information flows relating to human affairs, gender relations and the use of science and technology for betterment of life would be the common factor in all the three programmes.

43. The growing availability of communication media should be directed towards keeping up information flows and

portraying positive images of women in non-conventional roles. Audio-visual materials, combined with non-formal training arrangements, could impart to various population groups the kind of instruction they need in the use of new technologies. Involvement of mass media in motivating women to attend literacy classes is most essential.

44. Rapid strides in the development of technologies and tools for the reduction in women's drudgery and easy access to work places, water and fuel supply, child care, health services and population control can contribute significantly to the success of learning programmes for women. Women's literacy programmes would succeed better if they centre around women's concerns and also provide opportunities of recreation and sharing of experiences.

45. District plans should be prepared keeping in view literacy requirements of the learners and identifying agencies which can take up such programmes in districts.

46. All women working in industries or employed elsewhere should be made literate by the employers by allotting time from the working hours for their education. Place of teaching, teachers and teaching material should be arranged by them. Necessary legislation to this effect may be enacted.

47. At least 50 per cent seats in pre-service courses in all teachers training institutions should be reserved for women. Spatial planning to ensure that women from rural areas are selected as teachers is essential.

48. Provision of composite teacher training courses for women who have had insufficient education to improve their educational qualifications along with their training, should be made.

49. The existing Integrated Rural Development Programme, National Rural Employment Programme, Development of

Women and Children in Rural Areas, Training of Youth in Self-Employment Programme, Integrated Child Development Programme, etc., should have a component of literacy for their women beneficiaries. Training should be provided to the functionaries of various development departments by Directorate of Education in the States.

50. The State Resources Centres should produce suitable learning material for women on a priority basis. Literature for neoliterates should be suitably devised by experts, keeping in view the needs of different groups of learners.

51. Decentralization is the key to the successful application of the strategies outlined above in this decentralized approach, the village cluster or the block level is seen as most appropriate for the delivery of programmes. It is, therefore, necessary that the block is allocated a flexible budget so as to make funds available to village clusters/ villages for innovative educational activities and for equalization of educational opportunity.

52. An overall coordination of health, welfare and educational inputs would be most desirable. This would entail (a) Convergent policies in these sectors; (b) Coordination of delivery mechanisms; and (c) Pooling of allocations.

THREE

Education Denied

In this land, as centuries rolled on, Aryan culture was firmly entrenched. Indian women were trapped more and more in the web of myth and lost their sense of self and will. The goddesses were robbed of their glory even though they were still seated on a high pedestal. Men's obsession was to pull them down to earth by having the women sing their praises and do their will. Only when the women pleased them and satisfied their ego-needs, did they call them the goddesses of the household (Girhya Lakshmi). The moment women defied male idiosyncrasies, they were called devils. Men took upon themselves the responsibilities of protecting and feeding the women who were consequently destitute and completely dependent. The women were not allowed to move outside the household without male company since it was taken for granted that they were incapable of defending themselves. Women became frail and weak creatures and believed that if any man other than their husbands touched them or cast a lustful glance towards them they were defiled and dishonoured. Hence, their only path to an honourable existence was to give the men unflinching loyalty, submit to their care and deny their own self and will.

Perhaps in no other culture does such a duality exist where women have been mythically placed upon a high pinnacle while at the same time pulled down to dust in reality. In no other civilisation the women's status in the social milieu has been raised so high and simultaneously, so brutally lowered as in the Indian culture. In other cultures women are usually labelled as either saint or sinner, while in India she is both. Years of being enmeshed in the many strands of this web have deeply affected the position of the Indian women.

Ancient Period

Women of the early Aryan civilisation were highly respected. This society, however, as patriarchal, therefore, the birth of a girl was generally an unwelcome event. As early as in 2000 BC charms and rituals ensured the birth of a son in preference to that of a daughter. These charms are reported in the ancient Atharva Veda. Even though a son was desired and preferred, the birth of a daughter was a source of great pleasure to the family. Alteker points out that some scholars of this period were of the opinion that a gifted and well-mannered daughter might be a source of pleasure to the family. No restrictions were placed on girls in performing religious rites. The marriage of a daughter was not a difficult problem since she was free to choose her husband.

The marriage of girls used to take place at the age of 16 or 17 years. The women were not restricted and were allowed freedom of movement within the society, even in the company of their lovers. The wife occupied the honoured place in the family as the mistress of her household. Marriages were mostly monogamous. Widow remarriage was usually permitted within the family. Parents desired their daughters to marry the husbands of their choice. During the early Vedic period, the prayer of an anxious father used to be "May Saviter lead and bring to thee the husband whom thy heart desires". Pinkham notes: It is important for us to note that a wife was on a level of equality at the hearth which was the altar of sacrifice.

Around 1500 BC, the education of the daughters confined to the family. Religious and secular training was given only to girls from rich and cultured families. Men performed functions in the religious sacrificial rites, which had previously been the wife's domain. Girls were married at about the age of sixteen years, and divorce and widow remarriage were, still permitted.

Gradually circumstances changed. As ancestor worship gained popularity, sons alone were permitted to perform religious rites. Women became "valued only as the vehicles for bearing sons, and when they were unfit or unwilling to perform this function, they were considered useless". The value of the sons increased further, and they began to be regarded as investments for the future. Without a son, no man or woman could hope to go to heaven. The position of the daughter was greatly undermined. Still the women were not debarred from the study of the Vedas and there existed very few taboos regarding the rearing of girls.

During the Epic period in India, the birth of daughter became an exceedingly negative event because of the prevalence of marriage customs, which subordinated the position of women. Still, a daughter was regarded as a prized possession, and family took a keen interest in her rearing. In Mahabbarata, Draupadi is described as the common property of the five brothers. She was put at stake in a gambling bout. Sita, the ideal woman character of Ramayana, was put to fire ordeal to prove her chastity. She was denounced by Lord Rama to prove himself as an deal king. Draupadi did not accept her subordinate position and fought in an open assembly when Duryodhana the winner of the bout, sought to derobe her. Sita, on the other hand, took her humiliations with fortitude and goodwill toward her husband. However, by this time the right of the husband over his wife or a man over a woman has generally accepted by the society irrespective of whether women acknowledge it willingly or not.

This willing acceptance, even today, is considered as the ideal of womanhood. Sita is worshipped in most of the devout homes for her absolute obedience to her husband. Everywhere in India her example is exalted to be followed by all women. Sita had great strength of character and virtue. She pursued what she considered to be right. Her love for the husband was limitless. Her character was of utmost purity and chastity. If we for the sake of argument forget for the time being the divinity of Rama and Sita there arises a doubt in our minds that such a character might have been drawn to satisfy the male ego by the male poets. It might be possible that

Sita's character was enfolded in the myth of male supremacy and female subordination so that the women's sole aspiration in life became the loyalty and the service to her husband who was put at the level of God to her. This emphasis on chastity and service to the husband may lead to the conclusion that the women of this period were put on pedestal as goddesses only if they lived the ideal and the virtuous life according to the most rigid standards set by a male dominated society.

The witch type of the nature of women is demonstrated in the Ramayana through the story about Kaikeyi and Manthra. Kaikeyi tried through deceit to obtain the throne for her son. Manthra prompted her to do so. Hence both are branded as great culprits at the opposite end of the spectrum from Sita.

An aspect worth noticing in the character portrayal of Mahabharata heroines is the strong willed women. They are depicted as "resolute, full of fire, passionate in comparison with the often slackened, spineless men". Perhaps the Indians of this period were not in full control of their women and were frustrated enough to seek means of controlling them. One such means was to put an exceedingly high value on loyalty and chastity. Meyer points out that in Indian literature no ideal of a man is found; however, idealistic character portrayals of women are outstanding, especially in the Epic period". We may not entirely agree with this view as the portrayal of characters of Shri Rama, Shri Krishna and other heroes of Epic period cannot be ignored and yet there seems to be truth in this observation that women of this period were certainly of strong will.

During the post-Vedic period the age of marriage of girls was nine or ten years. Since the marriage was performed at such a young age, the choice then was not that of the girl but of the parents or other elders. A woman was debarred from revoking her marriage but the husband was free to throw his wife out of his household if she was not submissive. Widow marriage became unacceptable and was banned by 500 AD. The dictum that "the wife ought to revere her husband as a god even if he was vicious and void of any merit was accepted as applying to all women". The Law of Manu became the accepted way of life. It stated that the father should protect his daughter while she was young, her husband when she was married, and her son when her husband was no longer there. This law contributed to woman's inferior status in society and denied her all decision making rights.

Kautilya was in favour of marrying girls at a tender age. He advocated the marriage of girls when menses appear. He advocated the punishment of parents who did not marry their daughters at proper time. According to Jha: "Probably Kautilya advocates early marriage with a view to maintaining the chastity of girls, preventing 'women' from joining nunneries, check love marriages, utilising the fertile period of girls for bringing forth offspring, and increasing the population at a time when frightful wars of conquest reduced Hindu population by one-half". Kautilya propagates the subjection of women in married life. The wife must remain under the control of her husband. As the girls were to be married at an early age their education was totally neglected. Kautilya considered that a wife must be fully devoted to her husband and blindly follow him. The woman's freedom of speech was totally curbed and since her individuality was denied she was kept ignorant.

At this time, Buddhism developed in India as a revolt against Brahmanism, a too formal ritualistic religion prevalent about six centuries before the birth of Christ, Buddhism soon spread throughout India and dominated the nation until about 800 AD. Buddhists still maintained women in an inferior position through an emphasis on celibacy for men who made women appear unclean or as objects simply for men's pleasure. Women were admitted to the Buddhist order as a gradual change occurred. According to Altekar, "this change was the beginning of a movement, which led to new attitudes about female education among ladies in commercial and aristocratic familes". Several ladies from Buddhist families led lives of celibacy with the aim of understanding and following the eternal truths of religion and philosophy. Some women like Sanghamitra went to foreign countries to propagate Buddhism.

Also, many women of the Jaina faith devoted their time to learning and became famous scholars. However, these were early exceptions. For the majority of women, no educational gains were made between 300 AD and 800 AD because of either Buddhism or Jainism. The celibate Jaina monks considered women as the temptresses that perpetuated the misery that was life. This attitude certainly did not deter in general the Jainas from marriage or begetting of children. Women were given place of honour in the household. However, the monkish tales about celibacy did contribute to ambivalence among the Jaina men in their behaviour pattern with their women. Jaina men enjoyed their women in spite of the religious discourses about their evils.

The road back to educational equality was slow and difficult. By 500 AD the religious influence had obligated all education for women. The model women were exposed to re-modelled. Women were exposed to such literature, which highlighted dependence and punishment for breaking the norms of conduct imposed on them by indifferent priests. A blind faith developed among the women through a process of awe and forced reverence. The Puranic literature cites examples where the husband was carried on his wife's shoulders to the house of a prostitute. The wife's willingness to put her husband's needs above hers' proved that she was a sati.

This literature which seems to have been developed by male Hindu priests completely subjugated the will of women. It emphasised husband worship along with the notion that a woman's salvation was possible only by doing that which her husband desired. An abundance of stories about Pativarta Nari or the husband worshipping woman influenced women to perform every kind of unnatural act for the sake of their husbands. Women started taking pleasure in their morbid existence. Eventually they became even greater fanatics than men in opposing their freedom. Perhaps they were so removed from the idea of an independent existence that even the thought of such responsibility frightened them. It may be said that it is human nature that one wants to stay with the familiar even if it is destructive because the unknown is scary.

Medieval Period

Muslims considered marriage as a contract. In certain respects the Muslim law gave woman a higher position in the society than the medieval Hindu law. However, the purdah or veil as well as the women's ignorance of the law diminished this small difference. The Muslim men believed that their women would remain safe only if they were not exposed to temptation. Thus the women were denied the right to make choices.

The Muslims like Hindus believed that the women's only path to salvation lay in the service to their menfolk. Divorce was shunned and many myths were woven about the dutiful wife who was prepared to sacrifice her all for her husband. Muslim had put all types of restrictions on the movement of their women outside their households and by and large they were restricted from having any contact with men who did not belong to their immediate family. Chastity was valued and the husband considered it his conjugal duty to keep his wife away from temptation.

According to the Holy Quran women were respected because they bore children. Progeny was very important to the Muslims as defenders in warfare against unbelievers. Hence among Muslims there also developed ambivalent feelings towards their women. Women were respected for being mothers but at the same time they were restricted from having any freedom of action. They were completely subjugated by the dominant males. Due to a number of environmental factors affecting the Indian Muslims the feelings of respect were overcome by the need or restriction. Most of the legal rights of the women were virtually subjected to the male will.

The early Muslim period was one of great instabilities. Local feuds and conversions were dominating the social life. The fanaticism and religious intolerance closed the doors to rationality. The women were the worst sufferers of the irrationality of the ignorant priests and religious fanatics. Their spirit of inquiry was crushed, as they were not allowed any interaction with learned or open minded persons. The women were left with no option but to submit to their submissive role and suffer indignities and cruelties in silence. Dubey describes the personality and the character of the women that emerged during this period: They had no status in society; none in their own estimation. They were more like puppets, which move when someone pulls the strings than individual human beings with minds of their own.

At this time the patriarchal type of family in its perfectly developed state was generally in existence. The senior male in the family was the undisputed head. Hindu women could not claim any patronage since the law of succession did not give them independent right of inheritance. The inheritor of the property was made responsible for looking after the widow of the deceased. However, in spite of their low social status, women were still the ideal of conjugal devotion, and the family was the most intimate and enduring social relationship. Dubey considered that "the Hindu family was an ideal family, the Hindu parents .... Mothers were not equalled by any people on the earth in tenderness towards their progeny and attachment to the family ties".

This attachment to their families was not an exercise of free will for the women. They only knew to be dutiful wives and loving mothers. No other options were open to them. In most cases, motherhood was the only solace for them in their subordinate existence. As mothers, they elicited respect, and through their sons, they ruthlessly made attempts to dominate their daughter-in-laws and other poor and dependent relatives. The condition of the women in the Indian society continued to remain low. The disruption of the Mughul Empire in the eighteenth-century and the consequent confusion throughout the country added to the women's miseries. At the beginning of British rule, the marriage age was lowered to three or four years. Since hygienic conditions were poor and disease and famine were common, a large number of girls became widows in their early childhood. These child widows were ill treated and considered a curse to their families.

The use of the veil became popular, particularly among the Muslims. The higher-class women were kept away from the males by means of purdah even a glimpse of a woman's fully clothed and veiled body by a stranger was not tolerated. While travelling, dark clothes also covered the vehicle, and when the women entered it and left it, the male servants or the carriers had to be removed from their presence.

The observance of purdah was not only to safeguard the honour and chastity of women, it also kept them for special pleasure of the men. Certainly, the veil produced a special type of feminine beauty, which was pale and passionate with mystic eyes, and the mind of a child. Such women seemed to appeal to the morbid taste of the pleasure lovers. When a woman is unlimited and has free social interaction with the opposite sex, her sexual impulses are toned down. Perhaps those who put their women in purdah do so to obtain more sexual pleasure out of them.

During the period of Muslim rule, quite a number of upper caste Indian widows burned themselves on the funeral pyres of their husbands. This was known as the sati system. The Sanskrit word sati means "true wife" or "good woman." Thus a woman was considered true to her husband when she burned her body with him after his death. Akbar, the Mughal emperor, made efforts to stop this practice about 1600 AD. He, however, was unsuccessful. When the British became the rulers, they found this practice so firmly entrenched that they also had no luck in disrupting it. The magnitude of the tradition is further understood by noting that in the year 1803, 275 women were burned at their husbands' funeral pyres within 30 mile radius of Calcutta. Within six months of the year 1804 in the same area, the number was 115.

Modern Period

The British passed an Act in 1829 to stop the burning of widows. However, the practice continued in rural parts of India as late as 1905 when a few people participated in a sati ceremony in Bihar and were condemned to prison. The Hindu priesthood strongly resisted the British India law. They argued that Vedas, their holy text, sanctioned the practice, therefore, alien rulers could not suppress this practice. When the religious texts were examined, it was found that the Hindu priests had falsified them to support this rite. The prevalence of the sati system and the opposition of its abolition by the orthodox priests show the extent to which a society can degenerate in the name of religious law. It also shows the strong influence of myth which the men and women came to believe. The honour of a family became so strongly linked with the widow burning that the kinsmen of a widow could cruelly push her into the fire. Unfortunately, the abolition of sati system did not end the miseries of the Hindu widows. Their burning was stopped, but they were still treated worst than the pet animals of the household. They were not allowed to remarry and had to pass their lives depending on the charity of their kinsmen and serving them like domestic servants. The plight of the young widows was extremely bad. They were not only tortured but also many times sexually exploited by the unscrupulous males in the family or the neighbourhood.

Unfortunately sati system is still not completely wiped out. In September 1987, a young widow of 18 years Roop Kanwar was burnt at the funeral pyre of her deceased husband, a bare seven months after her wedding. The burning took place before a large gathering of people. The illiterate village folk endorsed the sati pratha and the rural women developed worshipful attitude toward the burnt widow. She became a deity. The myth woven centuries ago around the virtuous wives and self-destroying satis as goddesses seemed to persist in the minds of the people. It is worth noticing that all those women and men who supported and organised the burning of Roop Kanwar were not totally illiterate. They were some that were educated. Yet the type of education which they had received did not result in opening the vistas of their minds. This has in fact opened the question of quality of education, which these persons had received. In the case of these persons education which they had received had completely failed in developing in them a positive attitude towards modernity and a will to fight against orthodoxy perpetuated by a corrupt and ill formed priestly class.

The institution of prostitution continued to flourish as a respectable way of life and the dancing girls were patronised by the nobles and landowners of their villages or towns. Chakraborty writes that in 1853, the Chief Magistrate of Calcutta reported that his town with its 416,000 people supported 12,419 such women. Of these upwards of 10,000 were Hindus including several daughters of the Kulin Brahmins.

Existing along with the customary form of prostitution, which was quite common in large part of the country there was another form of prostitution that of Devdasi cult or temple prostitution. In early times, the practice of offering virgins to the deity was common. Some examples can also be found in the temple precincts of Sumerian culture in Mesopotamia. In India, the Dravidians who may have borrowed it from Egypt or Mesopotamia probably introduced this custom. In the Rig Veda there is a clear reference to the dancing girl. Usha, the goddess of dowri, is compared to a dancing girl wearing embroidered garments and baring her bosom. In the Atharva Veda there is also a reference to the existence of women called Gandharva grihtas (possessed or owned by Gandharvas). They do not marry and exist for the pleasure of gods and men.

The cult of Devadasi originated in the early civilisation and became prevalent in South India between the sixth and the thirteenth centuries AD. During the reigns of Pallavas and Cholas all big temples recruited girls for temple prostitution. The temple dancers were married to the temple deity at a young age. They were taught music, dancing and the classical literature. After seven years of practice, the rite of worship of anklets (gajjai puja) took place. This was the first wearing of the anklets for the dancer. It has been traditional for families to offer their daughters as Devadasis or servants of the gods. In spite of the Devadasi Protection Act of 1934, some families still continue with this tradition in Maharashtra and Karnataka. In most other parts of India, this practice has been abolished.

The courtesan in India has filled a need for the men, which the wives were unable to meet. It seemed normal to a wealthy male that wives are kept for progeny and prostitutes for pleasure both sexually and aesthetically. The high-class courtesans throughout most of India's history were the most learned women in the country. Santosh Chatterjee in one of his articles has observed that "Be she of heaven or this earth, the courtesan in India had dual purposes in her life. She was in one way an object of lust for men, in another way she was the repository of all the delightful acts of music, dancing and personal decoration'.

The cult of Devadasis supported the envelopment of women in the web of myth regarding self-sacrifice and negation of will for men's pleasure. Women lost their individuality partly due to the contrivance of men and partly due to their need for the advantages they gained by being submissive.

On Female Education

Many factors contributed to women's dependent state. Numerous pregnancies during their most active years left her unfit and unable for engaging themselves in any type of employment except in the case of very poor or destitute women. Men accepted the responsibility of looking after the material needs of the women but in return for this they demanded from them unflinching loyalty and devotion. They denied them any opportunity to develop them physically or mentally or to develop their own will power. Thus women became weak and inferior to men as human beings. This degeneration of the women in India was at its peak by the end of the eighteenth century. By the beginning of the nineteenth century the entrapment of the women in the mythical web was so complete that in almost all the spoken languages of India women were, described as evil, an appendage of men, and always open to temptation.

And so such sayings were quoted:

> "To educate a women is like placing a knife in the hands of a monkey".
> "Where there are women, there is trouble".
> "Woman is a poisonous creeper, avoid her company; her love destroys faith, caste, wealth and money".

PART — TWO

Determinants

FOUR

Physiological Factors

The education of the women should usher in an era of complete rationalism and equality. Equality between men and-women means equality in their dignity and worth as human beings as well as equality in their rights, opportunities and responsibilities.

A big question; Are women different from men because of their physiological development? This question is raised time and again. The men establish their superiority by pointing out the biology of the female sex. Whenever the question of the equality of sexes is put someone is sure to say: "But it's just a matter of biology. You know women are different from men-they are more intuitive, nurturing, emotional, but also weaker and subject to fits of weeping once a month." Women are born to be mothers. Men are stronger, both physically and psychologically and so are fit for work and to play role of dominant partners in the men-women relationships. It is because of such notions that the education of women is considered not of as much significance as the education of men. But is it the right conclusion? We will now try to focus our attention on this question.

There is much divergence in the opinions regarding the basic biological differences between sexes. One viewpoint is that sex differences are biologically determined while the other viewpoint emphasises that the only difference between the sexes is reproduction. Only men can impregnate women and only women can give birth and lactate. It is true that one is born either male or female (not talking into consideration a small percentage of those born with no explicit sex or as eunuch). But there are six determinants of gender: (1) Chromosomes, XX for females and XY for males, (2) Gonads, testes in males and ovaries in females, (3) Hormone level, more androgens in males and more oestrogens and progesterone in females, (4) Internal accessory organs, which are the uterus and the organ of menstruation in female and the prostrate gland and seminal vesicles involved in the secretion of seminal fluid in male, (5) External genital appearance. (6) Assigned sex and rearing, usually based solely on external genital appearance (Hampson and Hampson, 1961).

There is research evidence that indicates that after birth the brain regulates secretion of sex hormones. Puberty seems to be initiated by an interaction between the sex hormone and certain cells of the brain. In normal child, both male (androgen) and female (oestrogen) sex hormones are almost undetectable in the urine until the child is eight to ten years of age. At this point the male hormones sharply increase in both sexes, while the female hormones increase only in females. In girls the production of sex hormone becomes cyclic at about the eleventh year and is accompanied by the beginning of menstruation, the appearance of secondary sexual characteristics, and a growth spurt. Thus in terms of hormones there are no appreciable differences between males and females up to puberty. After puberty both adrogenic and oestrogenic hormones are present in both sexes but in different proportions. Males have high level of androgens and low level of oestrongens, while females have high level of oestrogens and moderate level of androgens.

A Relevant Question

A very relevant question that may be raised here is: Do hormones determine our personality and behaviour completely or in their determination social factors are also involved? The biological determinists consider that hormones give us energy and direct that energy into natural channel such as sex and fighting. Thus our moods and behaviour are related to our own body state and socialisation factor is irrelevant. But this view is open to controversy. Research has shown that even our private emotions and their interpretation are shaped by reaction of those around us. While visceral sensations such as heart palpitation, flushing and tremor tell us that we are emotionally aroused, we have to learn whether that arousal means that we are excited, angry or happy. All body chemical hormones produce a physiological state that must be translated into personality and behaviour through a specific social control. Thus sex role probably enters into the very way we perceive and interpret our own bodily sensation even those due to hormone. This is not to say that hormone levels are irrelevant to personality and behaviour. It merely suggests that even with such purely biological differences as hormones, we need to keep a sharp eye for ways in which social factors help to translate these biological factors into every day behaviour. We may say that the differences in personality and behaviour of male and female are not only because of hormones but also the process of socialisation of girls and boys creates such differential behaviour, which is known as typically male or female behaviour. We may give a few more research findings to establish our above-mentioned belief.

The hormone androgen is found in greater quantity in males than in females. This is then considered as a factor governing more assertive behaviour among males. But Moss (1967) found that mothers tend to comfort crying female babies more than they do crying male's. It may be that the male infant experiences visceral sensation, such as stomach contractions of hunger pains. He cries but mother's attention is not drawn. He then learns that crying is not enough. He has to assert himself physically to attract the mother's attention. When this situation persists for months or years the male child may then associate this visceral sensation with greater activity or aggression and he may show it in his emotion of anger. On the other hand the female infant when experiences the similar visceral sensation due to stomach contraction she may also cry but in her case the mother comforts her. Gradually the female may come to associate these visceral sensations with comforting which may lead her to the emotion of happiness. The mothers perhaps do not attend to the male infant's cries as quickly as that of female infants because they may feel that males ought to be tough and should not cry. The finding of Moss may be taken with a sense of skepticism, in the case of Indian male child. In this country because of too high aspirations for a male child more attention is given to him by the mother. But this might be leading the male child becoming too much attached to the mother and an entirely dependent individual to the parental wishes.

It cannot be said that hormone levels are irrelevant to personality and behaviour. It merely suggests that even in dealing with such purely biological differences as hormones, we need to keep a sharp eye for ways in which social factors help to translate these biological factors into day to day behaviour.

The Agression Factor

The controversy surrounding aggression is not about whether males act more aggressively than females but about the causes for these sex differences, for regardless of how aggression is defined and measured, males of all ages show a consistent tendency to be more aggressive than their female peers. The greater male aggression is expressed not only in a variety of behavioural modes but also in a variety of situation and culture. But how do female hormones affect aggression? Unfortunately we know little about the answer to this question. Most researchers have assumed that male hormones increase aggression while female ones decrease it. Bronson and Desjardins found that administering female hormones to newborn may decrease the aggressiveness of males but increase the aggressiveness of females. Thus in females the oestrogens may mimic the effect of androgens in males, when given to males, however, oestrogens may interfere with the action of the androgens.

Further more, male androgens administered shortly before or after birth seem to increase aggressive behaviour in females but not in males, while female hormones administered at that time also seem to increase aggressive behaviour in female while decreasing it in males. Thus XX hormones, whether androgens or oestrogens seem to increase aggressive behaviour in females more than in males. This conclusion then suggests that it is the absolute level of all hormones androgens and oestrogens together that underlies aggression in women, rather than a level of androgens relative to that of oestrogens. The basic argument is that both the sexes are actually equally aggressive in their underlying motivation but carry out desires to hurt others in different ways. This argument takes two basic forms. The first maintains that the two sexes are reinforced for different forms of aggression: Girls are allowed to show hostility only in subtle ways, while boys are encouraged to show it more directly by physical attack. The second form of argument maintains that aggression in general, is less acceptable and hence more discouraged for girls, leading to greater female anxiety and conflict over aggression.

It is now widely known that there are no sex differences in over all scores on intelligence tests. Some psychologists have, however, suggested that the sex hormones influence general intellectual capacity. The most popular view has been that male hormones enhance intellectual functioning and development in both sexes and, perhaps is based on the assumption that several social and physical behaviour levels of male hormones are related to aggressive or energetic intellect. There are also some psychologists who argue that female hormones may underlie intellectual ability.

The fact that males and females obtain similar overall scores on intelligence tests which does not mean that there are no sex differences in intellectual abilities. The pattern of intellectual abilities that make up the overall IQ score differs for the two sexes. In fact IQ tests are carefully constructed to weight the various portions on which men and women, typically score higher in such a way that their average overall scores will be equivalent. Females generally excel in verbal ability while males in visual-spatial and mathematical ability. The females superiority in verbal is found in both "lower level" measure (fluency) and "higher level" tasks (comprehension of different material and creative writing). The males' visual-spatial advantage is about equal in non-analytical tasks (matching similar shapes and completing routine numerical operation, perceiving and manipulating parts and performing complex numerical operations).

The idea of difference in male and female brains continue to have popular appeal and has been hotly debated and researched for many decades in spite of numerous contradictions in both theory and data. About the differences between the male and female brains the researchers are only able to find that the issue is extremely complicated and does not offer any conclusive evidence that biological sex differences exist in intellectual performance.

Tapping the Intellect

Can the sex difference in intellectual abilities be erased through altered social experience or specific training? If they can, these differences might be attributed to differences in the training that males and females receive in the usual course of growing up in our culture.

Our entire educational system is based on the premise that training is crucial, that without it children would not be able to reason clearly or to complete complex verbal and non-verbal tasks. Yet every teacher knows that there is limit to what the best instruction can accomplish with each child. There seem to be a basic intellectual capacity that sets the limit for the rate and perhaps for the total amount of learning. With no instruction only a few children will develop complex skills, yet with the best instruction no all children will become highly skilled. The issue is whether instruction helps a child use basic cognitive abilities he/she already possesses, or whether instruction can affect the development of these basic intellectual abilities themselves.

Research on the training effect has focussed on the Embedded Figures Test (EFT) and the Rod Frame Test (RFT) developed by Witkin, in 1950. These tests assess spatial decontextualisation, or the ability to extract key elements of a stimulus from a confusing background. They measure "fields dependence versus fields independence" that is one's ability to assess external or internal stimulation independently of the environment. It has been reported that women are more fields dependent than men are." In other words, women have lower spatial ability scores than men have. It was also reported that the field independence does not increase with training. But these findings and Interpretations have been challenged. Mazy Brown Parlee (1973-74) conducted a thorough review of all published studies and concluded that sex differences were not nearly so conclusive as usually reported. Parlee maintained that field independence scores tend to improve with practice or training.

Cross-cultural research results lead to the conclusion that the greater field dependence in women is an indication both of basic female dependence on others for emotional support and social stimulation and of a general lack of psychological differentiation" or development of a clearly defined and separate self-identity. Kogan and Kogan (1970) conclude that not only child rearing practices are associated with spatial ability scores in the predicted fashion, but sex roles are also implicated, i.e. men tend to score higher in spatial ability in those cultures with marked differences between the social roles assigned to the two sexes. The assumption is that greater sex role differentiation is associated with greater encouragement of dependence in females, and this dependence in turn interferes with spatial ability as measured by field independence and other measures.

The cross-cultural argument is organised around the theme of dependence and assumes that the trait of dependence interferes with the restructuring of external physical and social stimulation and hence inhibits abstract reasoning. When cultures begin to adopt a modern lifestyle, allow children more autonomy, or define the proper role of the sexes less strictly, they are increasing the independence of their population. This more independent population then scores higher on field independence and other spatial ability measures. But increased childhood autonomy, decreased sex-role differentiation, and increased technological innovation are all associated with higher levels of formal education for the population in general and for women in particular. Thus increase in visual-spatial ability scores may be reflecting increased formal education rather than a personality trait of independence.

To conclude the argument regarding physiological differences influencing the intellectual differences between males and females we once again raise the question: Do biological sex differences underlie any possible differences? It seems unlikely. Owing to traditional sex roles females are discouraged from being assertive and independent and therefore, their intellectual development and performance are inhibited. It is very well known that the parents treat male and female newborns differently. They encourage gross motor behaviour in males while viewing females as littler, cuter, cuddlier, and generally more fragile. The cross cultural research echoes this social theme by demonstrating that most cultures encourage males to be independent and assertive while encouraging females to be dependent, nurturing and responsible.

Psychology of Education

In 1912 in his book, The Psychology of Education Walton wrote that the profound physiological differences which distinguish the sexes are the correlates of equally important mental differences. While man lives by reason, women's outlook is molded and determined by feeling. In his opinion the advocates and promoters of equal education to the sexes sadly ignore the mental and intellectual differences between the two sexes. He is against coeducation. He emphasised that, as the psychological differences between man and woman are so intimate, so deep that the other cannot give the real training in character and in outlook in life of the one sex. A man cannot be a really sympathetic guide to a girl, nor a woman to a, boy, simply because the man has never been neither a girl nor woman a boy. But Walton clarifies that it must never be supposed that woman is an imperfectly developed man. That woman differs from man in intellect does not mean that she is in any way intellectually inferior to him. He proposes a different type of education for woman as her functions differ from that of man. He proposes a system of education which lays stress on preparation for an efficient woman.

Howard in 1928 drew attention to the prevailing educational system in which the boys and girls studied very much the same things even when their schools were separate. He advocated a separate system of education for boys and girls. In his opinion girls are liable to fatigue more readily after puberty when the amount of haemoglobin in the blood becomes lessened. With their thinner blood with lowered content after puberty, they are nearer to the threshold of anaemia. These girls in general are not so strong physically as boys are. They are also highly-strung and liable to nervous strain, which possibly is associated with the fact that physiologically they are liable to heavier drains upon the circulating calcium of the blood. These considerations of the physiology of the girl, Howard advocates, must weigh when laying down a particular system of education for girls.

Many other psychologists have also pointed out the physiological differences between men and women and recommended a different type of education for women. Geddes and Thompson in their book Sex (1927) argue that though certain differences between men and women are undoubtedly modification and natural, that is to say, the individual results of disparities or peculiarities in their education, training and occupations, many of the differences are constitutional, inborn and not acquired. They say that "the tenacity of life, the longer life, the characteristic endurance, the greater resistance to disease, the smaller percentage to genius, insanity, idiocy, suicide, and so on, are all correlated with the distinctively female constitution which may be theoretically regarded as relatively more constructive in its protoplasmic metabolism".

Stanley Hall (1920) has stressed the psychological differentiation between man and woman. Woman, he points out, are more emotional, altruistic, intuitive, less judicial, and are less able to make disinterested and impersonal judgment. He is of the opinion that woman thinks more in terms of the concrete, is slower in logical thought and has less patience involved in science and invention.

The psychologists, physiologists and social reformers till quite recently were pointing out the different physiological make-up of women as a ground for giving them a different type of education than that was to be given to men. They were emphasising that the existing female education was incompatible with the nature and need of woman. It had entirely ignored her function and mission in life, namely motherhood. The educational curriculum for her was a complete imitation of that of the man, as if like him she was going to be in future an office bearer. With only a few exceptions most of the women were going to be married and the motherhood was a undoubted fact. Hence they needed an education which would prepare them for motherhood. These persons were quite critical of the modern feminists whom they considered were criminally ignoring this vital fact in their zest of following the standards of male pursuits. According to them the girls should be given education in domestic economy, nursing of children, hygiene of pregnancy, general household management, and in all such subjects which would be intimately personal to them.

Dr. Saleeby in the Report of the Proceedings of the English Speaking Conference on Infant Mortality has remarked: "Education of a girl must be to prepare her for womanhood and not to show that at a pinch she would be a boy".

Truby King in the same report has mentioned that: proper education should be given but above all there must be a development of love of human life, and interest in children, and a development of proper womanly qualities".

The ideas expressed above are considered redundant now. The technological and scientific advancement has refuted all the arguments put as above in view of the women's physiology. It is now being said that because of technology, tomorrow's most challenging and rewarding careers will require the powers of mind, not muscles. The most modern psychological and brain research have made it very clear, despite all of yesterday's cliches, that women have all the intellect and ambition needed to go after these jobs. Science is also relieving the women from the tyranny of the biological clock, allowing women the freedom to delay bearing children until late thirties or sixties.

The changes in work and reproductive choices are women's family lives, encouraging "Parallel" marriages in which husband and wife both share the work inside and outside the home.

The study of biological and other sex differences is being carried out on many fronts by the anthropologists and psychologists, who catalog human behaviour, neuroscientists, who probe the brain, and endocrinologists, who trace the action of hormones in the body. It is still a very young science. But this science has given us new dimension regarding the biological and psychological differences between man and woman.

Male and female brains are different although not in ways that would support most of the stereotypes of the past. The distinction is certainly not one of intelligence, for the average female brain is as smart as the average male brain by whatever test we use to measure it. The difference lies in question of values, interests, style and Motivation. Different does not mean superior or inferior. We should also not deny biology in order to shake off the myths that have accumulated regarding female nature. Howard Gardner in his book Frames of Mind (1983) argues that the human intellect is not a single entity. Multiple forms of Intelligence exist, including musical, linguistic, spatial, logical ..... mathematical, interpersonal and bodily and kinesthetic intelligences. All individuals have an intellectual mix intellectual mix that includes all these types in varying Proportions. The mix may be weighted differently in each sex too.

The genetic engineering has revealed a number of facts regarding the physiological development of male and female. Now the scientists recognise that the creation of a male from thé arrival of the chromosome to the testosterone that floods the embryo, is a precarious business, the result at best, is a creature with a single survival advantage over females: greater muscular strength. At every stage of life, men pay dearly to gain this advantage; fall victim to every threat from genetic defects to heart disease. Women are biologically superior to men in every other category but muscles. Boys are more likely to suffer than girls from birth defects and genetic diseases. So called X-linked genetic diseases such as haemophilia and muscular dystrophy strike boys almost exclusively because they are carried on the X-chromosome to protect them. But Y provides no such back up to a boy with a defective X. Infant boys suffer more illness and infection and in the first month of life three of them die for every two-baby girl. At every age, women have lower death rates from heart disease and heart attacks than do men. Even women who have high blood pressure and high blood cholesterol do not die as readily as men do. Women are less likely to die of infectious diseases. The endocrinologist Estelle Ramey says: "So women are an extraordinarily viable sex, right from the moment of conception".

In the modern times medicine has reduced the perils of childbirth and the threat of infectious diseases. Women are simply better prepared mentally and physically, to meet the pace and challenges of life and work in a technologically advanced world.

Women of all ages have more responsive immune systems than men, giving them protection from bacteria and virus. Girls have higher levels of a protective blood protein called immunoglobulin M or IgM than males, and a gene on the X-chromosome seems to be responsible for the immune system. The X-chromosome also carries other genes that influence various parts of the defense system. And after puberty, oestrogens increase the efficiency of the immune responses.

It is becoming increasingly clear as the gap between men's and women's life expectancies grown ever wider that women have better ways of coping with stress, physically, socially. Some of the biggest risks to life today – heart disease, alcoholism, lung cancer, suicide- arise from the way we handle pressure and stress.

Although the same stress response takes place in both men and women it is more extreme in men because they need a bigger head of steam to get their larger muscles fueled for action. It has been found that women are about fifteen years behind men in accumulating significant heart damage. Men on average, start to develop heart disease between age of thirty-five and forty, women between the ages of fifty and fifty-five. Men between thirty-five and fifty-five are twice as likely to die of heart disease as are women. Today's women are entering into competitive athletics with the same intensity as men and their performance is improving dramatically. No doubt that there are some biological differences between the sexes that cannot be ignored, although they are not nearly as great as the myths about the women have been propagating.

Knowledge, the Commodity

Knowledge is the most precious commodity in the information age. The doors are now wide open for women to push against the frontiers of ignorance and it is very heartening to note that women have begun to take their mental and intellectual capabilities seriously. Keeton and Basrin in their book Women of Tomorrow (1985) write that women are forging new ways to care, applying their concern along with their intellect to much larger human goals. These authors emphasise that women can be system analysts and computer programmers, they can be hardware as well as software engineers; women can enter into the fields of infertility and test-tube baby research, of molecular biology and genetic engineering, women should prefer to study Bionics, (a field that's already produced artificial hearts, artificial pancreases to secrete insulin to diabetics, the first rudimentary artificial ears and eyes connected directly to the human brain, etc.). It's never too late for a woman to start to find a place for herself in any of these frontier fields. The country needs scientists and engineers to improve life on earth and help expand in space.

It can be said with confidence on the basis of the findings of various physiologists and the biologists that the women are not physiologically weak, rather they are by nature superior and their superiority lies in the power to give birth. It is argued that woman and woman alone have the capacity to give birth. Despite all the evolution of socioeconomic conditions and progress of genetic manipulation of medical knowledge, the fact remains that it is the woman and none else that carries the work of reproduction. It is this biological feature gifted by nature to woman, which is at the root of the existence of necessary minimal sexual division of labour.

The modern physiologists reject biological explanation of the inferior status of woman. They argue that the biological view does explain why men have been excluded from the task of reproduction, but it fails to clarify why women have been excluded from some activities, which are not reproductive. This implies that the inferior position of the women is not due to any natural deficiency in them but it has resulted from changing historical circumstances, which have always been tied to the reproductive role. Needless to say in the modern society women have been doing the same work that was once considered exclusively to be of men. For instance, women have gone to space, joined modern guerrilla groups and fought on the battle fronts, headed the country's administration, participated in sports and games and the like. To the chagring of men, women even surpass men in many of the so-called men's activities. Hence It does not stand to reason to attribute women's inferiority in society to biological or physical factors.

In view of the above mentioned facts we may suggest that the education for women must be as liberal and deep as for men. A woman must know the course of history, the rise and fall of different political systems, the co-ordination and contact of different cultures, the fundamental issues that this evolution in history involves. She must also know where she stands, how is she related to society, how can she promote solidarity in social life without injuring the growth of the individual. She must also know how life began. She must have knowledge of Botany and Zoology. She must learn Geography and Literature, which are the fountains of culture and civilisation. In short she must learn all, the areas of liberal education so that she knows her relations to the society and may thus prepare herself for real citizenship.

The woman must also have training in domestic hygiene and economy. She must learn the art of nursing children and decoration of home. She may also learn fine arts, dancing and music. Her education thus must equip her for twin task of keeping the household and involving in the world of work. We consider that system of education an ideal one which aims at making of each versatile artisan-versatile for changing conditions, a good citizen consciously playing a part in a generai scheme and a well-disposed, considerate person in full possessions of all his/her powers.

FIVE

Socio-Psychological Factors

Education, or profession, the Indian world is a male world with ambivalent attitude towards female. She is visualised as good and noble as well as bad and degenerative. Her reproductive functions are worshipped, but her sex is considered as a pull towards hell. She is respected as mother but hated as charmer. Still the Indian male wishes to enjoy her sex in every conceivable manner as is depicted in temple designs, architecture, erotic texts and in the pornographic material. Literature depicts his enjoyment; his keenness to impregnate her and to father many children even though they may be deprived of food and milk and live in abject poverty. The female submits herself to the male's demands because she believes she must serve him and raise the offspring she is destined to bear. She is absolutely dependent on male for her well-being. The willingness of the female for male domination, for letting him enjoy her body without her desire for it, for bearing children without having strength to endure pregnancy or money to feed them is explained by the fact that her life is woven into the myth of motherhood and service to man whom she has been conditioned to be economically dependent. Her weakness makes it obligatory for her to seek male protection and male in turn considers it as his birthright to hold the positions of power and authority over her.

The most vital questions which the modern psychologists and sociologists are concerned with are: Why are Indian women, even the educated ones, not prepared to emerge free from their mythical existence? Why are they submitting to the irrational male domination? Why are the Indian women still not prepared to lead a free and independent life? To seek answers to these questions we will have to peep into the psyche of the Indian women. To do so we will have to revert back to the women in ancient India.

There is no doubt in it that the ancient Aryan women were strong willed and dominating. The traces of domination can be found in the lives of the famous and respected women of ancient India. Hence it may be possible that the psyche of the Indian women is an offshoot of an urge to dominate. This may sound to be a view very much different from the prevailing opinion. But it has many elements of truth. We will present some arguments and facts in favour of this viewpoint.

The Ancient Intellect

The powerful and strong women of ancient India, when controlled by scheming males contrived a way to seek satisfaction. Pardweshi, the wife of blind Rishi Drighatamas, threw him in the river when he proposed legislation that a woman should have only one husband in her life. She was not prepared to subordinate her sexuality to the whims of one male. Drighatamas saved himself by clinging to a raft and lived long enough to put through his proposals. Later women were bound by this law and were unable to physically revolt, because of weakness due to frequent pregnancies and domestication. These women learned to achieve supremacy not by trying to break the myths, but by strengthening them. They did not make demands, but submitted to the demands of men. As the men continued to assert themselves, the strands of the web increased and women internalised their domination and externalised their subordination until their external life became miserable and their internal life gained expression through entirely different channels.

Indian woman serves her husband and rears her children and finds happiness in being half-clad and half-fed so that her husband and children get the best. Then her son marries and she demands a great price for rearing him up in the form of dowry. When the daughter-in-law enters the house, the mother-in-laws dominant attitude becomes explicit. Many stories depict the harshness with which the mother-in-law treats her son's wife. In some marriage customs, the mother of the son runs out of the house and sits on the edge of a well ready to jump in until the son and daughter-in-law offer their devotion and shower her with gifts. Thus the urge for domination which she has repressed when she entered the house as a young bride now finds as outlet, as she becomes the domineering mother-in-law.

The strict supervision and harsh moral codes under which women rear their daughters may also be outlets of the dominant urge. The Indian woman judges other women's behaviour patterns under strict social norms. Any failing on the part of another woman is a delight because it establishes her own moral superiority. By scandalising other she obtains a sense of power. No wonder that women gossip has become such powerful instrument for the maintenance of the status quo. Any change in existing norm releases dormant energy for domination.

We have made an earlier reference to the predominance of an element of masochism in the Indian female. This element is her weapon for dominance. She stoops to conquer and often become successful. Consequently, her husband becomes more sadistic and tries to crush her further. She submits to his cruelty and thus shows superiority in endurance, thus, a vicious cycle ensues.

Women's desire for dominance is a secret hidden desire. It is not evident at the external level of her existence but an analysis of her behaviour pattern throughout her life reveals it. Woman learns from early life that she is liked if she is helpless and dependent. She gets her needs met from her father and brothers when she subordinates herself completely and serves them devotedly. She learns that her path to any type of fulfillment lies through them. She also notices that her prestige and way of life depend on her docility. She, therefore, represses her will for independent thinking. She becomes completely domesticated and all her desire for dominance finds an outlet in leading a subordinated home life.

Carstairs while carrying on her study of "village women of Rajasthan" was warned by the men of the village that their submissive women were really quite strong-minded and often get their own way. The women even employed witchcraft. Carstairs says: "At first, I found it almost inconceivable that these meek, seemingly unassertive women could be seen as powerful agents of the supernatural; but on 7th March, 1950, 1 witnessed a scene which revealed them in a rather different light". ' That night when all the men of the village, except Carstairs and an invalid old man, left the village for joining a wedding party the women came out of their houses and with gay abandon indulged in dancing, singing, abusing and rehearsing many of the sexual acts. They were unbridled, strong in their expressions; and as fully emancipated as women in any part of the world can be. The next day Carstairs found their behaviour dull and demure. Carstairs writes: "Next day the wedding party returned from Togi, and the women of Sujarupa resumed their normal demure behaviour, but I felt that I had been shown a glimpse of quite a different side of their nature, one rarely given free expression".

It must be noted that Indian women have developed the art of concealing the extrovert side of their nature. From their external behaviour it is difficult to fathom their psyche. One must patiently go deeper into the analysis of their behaviour pattern. It is firmly asserted that they are neither treacherous nor evil. There has, however, developed some complexity in their behaviour promoted by the sadistic attitudes of the men and suppressed feelings of the women for, the ages.

In all the normal human beings, both the attitudes of dominance and submission may be found. Both are necessary for survival. In women, submission is overt, while in the men, dominance is external. But covertly, neither the domination in women nor the submission in men is completely lost. Women learn to submit in order to dominate, and men learn to dominate in order to submit. Thus it may be wrong to contend that the Indian world is absolutely a male world. It is true that men have the economic power but this is what the women desire. Until they learn to desire overtly their own freedom and independence the situation regarding their status and position is not going to change.

Here is then a challenge for those who plan for women education in our country. They have to plan, for a different cultural training than that which is prevalent today.

We may again repeat that domination and submission are a universal parts of nature. When one is confronted by physical danger, the instinct of self-preservation leads him to choose either to fight or flee. Some animals play possum" and pretend they are dead until their predator leaves. Others attack ferociously. Pardweshi made an attempt to fight. Women after her learned to be more careful and played possum. They took flight in the inner dorms of their psyche and wage a battle in which their unconscious played the part of warrior who fought not with weapons of destruction, but with the weapons of seduction and devotion. If the Indian women are satisfied with the situation as described above then why bother to change it? If she is dominant in her own way why consider her the weaker sex? To find satisfactory answers to these questions the following consequences of her above described behaviour pattern must be taken into consideration. The most important consequence is that the development of the psyche of the Indian woman takes place in the direction of creating a split personality. The person who is responsible to subdue her becomes her passion. She becomes too ritualistic, superstitious and superficial. She becomes too modest and looses all her initiative in taking decisions. Her life becomes one, of rigidity and ignorance. She curbs independent thinking not only in herself but also in her daughter and other female relatives. She develops intolerance to any deviant member of her own sex. She becomes ruthless with her dependent relatives, particularly towards those women who are either divorced or widows.

Indian men respect motherhood in their women folk while women seem to want to turn their husbands into little boys so that they can "mother" them. The women want their men to be completely dependent on them to fulfil their needs. This type of behaviour pattern may be at the root of Indians lapses in taking bold decisions in the hours of crises and in the development of the "killer instinct" in the competitive games and competitive enterprises. They very often lose control even in the win-win situations.

The subordination of the Indian women served the purpose of securing for them the protection they needed so that they might avoid hardships for themselves and their children. Aileen Ross writes:

> "The attitude of Hindu women to this subordinate position has not often been understood by Western observers, for they have seldom seen it in the context of the total family setting. Bachmann interprets the satisfaction, which the Hindu women did, in fact, derive from her seemingly 'low' position. He describes Kasturbai, Gandhi's wife: 'Whoever knows her is bound to believe that the self-surrender of the widow which led to the custom of self-immolation on the funeral pyre, must in certain cases have been quite voluntary".

Despite Education

Despite being educated the Indian women are considered downtrodden, but to a great extent they are exercising their own will to this effect. They must now understand through proper education and training that the subordination might have been prudent in the past and the tension relieving in the present, but it is no longer necessary for the Indian women to submit to it. They must reflect upon on to what they desire and develop enough strength to achieve their goals of life. They must purge out old orthodox traditions and adapt to the modern world. It is satisfying to note that quite a few modern educated women are taking initiative in achieving their economic independence and in the free exercise of their will power. They are showing their excellence in very diverse fields. There are at present almost all the avenues of work or activities in which they are competing with men and achieving success. No doubt there are still a large number of women who are living the life of drudgery and toil mostly because of lack of initiative on their part and due to their ignorance. Hence the educational system in this country is facing the gigantic task of emancipation and empowerment of such women.

Eleanor Maccoby and Carol Jacklin (1974) reviewed and integrated the extensive research literature on psychological sex differences, reading through some 2,000 books and articles in the process. Most of these studies were comparisons of male and female behaviour in infancy and childhood, rather than in adulthood. On the basis of their review, they concluded that many of the differences that are commonly believed to exist between males and females are in fact myths. For example, there is no good evidence that boys are more independent, ambitious or achievement oriented than girls or that girls are more nurturant, sociable or suggestible than boys are. On the whole Maccoby and Jacklin conclude that male and female are much more similar to one another than they are different, and they share the same fundamental needs, emotions and abilities.

If many of the stereotypical differences between the sexes are myths, then why are they perpetuated? The main reason for the perpetuation of the myths seems to be the different opportunities that society provides for men and women. In fact, as children grow up, boys undoubtedly become more politically and professionally ambitious than girls, and girls become more interested in taking care of children. The differences that we observe probably result from social values and opportunities, rather than from basic psychological differences.

Our expectations about what men and women should do and what they should like are called sex roles. Boys are encouraged to be ambitious and assertive and discouraged from expressing their weaknesses or their tender feelings. Girls on the other hand learn to play a more submissive and dependent role. They are taught to be well-behaved and co-operative and to act as if they have no aggressive impulses at all. Girls are also expected to be tender and nurturing. These expectations are effectively communicated to the sons and daughters. This communication is sometimes done directly by suggesting the desired behaviour to the child and by rewarding the child for performing it. In addition, once the child learns his or her sex which all children do by age three, the child invariably wants to demonstrate that he or she can behave like a member in good standing of that sex.

Changing Sex Roles

As we are marching towards 21st century, the growing age of computer technology, the psychologists and sociologists are coming to the conclusion that traditional sex roles are in need of change. They have come to believe that by putting people in slots labelled 'male' and 'female' and shaping them to fit the slots we are limiting their full development as human beings. Instead they propose that each child should be treated as a total person; without regard for the traditional notions of what a boy or girl should be.

It may, however, also be noted that as the idea of breaking down traditional roles has gained force, there has also been a great deal of opposition to it. It is argued that sex roles are based on biological differences that have evolved over the course of millions of years and, therefore, should not be tempered with. In his book Sexual Suicide, George Gilder (1973) writes:

> "When reforming the roles of men and women, we must always be careful to avoid gibberish-patterns of activity that so violates the inner constitution of the species that they cannot be integrated with our irreducible human natures"

Gilder's warning 'may have some validity, but recent research findings reduce the force of his arguments. Maccoby and Jacklin emphasise that psychological differences between men and women are small, and they are based on only a slight degree of biological predispositions. Considerable change in sex roles could be accomplished by changing our values and expectations, without negation of our biological nature.

A second argument against sex-role changes is the notion that if boys and girls do not develop the pattern of traits that are appropriate for their sex, they may become confused about their sexual identity and thereby run the risk of serious maladjustment.

But recent research provides little cause for such alarm. Virtually all girls and boys learn without much trouble which sex they belong to and they do this by the time they are three years old. The extensive sex-role training that follows is not necessary to develop a stable sexual identity. In addition, highly 'masculine' males and highly 'feminine' females are not better adjusted or healthier than people who are less highly sex-typed.

Sandra Bern (1975) has called the ability to behave in ways, traditionally associated with both sexes Psychological androgyny. An androgynous person is one who combines 'masculine' and 'feminine' behaviours. Bern has, measured androgyny by asking students how often various adjectives are descriptive of themselves. Some of the adjectives were traditionally masculine, as for example, ambitious, self-reliant, and independent. Some were traditionally feminine like affectionate, gentle, sensitive. Subjects were categorised as androgynous if they indicated that they are about equally well-described by masculine and feminine traits. Bern found that androgynous students of both sexes behaved more effectively in a variety of laboratory situations than students who were highly masculine or highly feminine. The androgynous men and women could be independent and assertive when they needed to be men or women. They were also responsive in appropriate situations. They were able to behave in a more flexible and humane manner.

The above finding has very significant implications for schooling. Some schools keeping in mind the value of androgynous personality have started to provide work experiences for boys and girls in order to develop the dignity of labour in them and to accommodate reciprocal roles. Some co-educational institutions have introduced cooking, homecraft and embroidery for both boys and girls in their curriculum. They are providing the same type of curriculum for both boys and girls. It is desirable that almost all the schools should provide such a curriculum, which do not discriminate between the two sexes.

In spite of various measures, which have been taken for ameliorating the conditions of the Indian women there is still much scope for reforms. Unless such customs, traditions, rituals and values and attitudes which view and treat women as inferior beings and less desirable than men are discarded and changed, the status and position of the Indian women are not going to improve. This change can be brought about through equalitarian, formal and informal education. Education must prepare both the sexes for becoming all that they can be without any discrimination or prejudice.

Case of Dalit Women

We have described the socio-psychological factors which are influencing the education of the Indian women. In considering Indian women we have kept in our frame of reference a Hindu middle class woman. But Indian society is a very stratified one. There are many castes, classes and religions. The women belonging to upper and lower castes, rich and poor classes and Hindus, Muslims and Christians have their own specific problems even though as women they suffer from all those limitations with which the average woman of Hindu middle class suffers. In the present and the next chapters we are paying special attention to the problems concerning education of Dalit women and the women of the minority communities specially the Muslim women.

We are using the term Dalit women for all those women who are either put in the category of Harijans or Schedule Castes. These women suffer from many types of social disadvantages. Some of them were considered, untouchable while in the case of most of them the food touched by them was considered as defiled by the caste Hindus. Many of these indignities have now been sought to be abolished by the legal measures, but still their lot is far from satisfaction. One of the important reasons for this state of affairs is the woeful neglect of their education. Their ignorance is the major threat to their existence. Why has their education suffered ? What were the factors are still existing which have pushed them into a miserable existence? What factors which are putting hindrances in their respectable right of living? The thesis of this book is that these factors have to be searched out in the socio-psychological make-up of the women, particularly in relation to their education.

The Dalits have been put at the lowest level in the caste hierarchy of the Hindus. They were required to serve the higher castes. We are not entering into any discussion here as how and why this happened. This has already been a subject of a large number of investigations and discussions. Our concern here is that how this has affected the psyche of Dalits as well as the upper castes.

The Dalits were constantly reminded that they were the objects of hatred and their salvation lied in the service of the upper castes. This was done sometimes by persuasion but most of the times by force by the Brahamanical order of the Hindu society. They were told that they must have committed some heinous crimes or evil actions in their past life and hence they are born as "untouchables". This developed in them a feeling of inferiority complex and they began to consider themselves as the inferior specimen of the mankind. This feeling was much more aggravated among the females of the Dalits since they were considered inferior to their own men. The Dalit women accepted their lower status and position and started believing that it was fated that they involve themselves in doing menial tasks. Since these tasks required no education or training they developed a mentality that education is meant for the upper and richer castes and not for them. They thus never made an attempt to send their children to the schools. Also the higher castes did not allow Dalit children to sit with their own children in the schools and there were no schools exclusively set up for Dalit children.

The literacy rate in India according to the census of 1991 was 52.11 per cent. The percentage of male literacy was 63.86 while that of female was 39.42 only. According to the census report of 1981 the general female literacy percentage was 24.82. The literacy percentage of scheduled caste females was as low as 10.93 and of scheduled tribe females was 8.04 (Census was not conducted in Assam and no castes were scheduled by the President of India for Nagaland, A and N Islands and Laskhadweep and no tribes were scheduled in Haryana, Jammu and Kashmir, Punjab, Chandigarh, Delhi and Pondicherry). These figures show that the education of the Dalit women was totally neglected.

The Dalit women were mostly working in the unorganised sector. In the organised sector their percentage Was quite low. There were only two scheduled caste women in Indian Foreign Services in 1987 while the number of male scheduled castes was 65. The male scheduled tribes number was 30 while that of the females was 5 only. Similar was the case in most of the other Central services. In all the Central services while the total number of the women employed was 994 in the year 1987 only 31 were scheduled caste women and 31 scheduled tribe women.

The employment prospects for Dalit women in the organised sector are very few. These women neither have the educational, nor technical qualifications and nor have contacts or social connections. They have also to face discrimination from two directions. One is that they are women and the second that they belong to low strata of the society. Hence in spite of the reservations for schedule castes and backward classes the benefit do not reach up to them. Hence most of the Dalit women in the urban areas are self-employed in the areas like hawking, scrap collection, domestic help, petty trade, etc. The women have to undertake such employment for their survival and for supporting their families. The income from such jobs is very meagre and also has uncertainties. There is no security also in these types of activities. Some Dalit women are also employed in wage employment activities. These activities include construction labour, earthwork, petty manufacturing activities like beedi making or candle making etc. They are employed by some traders in these activities and are being paid very low wages. In the rural areas the Dalit women are engaged for labour in agriculture and agro-based industries.

From the brief account of the education and employment of the Dalit women it may be evident that in spite of more than 50 years of our independence they are in miserable plight. It is, therefore, necessary for the government as well as the general public that serious efforts are made towards their betterment. We can tackle this problem only when we make all out efforts for their education. One way to do it is to open more and more schools for them and give them incentives like free tuition, dress and mid-day meals. But this is a very simple solution. The women may still not go to attend the school. The majority of the Dalit households will not send their girls of school going age to the schools as this may mean the loss of income for the family as these girls might have been employed in some type of wage earning work or these girls might be busy in looking after their younger siblings, etc. when their parents have left for work. If we wish to educate them and provide help in their social and economic progress we must understand their psychology and the sociological problems which they face.

Psychological Aspects

The Dalit women suffer from extensive inferiority complex. The indignities that they have suffered in the past have left such a deep mark on their psyhe that they had started considering themselves as persons meant to lead a miserable life. This complex has not been altered till the present times. Hardly they take interest in raising their pattern of life. The Dalit leaders have recently made very powerful efforts to bring changes in their thinking. Mayawati and Phoolan Devi are the present day examples of such leaders. But still there is a long way to go before the mentality of Dalit women as the scum of the society is going to change. The efforts of social workers and political leaders are undermined from time to time by the atrocities being committed on them by the upper caste and affluent members of the society. The tradition bound society in India do not relish that the Dalit women should think themselves as equal to them. They are prepared to commit all sorts of acts of aggression on them if they express any desire to achieve equality with the higher caste women.

The daily newspapers are full of incidents describing rapes, murders, and beatings of both the Dalit males and females. These have two types of reactions. One is that the Dalit leaders raise Dalit Sena and try to retaliate by attacking the citadels of the upper castes and the seconds that they take it as a matter of their fate. Both are wrong approaches. The Second approach increases caste tensions without offering any solution. The other approach of it being their fate is the pessimistic outlook that throws them back to square one. A better approach is to educate them in terms of their importance. They should not feel marginalised. It is the duty of their leaders to educate them in terms of their importance in the present day social and political order.

One of the factors responsible for their poor economic condition is the large number of children, which they produce. They do not realise that more children mean more mouths to feed. Unfortunately the Dalit leadership has failed to develop among Dalit women the value of family planning. The syndrome of what is fated will happen need to be altered. We may call such a syndrome as "fatelinked proverty syndrome". Unless the Dalit women are prepared to discard this syndrome their plight will remain the same.

Sociological Aspects

As we have already pointed out the Dalit women's low status and position is due to their poverty and involvement in menial tasks. To improve their lot it is necessary that they should get better education and training. Now no task may be taken as menial. The technology has created a situation in which even the most menial task can be performed with machines. The handling of machines is the task of the technologists. The technologists are those who have got training in the handling of the machines. Thus the women are to be trained in handling machines and in the use of gadgets. One example may be given to clarify the issue raised here. We all know that Barber or Nai caste was considered among the low castes. His job was hair cutting, etc. Today this role has been taken up by the so called beauticians or by the owners of "air conditioned hair cutting saloons." The hair grooming is no more considered as a low task. Similar is the case with cooking. Now

Chef is an honourable member of the society. The change has been brought about by the introduction of the specialised training being associated with these professions.

The Dalit women's aspirations and the motivations have to be increased manifolds. For this the social workers have to strive hard. The politicians cannot perform this task because they only want to keep their leadership intact or to get Dalit votes in the election. They have a vested interest in keeping the electorate ignorant and keeping it in the state in which it is so that these leaders can always exploit it by arousing its emotions for caste or class struggle. The enlightened electorate may question their leadership and may ask them to be accountable to the electorate. Only the leaders gain by creating hatred among different castes and classes. We may say that all the leaders are not like this. There are many selfless workers. It is to them that an appeal to bring a change in the psychology of the Dalits should be made.

The role of teachers in bringing attitudinal changes among the Dalit women cannot be ignored. Education does not mean simply learning the language or some other subjects. Real education is that which has a bearing on a better personal and social life of that individual who is getting education.

PART — THREE

Perspective

SIX

Paving Way for Education

Before educating a nation, we need a healthy and developed community, ready to be educated that's why, the first Prime Minister of India had said :

> We talk about a welfare State and direct our energies towards its realisation. That welfare must be the common property of everyone in India and not the monopoly of the privileged groups as it is today. If I may be allowed to lay greater stress on some, they would be the welfare of children, the status of women and the welfare of the tribal and hilly people in our country. Women in India have a background of history and tradition behind them, which is inspiring. It is true, however, that they have suffered much from various kinds of suppression and all these have to go so that they can play their full part in the life of the nation.
>
> —Jawaharlal Nehru: Foreword to *Social Welfare in India*

Indian planners have generally seen development as a process comprehending the entire social system. According to the Planning Commission on the First Five-Year Plan:

> Maximum production, full employment, the attainment of economic equality and social justice constitute the accepted objective of planning ... plan for development must place balanced emphasis on all these.

> Development touches all aspects of Community life and has to be viewed comprehensively. Economic planning thus extends out into extra economic spheres- educational, social and cultural. Second Five-Year Plan.
>
> This broad approach to development was to give shape to the policy of transforming India into a welfare State, as directed by the Constitution.

The overall development process envisages a share in the development generated by the Plan equally for women and men. Since the Constitution stresses the need for promoting with special care the educational and economic interests of the weaker sections of the people, the welfare and development of women received particular attention from the beginning.

The Planning Commission's 'Plans and Prospects for Social Welfare in India, spells out social welfare services as intending to cater for the special need of persons and groups who by reason of some handicap-social, economic, physical or mental-are unable to avail of or are traditionally denied the amenities and services provided by the community. Women are considered to be handicapped by social customs and social values and therefore social welfare services have specially endeavoured to rehabilitate them.

The Planning Commission defined three major areas under which they have paid special attention to women's development: (a) education, (b) social welfare, and (c) health. The development of education for women has been already discussed. In this Chapter we shall examine the policies, provisions and programmes for women's development, in the fields of social welfare and health including the administrative agencies created by the Government of India to implement the overall policies regarding women's development, in order to assess the achievements in this regard.

The *First Plan* emphasized that, in order to fulfil women's legitimate role in the family and the community, adequate services needed to be promoted for her welfare. Well organized social service departments were needed in the States to initiate comprehensive programmes of women and child welfare. It recognized that the problem of high infant and maternal mortality was mainly due to malnutrition and undertook to develop (a) school feeding schemes for children and creation of nutrition sections in the State Public Health Departments; (b) maternity and child health centres; and (c) family planning.

The *Second Plan* emphasized the need for special attention to problems of women workers, since they were comparatively less organized and suffered from certain social prejudices and physical disabilities. They were also paid less because of the feeling that they were less suited to heavy work and were more vulnerable in situations which produced fatigue. The Plan stated therefore that women should be protected against injurious work, should receive maternity benefit and creches for children. It also suggested speedy implementation of the principle of equal pay for equal work, provision of facilities for training to enable women to compete for higher jobs and expansion of opportunities for part-time employment.

The main thrust of the *Third Plan* as regards social women's development was on the expansion of girls' education' in social welfare, the largest share was provided for expanding rural welfare services and condensed courses of education for adult women. The health programmes for women mainly concentrated on provision of services for maternal and child welfare, health education, nutrition and family planning

The approach in the *Fourth Plan* was a continued emphasis on women's education. As regards social welfare, the approach was to let the voluntary sector operate the bulk of departmental Programmes. Governmental efforts were confined to the provision of institutional services for destitute women and women rescued from prostitution. The basic policy was to promote women's welfare with the family as the base of operation.

The outlay on family planning was stepped up to reduce the birth rate from 40 to 25 per 1000 through mass education and motivation, and with cooperation of voluntary agencies and local leadership. High priority was assigned to immunization of pre-school children and supplementary diet for children and expectant and nursing mothers.

The *Fifth Five-Year Plan* indicated that priority was given to training women in need of care and protection, women from low income families, needy women and dependent children and working women. A programme for functional literacy to endow women with necessary knowledge and skills to perform the functions of the housewife (including child care, nutrition, health care, home economics, etc.) will be launched for the age group 15-45. Special steps will be taken for the Placement of follow-up of successful candidates under the exciting scheme of condensed courses, of education and the socio-economic programmes.

In addition to production-cum-training units, managerial and sales training will be introduced to promote the marketability of goods produced in different units. Under the Health programmes, the primary objective is to provide minimum public health facilities integrated with family planning and nutrition for vulnerable groups, children and pregnant and lactating mothers. The plan emphasizes the need to correct regional imbalances and provide services to meet the minimum needs of the community.

An examination of the Five-Year Plans reveals that in spite of the policy emphasis on welfare or investment in human resources, the share of investment in the social services in terms of the actual allocation has been steadily declining in successive plans. The objectives emphasized in the various plans, as well as the share of allocations indicate that among programmes specifically designed for women's development, the order of priorities up to the Fourth Plan has been education, then health, and lastly other aspects of welfare because it was generally assumed that all other programmes will benefit women indirectly, if not directly.

Welfare and Development Programmes

Programmes for women's welfare and development may be classified as follows :

Programmes under Statutory Obligations: The suppression of Immoral Traffic in Women and Girls Act, 1956 provides for institutional custody and after-care programmes. The Maternity Benefits Act, 1961 has a provision for leave and cash benefits. Under the protective laws, women in organized industries are entitled to provision of creches and family welfare facilities.

Programmes for Development: Under this category can be included the largest number of programmes which provide essential services and opportunities to women for development, such as education, health, maternity and child welfare, family planning, nutrition, socio-economic training and certain community organizations.

Programmes for Special Group: These vary from State to State. Some special assistance programmes have been initiated to serve groups like widows, the aged and the destitute, in the way of pensions or homes. A programme to provide hostels for working women in urban areas was initiated in the Second Plan, and has been continued over all successive Plans. For girls from backward communities, Scheduled Castes and Scheduled Tribes, there is provision for scholarships, and free residential schooling in Ashram schools.

While there have been additions and shifts in emphasis regarding the concept of women's welfare and development under the various Plans, and in some cases programmes have been expanded or integrated with others under a new nomenclature, the nature and content of the programmes have not changed.

Welfare and Development Agencies

In pre-independence India, while provisions of health and educational services had been increasingly demanded from the State, social welfare programmes were administered mainly, by voluntary agencies. There was no comprehensive nation-wide programme to provide welfare services. After the attainment of independence, it was felt that social and economic uplift of the masses required Government assistance to strengthen the services rendered by voluntary agencies. The administrative structure inherited from the colonial Government was clearly not equipped for this task. The Central Government therefore created a new agency-the Central Social Welfare Board in 1953 to promote welfare and development services for women, children and other underprivileged groups by providing assistance to voluntary agencies, improving and developing welfare programmes and sponsoring them in areas where they did not exist. Following the creation of the Central Social Welfare Board, the State Government set up, at the request of the Central Social Welfare Board, State Social Welfare (Advisory) Boards for the same purpose. This was necessary, as welfare is a State subject.

Even after creation of these Boards, there is no clear pattern in social administration. The responsibility for planning and administering women's welfare and development is scattered in various departments and other agencies of the government. The federal framework, and the need to involve voluntary or community organization in this task generally results in a three-tier structure of administration, with agencies at the centre, the State and the local level.

Agencies at the Centre: At the Centre, the major responsibility for planning and implementing women's welfare and development programmes rests mainly with the following:

(i) Planning Commission;

(ii) Ministry of Education and Social Welfare with its two specialized agencies - the Central Social Welfare Board and the National Council for Women's Education;

(iii) Ministry of Health and Family Planning;

(iv) Ministry of Home Affairs;

(v) Ministry of Labour and Employment.

Agencies at the State Level: At the State level, there is no uniform pattern. Programmes for women's and children's welfare and development are administered by a large number of departments. All States have separate departments for Health, Family Planning and Education. With the exception of a few States, the Department of Agriculture and Community Development also is responsible for some women's programmes. In some States, the department of Local-Self-Government is involved in these programmes. Social Welfare departments or directorates as well as Social Welfare (Advisory) boards have been set up in most States. In some cases, they exist independently while in others they have been combined with education, tribal welfare, etc. A few States have set up separate directorate for Women's Education, or Women's Welfare.

The Committee endeavoured to collect information from all Central and State Departments concerning their special programmes for women's welfare and development. 12 Ministries of the Central Government indicated that they have some programmes for women's welfare. 19 States and one Union Territory indicated the existence of similar programmes. The replies were not comprehensive and often did not provide full answers to our questions. Two things, however, clearly emerge from these replies:

(a) These programmes, even when they have common objectives, are supervised and implemented by many Government departments without any effective machinery to coordinate their functions.

(b) Government departments, by and large, are not at all clear in their understanding of what constitutes welfare or development for women. Some adopt a comprehensive view, some a very limited one. A few regard improvement of earning power as essential for any development. Most are, however, content to adopt a somewhat charitable approach to welfare and equate it with assistance to women in distressed condition.

Since the major responsibility for social welfare and development lies with the Ministries, of (a) Health and Family Planning and (b) Education and Social Welfare, we have examined them in some detail. The rest are only briefly enumerated.

Evaluation

It was impossible to use quantitative indices to measure progress in the implementation of these programmes. Owing to data particularly in the field of development, programmes specifically meant for women are very few and do not give a total view of governmental effort to improve the condition of women. The general programmes, designed for all sections of the population, do not maintain separate records of allocations or expenditure for women, nor has any attempt been made so far to evaluate their impact.

We were, however, surprised to note that with the exception of the Second Plan, all the others have confined their concern for women's development to only education, health and welfare. Conspicuous by its absence is any reference to the need for generating and improving employment of women. Even the Fifth Plan, which gives highest priority to employment generation, appears to accept the present low representation of women in the labour force as a natural order of things, which will continue unchanged in the years to come. This expectation appears to be in direct contradiction to the Planning Commission's own view, that utilization of idle manpower would be a tremendous force to speed up the process of development. It is also a denial of the Government of India's stated objective of the total involvement of women at all levels of national development.

It is interesting to note that all the agencies engaged in programmes exclusively for women, inevitably attach the highest priority to increasing women's earning power. But since these programmes are classified as welfare and therefore non-productive, they invariably enjoy lower priority.

This ambiguity and confusion springs from traditional middle class attitude regarding women's roles in society. It will continue to affect both planning and administration of women's welfare and development unless the objectives of such policies are clarified and given concrete shape.

Health Schemes

According to the World Health Organization, health is "a state of complete physical, mental and social well-being and not merely the absence of disease and infirmity." Health is both an important factor in the achievement of status as well as indicator of social status, particularly for women, whose health is conditioned to a great extent by social attitudes. The health status of women includes their mental and social condition as affected by prevailing norms and attitudes of society in addition to their biological and physiological problems. Societies delineate women's roles partly according to their biological function and partly from prevailing attitudes regarding their physical and mental capacity. These social attitudes also influence the provision and use of preventive and curative health care, including maternal care. The health care facilities offered by a community in the form of medical, particularly maternity services for women, is a significant index of the emphasis that community places on the health of its women. Some studies in both the developed and developing countries have shown a definite link between low status of women and deficiencies in the knowledge and utilization of preventive health services.

In 1957 a study was made of the percentage distribution of ailing males and females both adults and children according to expenditure for treating the illness in six rural communities covering six districts in Maharashtra State with a total population of 37,000. The survey revealed that in the year under study there were 730 ailing females and 513 ailing males in the age group below 15 years. The percentage of males getting medical treatment was higher than females. The study also showed that more adult women had to be content with free or traditional treatment or no treatment as compared to the medical facilities used for the males.

Cultural Norms and Attitudes: The cultural norms that particularly affect women's health are the attitudes to marriage, age of marriage, the value attached to fertility and sex of the child, the pattern of family organization and the ideal role demanded of the women by social conventions. They determine her place within the family, the degree of her access to medical care, education, nutrition, and other accessories of health. In India, marriage is almost a universal function because of cultural and religious influences. The age at marriage and fertility rate have important demographic implications. The largest number of children are born to women who marry at the age of 19 years. Cultural insistence on the marriage of women in the early phase of their child bearing period leads to high fertility rate and each additional child is a burden on the mother, affecting her physical and mental health. Barrenness is regarded as a curse and the woman is always blamed for this. Though the desire for many children may not be, the desire for sons is widespread. The joint family system also has in many ways contributed to high fertility in India. It encourages early marriage and large sized families which appears as a source of collective economic security as well as emotional security.

The lower status of woman is the result of her dependence and lower educational and social position. Tradition idealizes her role as the mother, housewife and the distributor of food.

It is customary in all Indian households for the women to serve the family first and then to eat whatever is left. According to our survey, 48.53 per cent of persons stated that in their families males eat first. In families affected by poverty, this generally results in still greater malnutrition for the women. The young girls as they grow up are taught subservience and self-effacement.

The process, therefore, starts at an early age and has very adverse consequences on women's health particularly at the time of pregnancy and child-birth. From their childhood, girls are taught to be uncomplaining and to maintain strict secrecy about their physical troubles. With menstruation, taboos are enforced and restrictions placed on their movement. They are unable to either discuss their health problems, if any, or even visit the doctor. Later as a mother, with children depending on her for care and attention, the woman has a tendency to carry on until ailment overtakes her. Reluctance to visit a doctor, particularly a male doctor, arises out of these restrictions imposed on women from the beginning. Such social attitudes, therefore, lead to a general neglect of women's health and in view of their child bearing role, they are the greatest sufferers as compared to men.

A study of data from particularly the developing countries indicates that other health problems of women-the higher maternal and infant mortality, maternal morbidity, lower expectation of life at birth, malnutrition, mental disorders, suicide rate and certain sex-selective diseases are linked to their status and role in the society. Child bearing and rearing is still the dominant role assigned to most women in developing nations. In the context of low socio-economic status of the bulk of the population, this factor becomes adverse to good health-in the case of women. All the developing nations are faced with rapidly growing population. Inadequate housing sanitation and poor medical facilities adversely affect the vulnerable segment of the community. Maternity, therefore, constitutes a special problem. The bulk of the stress and strain falls in the women who suffer from extremely poor health.

Indicators of Health

The indicators of women's health status in India are drawn from two sources: (a)Demographic trends, and (b)Access to health services. They should be examined separately.

Demographic Trends: We have already drawn attention to the adverse and declining sex-ratio, higher mortality rate and lower life expectancy of women. The high birth and fertility rates, beyond doubt, contribute to the low health conditions of women. Starting with 1871, almost every census report has emphasized: (i)The crucial role of female mortality; (ii)The significant contribution of mortality in the age group 15-44 to aggregate female mortality; (iii)The crucial role of neglect of female health in determining female mortality; and (iv)The insignificant role of under numeration to explain the adverse sex-ratio.

Neglect of women was proved by customs like female infanticide then prevalent in certain parts of the country. Child marriage, premature consummation resulting in early childbearing, overwork and malnutrition were cited as other causes of women's poor health. The census of 1931 drew attention to higher female mortality in the age group 5-10, and "at the reproductive age".

The apparently low sex-ratio of deaths (female deaths per thousand male deaths) is actually due to large under-reporting of female deaths as compared to male deaths. The doubtful accuracy of SRS data on age-wise and sex-wise mortality rates has been demonstrated in a recent study. The difference between estimated and reported deaths of females is sometimes said to be as high as 75.69 per cent for rural areas and 59.07 per cent for urban areas in the lowest age group; 46.57 per cent and 35.47 per cent in the age-group 1-19; 58.56 per cent and 37.94 per cent in the 20-49 age group; and 50.2 per cent and 28.54 per cent in the 50+ age-group. This difference in the case of males is consistently lower.

All the available evidence leads us to conclude that female mortality infact is higher for all the three age groups, namely, during infancy, childhood and during the productive age particularly in rural areas. The inference from this is that female mortality is due to the consistent neglect of female health.

It is observed that the maternal mortality rate is high enough to raise the overall death rate for females and accounts for the low sex ratio. It was reported to be 252 per 1,00,000 live births in 1964 for the country as a whole, but for rural areas, it is as high as 573 in 1968. It is unfortunate that no later figures are available for this.

The SRS data for 1968 and 1969 also reflects the same pattern as reported in the various censuses, namely that female mortality continues to be higher in the age groups 0-4 and 15-34.

Factors Contributing to Women's Ill-Health: Recent medical research has tried to identify particular contributory factors to the problem of women's ill-health and higher mortality. Since maternal mortality in India continues to be so high, it is understandable that the bulk of this research has concentrated on this aspect of women's health. The specific factor that has been identified by various studies is firstly pregnancy wastage, caused by abortions and still births. The incidence of this phenomenon has remained constant over the period 1957-68, a period which witnessed intensification of family planning activity. In fact there was even an increase in actual numbers. Such foetal wastage prevails more in low income groups. One study reported that pregnancy wastage of malnourished mothers was 30 per cent as late as in 1972. Still births are reported as constituting 11 per 1,000 live births. Much of this pregnancy loss and prenatal mortality and still births result from premature births, itself a consequence of maternal malnutrition, particularly iron deficiency during pregnancy. Haemoglobin estimations carried out on about 5,000 pregnant women in different parts of the country show that 30 per cent of them are anaemic, i.e., they have haemoglobin levels below 10 per cent. There is evidence that this is largely due to iron deficiency. Premature births have consistently been a very high proportion among the cause of infant deaths.

A second group of causes for both infant and maternal mortality relate to higher birth orders. Frequency of pregnancies causes protein malnutrition of the mothers. As it is, the majority of Indian women are victims of malnutrition. 10-20 per cent of maternal deaths are known to be due to nutritional anemias. This has been borne out by a series of studies of the National Institute of Nutrition.

It has been estimated that if causes of maternal mortality are eliminated female mortality will decline substantially, since pregnancy complications still constitute 16.44 per cent or the second highest contributor to female morbidity. The Bhore Committee had observed that even psychiatric morbidity among Indian women was the result of malnutrition, frequent pregnancies and anaemia. While data on this aspect of women's health is scanty, a WHO Report indicates that psychiatric morbidity is more prevalent among women than men.

All the demographic indicators thus point to a low health status of women. In particular they suggest that child bearing in India, for the majority of women, is more a health hazard than a natural function.

Access to Health Services

The broad objectives of the health programmes so far have been to control and eradicate communicable diseases, to provide curative and preventive health services in rural areas through the establishment of primary health centres in each block, and to augment programmes for the training of medical and para-medical personnel. In the Fifth Plan the main thrust was to improve the deficiencies in building, staff, equipment, drugs and medicines in the primary health centres and to integrate family planning and maternity and child health services. Health is a basic component of the proposed minimum needs programme. Any assessment of the impact of these programmes on the health of women has to take both quantitative and qualitative factors into account. A comparative assessment of available basic medical facilities in selected countries of the world indicates that India's position is more backward than even some of the developing countries.

In spite of the achievements during the last Four Plans figures indicate that medical care remains inaccessible to a large section of the population.

Any increase in personnel or medical facilities is nullified by increase in the population. The quality of the existing health services is reduced by inadequacy of staff, medical supplies and equipment, by overcrowding. In rural areas not even the minimum medical facilities by trained personnel is available in all districts. Distance and inaccessibility remains a major problem, particularly in hilly and difficult areas.

The lowest unit of the Health Service structure or its rural arm is the Primary Health Centre which is supposed to provide integrated and comprehensive curative and preventive health services in rural areas. The Bhore Committee which proposed the setting up of primary health centres had recommended that, to start with, each centre should cater to a population of 40,000 with a 30 bedded hospital to serve four Primary Health Centres. It visualized district level hospitals with a strength of 500 beds. Among other staff, primary health centres were to include four public health nurses, two medical officers, four midwives and four trained dais. Describing these requirements as the irreducible minimum, the Committee had recommended the key importance of developing preventive health services, with 'the country-side as the focal point.'

The Mudaliar Committee reiterated these recommendations, adding further the provision of three specialists in medicine, surgery, obstetrics and gynaecology, and 75 maternity and 50 paediatric beds to each district hospital.

In fact, when the primary health centres were established, the 'irreducible minimum' requirements were not provided. They had to serve a far larger population of 60 to 70,000 with only one lady health visitor and four auxiliary nurse-mid-wives (ANM), six beds and three sub-centres. Each sub-centre was put in charge of one ANM. Their functions were wide, including medical relief, maternity and child-health, control of communicable diseases (including the major national programme of Malaria control), school health, environmental sanitation and health education. By 1961, 2,800 primary health centres had been established.

Though the recommendations of the Mudaliar Committee were not implemented due to shortage of trained personnel and funds, from 1963 family planning services were initiated with additional staff (one woman medical officer, one extension doctor, one ANM, and two family planning workers to supervise four sub-centres). The sub-centres were to cater to a population of approximately ten thousand and were more than doubled in number, but with family planning as their major activity. The emphasis on family planning was strengthened further in 1966 by treating it as a crash programme, providing additional staff, and delinking it from Malaria control activities. In most States, the existing four health assistants were transferred to the family planning side.

Though the number of primary health centres increased from 67 to 5195 and the sub-centres from 17,522 to 32,218, their impact on the health of the rural population has not been substantial. An expert Committee observed that apart from West Bengal and Kerala, where utilization was 50 per cent, in other States like Bihar, Rajasthan, UP, Orissa, Madhya Pradesh and Jammu & Kashmir, the net utilization in primary health centres was hardly between 5-15 per cent. The reasons for this under utilization were: (a) apathy of the staff, (b) the status barrier that separates the doctor and his team from the village population, particularly the lower socio-economic groups, and (c) absence of lady doctors in many centres. Emphasizing the need to improve maternity and child health services, the committee recommended the provision of domiciliary maternity services as essential.

Critics of the present pattern of health services feel that they have deviated from the basic recommendation of the Bhore Committee, to emphasize preventive services in rural areas as the keystone of public health. Under the present system, the expenditure on curative services is thrice that on preventive services, but most of it is concentrated in urban areas. The 10 per cent of hospital beds meant for the four-fifths of the population living in rural areas are ill-staffed, ill-equipped, and ill-financed. In the sphere of women's health in particular, while all the expert Committees emphasized greater attention to maternity services, the actual position shows wide regional variations in the provision of this crucial service.

According to the estimate of the Study Group on Hospitals, earlier there were only 45,000 maternity beds in 493 maternity hospitals and wards of general hospitals. The total number of beds at that time was 2.75 lakh, i.e., maternity beds constituted less than 17 per cent of total hospital facilities. It should also be noted that most hospitals in India provide no separate beds for women.

The All-India Statewise life expectancy at birth, during the years 1951-95, projected that Kerala, which stands out for provision of maternity services also, has the highest expectancy of life for women, which was 60.7 for 1991-95, and the lowest infant mortality rate. Uttar Pradesh, with the lowest provision for such services has a female life expectancy of 53.7, which is nearly the lowest in India, and the highest infant mortality rate.

There is no doubt that improvement of maternity services has a definite impact on life expectancy of women. States like Tamil Nadu, Andhra Pradesh, Punjab, Assam, Karnataka and West Bengal which have given some attention to these services, have helped to improve their women's expectation of life. The impact, however, cannot be uniform, because of the operation of other factors, like education, employment, general cultural norms, etc., which exert considerable influence on women's utilization of these services.

An important cultural norm which has a direct impact on women's health is the age of marriage. No district in Kerala has below 15 as the average age at marriage and only 3 districts (33 per cent) have an average below 20. In the case of Bihar, Rajasthan and UP, the picture is just the opposite, where 71 per cent, 65 per cent and 48 per cent of the districts respectively have an average below 15 per cent, 35 per cent and 31 per cent of the districts in Andhra Pradesh and West Bengal also come into this category.

Kerala also has the highest female literacy rate which is 53 per cent in rural areas, and 60.6 per cent in urban areas. Tamil Nadu, though well behind Kerala, is still the second highest State in female literacy, which is 19 per cent in rural areas and 45.4 per cent in urban areas. Uttar Pradesh, Bihar, Rajasthan stand out for their low female literacy rate.

We may infer from this that the availability and utilization of medical care for women reflects the general social attitude to women in a region. There is also no doubt that the female literacy rate is an important determinant for utilization as well as supply of medical and health care for this section of the population. This is particularly true of maternity and child care.

Apart from regional variations, the accessibility of health services is also affected by rural-urban and social-economic differentials, including a broad pattern of sex differentials. For example, uncontaminated water is available to 40 per cent of towns, but only 9 per cent of villages. Since about two-thirds of the total number of doctors and nurses, and most hospitals are concentrated in urban areas, the four-fifths of the population living in rural areas get a much smaller share of these services. The National Sample Survey (19th Round, 1964-65) found that 46 per cent of all births in urban India are attended by trained medical personnel, as compared to 9 per cent in rural areas. The household consumption data of the same Round also shows that average per capital private monthly expenditure on medicines and medical services is Rs 1.01 in urban areas, and about half that in rural areas. Majority of doctors in urban areas are private practitioners, charging high fees. Their services can be used only by the upper and middle income groups. Private nursing homes and paying hospitals, with private doctors, are almost totally out of reach of the poorer sections of society.

A recent study on rural health services brings out the peculiar tension created by scarce supply of medical personnel in the villages. On the one hand is the unmet felt need for the services of the Auxiliary Nurse Midwife at the time of child birth. Villagers are keen to have the ANM's services because they consider her to be more skilful than the traditional *dai*. Whether the ANM's have provided the services, the dais' role has become less significant. During our tours we were repeatedly informed of the inadequacy in the number and services rendered by ANMs. Apart from their small number, the area covered by these personnel is too large, with consequent transport and accommodation difficulties. Nighthalts and the problem of security create difficulties for most of these workers in rural areas, and effect their functioning.

Such problems very often obstruct an ANM from really attending to her duties in all places under her charge. Secondly, for an outsider to live and work in rural areas, a degree of social acceptance and security is essential. Protection extended by influential members of the village community ensures this, and prevents her from being handicapped by their hostility. The result very often is that her services are monopolized by the dominant, or relatively well-to-do section of village society. It should also be remembered that the social and educational background of the NMs is likely to be closer to the dominant, or well-to-do groups in the village, rather than the poorest.

This sort of cornering widens the gap between the ANM and the masses of women who need her services. The overall image of the ANM in villages, particularly in North India, is that of a person who is distant from them, meant only for special people or for those who can pay for her services. She is not for the poor. She can be called only when there are complications and then also she has to be paid.

As for sex differentials, they are deep rooted in social attitudes regarding the needs of women for care and assistance during ailments. In many areas we were told that rural society does not always care to report women's ailments, or seek medical aid. Women themselves often prefer to be silent in such matters. The studies in nutritional deficiencies of women indicate that their requirements are often sacrificed to provide a little more nutrition to others in the family. The incidence of diseases caused by malnutrition is higher not only among adult women, but even among female infants. At the same time hospital records reveal that more male children are treated for such diseases.

The two sets of indicators demographic trends, and access to medical care, both reveal the same situation regarding the health status of women.

This increase in comparative neglect of female lives as an expendable asset, observed to persist and increase over several decades, is a matter of serious concern.

Family Planning

If the masses of Indian women are to be freed from their status as 'expendable assets', some of the obvious and immediate answers lies in releasing them from the bondage of repeated and frequent childbirth, providing them with some choice in the size of their families and in ensuring adequate medical facilities to protect them during and against maternity.

Propagators of the family planning movement in India have been keen to emphasize the improvement in the status of women as one of the direct consequences of acceptance of family planning. The birth control movement in India, from its inception, was associated with the feminist movement, and women's organizations were among the first to start a voluntary campaign for spread of birth control techniques among women. Even now they are active partners of the government's programme to persuade more and more women to accept family planning methods.

Recent researches in this field however make it extremely difficult to establish such an *a prior* relationship. All recent studies seem to agree more on the obverse of the relationship, viz. that improved status of women, with rise in the age of marriage, education, employment, better living conditions and greater general awareness, have a direct impact on the adoption of family planning methods.

There is no doubt that knowledge of family planning methods enables a woman to regulate her biological function and thus gives her a greater control over life and future. This certainly helps to build up her confidence in herself and can enable her to pursue various other ways to develop her personality, e.g., training, career interests and fulfil responsibilities to herself, her family and the wider society. Above all, such control has a direct impact on her health, Ability to prevent frequent and excessive drain on her physical resources undoubtedly helps to preserve her health, and since health is a basic necessity for any kind of development for a person, ability to plan her family ultimately contributes to such improvement of a woman's personality. A third consequence, which is sometimes emphasized is the possible change in husband-wife relationship, leading to improved position of the woman in decision making within the family.

All these results could certainly lead to a general improvement of a woman's status. But each of them are integrally connected with other socio-economic factors and developments, and the relationship between family planning and status improvement depends, in the ultimate analysis, on the presence and behaviour of such variables as social attitudes and opportunities for women's education, employment, pursuit of independent interests and career, size and sex of the family, accessibility of health services, and general economic development.

If the sexual role were the main determinant of male dominance and authority in a society, there would have been no communities in the world where the women are dominant, or equal members. The status of women in any society depends on a complex set of social, economic, demographic and political variables, among which the woman's ability to control the size of her family could be a contributory factor. But in our view, emphasizing it as a direct cause of improvement of women's status is somewhat exaggerated, and ignores the evolution of women's status in different societies. The matriarch of many ancient civilizations and primitive communities certainly enjoyed a much higher status than the women with complete control on the size of their families in the developed, modern societies of the West today. Knowledge of family planning techniques may have liberated Western women from excessive pregnancies, but it has not basically changed their status in these societies either economically or politically. Even in the sphere of social attitudes, with all the progress in education, and different types of social freedom and changing roles, their image as sex-symbols has been intensified, not eliminated.

In India, there has been an enormous volume of research on degree of acceptance of family planning, to assist the continuous evaluation of the Family Planning Programme. In one such research by the Ministry of Health and Family Planning, it was concluded that:

> The focus of evaluation of the Family Planning Programme at present is on the purposive assessment of impact of the programme, identification of areas of success and failures and reasons thereof, and feeding back this information for motivation and improvement or programme implementation. Family Planning Programme can be evaluated in terms of its objectives, viz., (a) the immediate objectives, including efforts and performance, objectives set for developing resources and activities for achieving the decision made; (b) the intermediate objective of spreading knowledge, developing favourable attitudes towards encouraging practice of family planning methods; (c) the ultimate objective, which is reduction of fertility so as to bring down the birth rate to 15 per thousand.

Apart from continuous assessment of information received from the States, regarding the success of the programme in quantitative terms, i.e., actual number of couples protected by various methods, provision of services in the way of personnel and equipment, etc., the evaluation includes field surveys on knowledge, attitudes and practices (KAP Studies). The Central Family Planning Institutes, the National Sample Survey, the various demographic and communication action research centres in the country, as well as a large number of individuals and institutions in the university system have been engaged in periodical assessment of the impact of this programme at both local and national levels since its inception. As a result, family planning is now the most heavily documented and evaluated among all major programmes of the Government of India.

One common trend in the results of these studies has been to expose the differentials in knowledge, acceptance and practice of family planning methods between different sections of the population. The results from the national survey conducted by the Operations Research Group, Ministry of Health and Family Planning indicate that the percentage of couples using any family planning method increases with:

(i) Age of wife (from 7 per cent among those below 25 years of age to 17 per cent among those aged 30 years or more);

(ii) Number of living children (from 2 per cent among those without any living child to 25 per cent those with 5 or more living children);

(iii) Education of wife (from 10 per cent among wives without any education to 56 per cent among those who have gone to college);

(iv) Family income (from 10 per cent among those with monthly income of Rs. 100 or less to 30 per cent among those with monthly income of Rs. 1,000 or more);

(v) Size of city or village (from 10 per cent among those living in villages of 5,000 or less to 32 per cent among those living in cities of 1 million or more);

(vi) Community trends that the percentage of current users among the Hindus is higher than among the Muslims.

The survey revealed notable differences in the characteristics of current users, past users and non-users of contraception.

In our discussions with Muslim women in different parts of the country, we did not get the impression that there was any organized resistance to family planning on religious grounds. Some of the very poor women told us that they had heard about the religious propaganda but they could not see their children starve. In every state we asked the lady doctors about the response to family planning from different sections of society. The answers were interesting. Those doctors who had some kind of social commitment and sympathetic attitude invariably said that women from all classes and all regions came to them for advice while the others complained that Muslim women and women from the poorer sections of society were not interested.

Our general impression has been that men, particularly, Muslims, are not very much concerned about family planning, though in Kerala an enthusiastic collector informed us that in the Family Planning Camps a number of Catholic and Muslim men came to him for vasectomy but they did not want anyone to know about it and requested that the operations may be performed at night. He agreed to make the necessary arrangements and the response was good. According to him there was no significant difference in the percentage of acceptors from different communities. In a village in West Bengal while a B.D.C. was complaining that Muslims were not coming forward for family planning, an old, poor Muslim woman came up and asked where she could take her daughter-in-law for advice, so that she would stop having any more children. She already had 5 children. In Kashmir, the educated and working women are very much interested in family planning and we did not come across any group of women expressing disapproval on religious grounds.

An analysis of variance in five factors, viz., educational level of spouses, family income, number of children, urbanization and exposure to mass media simultaneously has shown that the effect of each of these factors on the use of family planning methods is significant at 1 per cent level. Some studies have suggested that the differential in adoption and use of family planning methods between States may be due to the differences in socio-economic characteristic of couples in actual implementation of strategies or combination of both.

While some of the studies occasionally contradict findings of previous research, one factor which is generally emphasized by most is education, particularly the education of women. The Regional Fertility Survey conducted by the Demographic Research Centre, Lucknow, indicated that mean number of live births varied inversely with the mother's education. The educational level of both husband and wife was found to have a very large influence on their attitudes towards family planning.

The Delhi Fertility Survey conducted by the Demographic Research Centre, Institute of Economic Growth, Delhi based on a total sample of 9,000 households, indicated the inverse relationship between a couple's educational level and average number of live births in a pronounced way only when both husband and wife were educated beyond matriculation level, the variation being 2.73 for this group and 4.47 for literate couples. The Mysore Population Study reported that among the social and economic factors studied, the one which appeared to be the most significant in relation to fertility in Bangalore City was educational status, but education below the high school or university stage was not found to be related significantly to the average number of children born.

Education may affect fertility in two ways: (i) by increasing knowledge and advantages of family planning; and (ii) by generating deliberate efforts for a planned family.

The first is effective at lower educational levels, while the latter operates probably when a sufficiently high level of education is achieved by the couple. The National Sample Survey indicated that the percentage of husbands desiring additional children after 2, declined from 60 when they were illiterate to 41.59 when they were intermediate and above. However, the decline was neither consistent nor pronounced when the educational level was below intermediate and above.

The Dharwar Surveys on the attitudes towards family planning undertaken by the Dharwar Demographic Research Centre indicated that educational level was the most important factor associated with awareness about family planning.

Role of Education: While all the major surveys found a positive relationship between education and knowledge, acceptance and practice of family planning, most of them have revealed the existence of other associational factors which may have influenced this relationship. Education is generally associated with one or more of the following: (a) rise is the age of marriage; (b) diversification of consumption pattern of people, involving both material and non-material aspects which can lead to a decline in the psychic utility generated by the birth of children; (c) urbanization; (d) possible increase in work force participation of women; (e) higher socio-economic status of the couple; (f) higher mobility; (g) higher exposure to mass media and (h) more diversified knowledge of family planning methods. It has been found that couples with primary level education or below have very limited knowledge of family planning and are most often aware only of sterilization and IUCD (Intra Uterine Contraceptive Device).

Methods of Contraceptions: Most of the methods for contraception affect women directly, and acceptance by them would indicate the success or failure of a method.

IUCD: This was introduced in 1965 and initially was very popular. Later the level of acceptance showed a reverse trend. Various studies indicate that the failure of IUCD was largely because enough information on certain side effects of the insertions was not adequately published.

During our tours, the doctors and field workers told us that this method was unpopular and it was a failure. Their observations were as follows: (1)The careless handling of IUCD insertions by the paramedical staff led to complications and there was a whispering campaign everywhere that it was harmful for the health of the women. (2)Proper arrangements were not made for a follow-up treatment in case of bleeding or other side effects.

We found, however, that wherever it was handled by properly trained personnel, e.g., in Haryana and Punjab, it was found to be the most successful method, specially because it was reversible and inexpensive.

Sterilization: This has been performed as part of the family planning programme. Tubectomies accounted for two-thirds of all sterilizations and they exceeded the number of vasectomies, but since then the number of vasectomies has increased more rapidly, and they accounted for more than 80 per cent of all sterilizations. We would like to point out, however, that the validity of these figures has been often questioned.

Since sterilization is a terminal method which is often believed to have consequences on the health of the woman, the possible constraints that may develop in taking recourse to this method are obvious. During our tours we received evidence of this apprehension from a large number of women. They were reluctant to end their chance of child bearing because of an underlying fear regarding the survival of their existing children. They were also apprehensive of the possible consequence of their health. This fear has occasionally been aggravated by the experience of the mass tubectomy camps which very often did not provide adequate medical care or follow-up measures.

Two specific arguments regarding sterilization were brought to our notice by women doctors. A group of these doctors in West Bengal mentioned a number of cases of 'post ligation syndrome' where the women developed psychological disturbances after tubectomy, particularly if any untoward incidence like illness or death of a child happened in the family. In their view, this was due to the tremendous hold of traditional values on the minds of these women, who developed a sense of guilt and regarded these tragedies as being the consequences of their 'unnatural' act. Yet another argument by doctors in the rural areas of Rajasthan was the impossibility of undertaking sterilization for a large number of women, particularly tribal ones, because of their extremely anaemic condition.

Other Methods: About 2.3 million couples are estimated to be using various other types of conventional contraceptives. This is 2.3 per cent of the estimated couples protected in the reproductive age group. For women the most significant is the use of oral contraceptive pills. A number of trials have been conducted to study the medical and social acceptability of oral contraception among Indian women. The pill as a method of oral contraception is useful for the educated urban rather than rural women. It is also comparatively more expensive and constant medical supervision is necessary to check the side effects.

Abortions: The objectives of the Medical Termination of Pregnancy Act 1971 is to reduce the incidence of criminal abortions which pose grave risks to pregnant women by liberalizing the provision of the Indian Penal Code which restricted medical practitioners from terminating pregnancies legally. The Shanti Lal Shah Committee has estimated that for every 73 live births, 25 abortions take place of which 15 are induced. "In a population of 500 million, the number of abortions per year would be 6.5 million, 2.6 million spontaneous and 3.9 million induced." From hospital records it has been observed that 15 to 20 per cent of the direct obstetric causes of maternal deaths are from abortions. Of these, 98 per cent were from septic abortions usually resulting from abortions undertaken by unqualified persons. According to the Registrar General Census (vital statistics); abortions form a high percentage of causes of all deaths due to child birth. According to two studies of the National Institute of Nutrition, Hyderabad, pregnancy wastage from miscarriage and abortions ranges from 16 to 19 per cent to 32 per cent among poor income groups.

The Act allows termination of pregnancy on: (a)Therapeutic grounds where the continuance of pregnancy would involve a risk. (i)to the life of the pregnant mother or, (ii)of grave injury to her physical and mental health. (b)Genuine grounds where there is substantial risk that the child, if born, is likely to suffer from such physical or mental abnormalities as to be seriously handicapped. (c)Humanitarian grounds, where the pregnancy has been caused by rape; or (d)Social grounds: (i)where the pregnancy in a married woman is the result of contraceptive failure, or (ii)that the environment of the pregnant woman during the continuance of pregnancy at the time of childbirth and thereafter, so far as is foreseeable, would involve risk of injury to her health.

Termination can be done only by registered practitioners certified for the purpose in approved places, mainly government hospitals.

While the Act emphasizes its importance as a health measure, the permission granted under section 3(2) to permit such termination for married women in cases of contraceptive failure, has emphasized its importance as an instrument of population control. This has given rise to a strong difference of opinion among medical personnel who are averse to using abortion for such a purpose. Many of them insist on tubectomy as a condition for abortion. In their view, based on experience, abortions often lead to frequent pregnancies, apart from its health hazards.

There is considerable evidence that the measure is being used more for birth control than for other reasons. According to a study undertaken by the Government and Children Hospital, Egmore, Madras, out of 7,957 abortions only 11 were for therapeutic reasons and 617 were cases of induced abortions admitted to the hospital only after complications had set in.

A study undertaken by the International Research Fertility Programme revealed that 88 per cent of abortion cases were among married women, of whom 55 per cent were between the age of 25 to 33, 81 per cent were urban, 19.1 per cent rural; 37 per cent had three or four children. In another study it was found that 72 per cent were married, of whom 60 per cent were in the 20 to 29 age group. The average total pregnancy of these groups was 4.3, where the average number of living children 2.5 and 0.8 had previous abortions. 50 per cent of all the patients had a previous abortion in their record and 17.8 per cent had 2 to 5.

All the studies indicate "that most pregnant women who go in for induced abortions are fully motivated for small family norms if not planned parenthood. These people are very amenable and can be fully motivated for adoption of family planning methods, more often sterilization, if they have two or more living children or other temporary methods of spacing children."

We have given serious consideration to this matter and discussed it with several representatives of the medical profession. While we appreciate the ethical considerations which make some of them reluctant to perform this operation, we feel that it is a woman's right to have control over the size of her family. At the same time it is important that doctors should have the authority to discourage such operations when it possesses a definite risk to the health of a particular patient.

We, however, feel that the condition being imposed in many hospitals, that abortion will only be performed if the patient agreed to sterilization, should not be compulsive, particularly where a woman has only one child. It would be far better to adopt methods of persuasion through expert counselling rather than compulsion. Compulsive conditions of this kind will only drive women to unqualified persons, thus defeating the main purpose of this Act.

We have been informed that there are serious psychological hazards posed by both pregnancies as well as sterilization. It is, therefore, imperative to organize systematic research on this field, to ascertain the impact of these situations and operations on the physical and mental health of women.

The difficulties placed before us by medical personnel regarding the recording procedure and paper work involved in these operations, lead us to suggest that these procedures need to be simplified. It is also necessary to extend facilities for authorized termination of pregnancies, particularly in the rural areas. We have also been informed that though the law does not require it, many hospitals insist on the husband's consent before performing these operations. A special effort needs to be made to convince the medical profession of the social value of this law, from the point of view of both individuals and society.

We have also been informed that most doctors are reluctant to perform these operations in the case of unmarried girls. It is necessary to clarify the point that rape is not the only ground to justify termination in cases of unmarried girls nor is there any legal obligation on the doctor to inform the police of an abortion done in a rape case. We note that the All India Medical Council has introduced this Act in the syllabus for medical jurisprudence, with the object of setting up new norms for the medical profession. This will go a long way in breaking down the resistance of doctors.

Recommended changes in Law: We would also like to recommend the following changes in the Law: (a)According to Section 4(a) of the Act - consent of a minor girl is not required for operation, while in other surgical operations on children above 12, such consent is necessary. In our view this distinction is uncalled for and may lead to guardians' compelling young girls to undergo this operation even when they do not want it. The consent of the patient should be essential. In the case of a minor girl nearing majority if the doctor and the patient are in agreement, the consent of the guardian may be dispensed with. In all such cases, greater discretion should be permitted to the doctor; (b)Section 8 of the Act provides an overriding protection to the doctor for any damage caused by the operation. Since no such protection is given for other operations, this seems an unnecessary clause and may lead to negligence. It may, therefore, be dropped.

Policy Changed

During the First and Second Five-Year Plans, Government's

approach to the problem of population growth, and the need for family planning, was a long-term objective, depending as much, if not more, on 'improvement in living standards and more widespread education especially among women', as positive measures for 'inculcation of the need' and techniques of family planning. Admitting that rates of population growth could only be altered over a period, it was agreed that programmes to restrain population growth had to complement a massive development effort.

From the Third Plan, however, restraint of population growth received a much greater emphasis and priority, with time-bound targets for reducing the birth rate and heavy investment in the administrative network to mount the programmes on the lines of a military operation, and the adoption of practices like mass sterilization camps, financial incentives and appointment of promoters, to make sterilization acceptable to the people. The legalization of abortions in cases of contraceptive failure was also a step to promote reduction in the birth rate. Some State Governments even adopted measures to deny maternity benefits to Women Government Servants after the third child. We feel strongly about this measure, for the denial of maternity benefits to a working woman is likely to affect both the health of the mother as well as that of the child. In Madhya Pradesh, we met a group of women teachers who complained bitterly that this measure has resulted in a number of them having to work till the day before the child was born. We have already pointed out the results of the absence of this benefit to construction workers.

The result of this change in emphasis was to put excessive reliance on the clinical rather than the welfare approach to family planning. Heavy investment in services, personnel and propaganda, exclusively devoted to family planning, led to a relative neglect of the other health and welfare services. In the case of women, the maternity and child health services, family welfare, adult education, and economic progress, all suffered relative lack of attention and resources, and Family Planning came to be described as the most important governmental programme for women.

The Fifth Plan had changed the emphasis again, mainly in view of a growing realization that the programme is becoming increasingly unpopular among many sections, and is failing to achieve the unrealistic targets. It is also admitted that a purely clinical approach cannot overcome the socio-psychological resistance caused by poverty, ignorance, low survival rate of children among the poor sections, and the economic and social dependence on children.

Though integration of family planning with maternal and child health care was suggested in the Fourth Plan, the policy of integration could not be achieved, since the family planning services had been already placed under a different administrative machinery from the other health services. A new strategy evolved for the Fifth Plan visualizes the integration of family planning into the general health services, particularly its maternal and child care component including nutrition. The principle of integration will be extended to other fields, in particular to efforts at mass motivation through the existing channels for functional training programmes to train multipurpose health workers to deliver the integrated health care services under the Minimum Needs Programme. The impact of this decision to see family planning in its proper perspective is clearly visible in the allocation of resources proposed for the next Plan. According to the Draft Five-Year Plan:

> The primary objective during the Fifth Plan is to provide minimum public health facilities integrated with family planning and nutrition for vulnerable groups - children, pregnant women and lactating mothers. It will be necessary to consolidate past gains in the various fields of health, such as communicable diseases, medical education and provision of infrastructure in the rural areas.

During our tours we found that wherever the medical personnel and the village level workers were mature and sympathetic in their approach and worked with a sense of social commitment, their persuasive power evoked a great degree of response. On the other hand there was considerable criticism of the 'motivators', most of whom are very young and inexperienced as well as purely untrained persons. It was a frequent observation that they were responsible for criminal mistakes like persuading extremely young persons both male and female to undergo sterilization, or bringing elderly women who were long past the child bearing age for the same, entirely because of the financial incentives. According to Banerjee:

> Perhaps the greatest mistakes in the formulation of family planning programmes has been a gross overestimation of the effectiveness of the motivators and equally gross underestimation of the resistance to be encountered motivating a community as a whole.... Motivation techniques were viewed as some sort of a magic which would be applied by a person to induce another to accept family planning.

We understand that it has been decided to introduce community incentives and group awards for the programme personnel with a view to increasing the involvement of the community and strengthening the commitment of the staff and institutions in order to improve the quality of the services. Most of the doctors and the women with whom we discussed problems of family planning were of the opinion that while payment to acceptors should continue particularly for daily wage workers, the payment to motivators is not only a waste but has been responsible for much of the unpopularity of this programme. There were also severe criticisms of the lack of adequate follow-up measures. We also came across large gaps both in areas and communities where the family planning services have not reached. One group of women whom we met in Bangalore had never heard of family planning.

During the course of its tours in the States, the Committee met a number of health and family planning officials, social workers, as well as a cross-section of rural and urban women. An analysis of the tour reports reveals that the message of family planning has reached almost everywhere, but access to health and family planning services was most inadequate. Even in slum areas of big cities, there were no family planning clinics in the vicinity, and the women did not know where to go though they were anxious to avail themselves of the information. In the rural areas, there was an acute shortage of maternity facilities, and trained medical personnel.

In Bastar district, and in some tribal areas of Himachal Pradesh, we were informed that the birth rate is 29 per 1000, which is well below the national target for the Vth Plan, and yet we found money being spent on family planning projects in these areas. There were huge hoardings and posters advocating the small family norm, when this money could very well have been utilized for other welfare activities in these extremely backward areas.

In our view, the inadequacy of qualified medical personnel and mature counselling presents the greatest internal drawback to the success of this programme. We are entirely in agreement with the Draft Fifth Five-Year Plan, that integration of family planning with more positive health services like maternal and child health and nutrition, and improvement in the life expectancy of children and mothers, will provide a far greater incentive to the adoption of family planning measures than the hitherto adopted negative approach.

Programmes for Welfare

Programmes for women's welfare and development can be classified under the following broad base

A. Programmes in the rural areas: Welfare Extension Projects, Family and Child Welfare Projects, Organization of Mahila Mandals, Training Schemes for Workers.

B. Programmes in urban areas: Welfare Extension Projects, and Working Women's Hostels.

C. Other Programmes: Grants-in-aid to voluntary organizations, Condensed Courses of Education for Adult Women,

Adult Literacy and social education for women. Craft training centres, Socio-economic programmes, Nutrition Programmes, Social Defence Programmes, Border Area Programmes, Homes for Women.

Rural Areas: The concept of rural development as conceived in India covers a wide field and history. Both Mahatma Gandhi and Rabindranath Tagore had seen rural development as an important method of social mobilization which could build the social infrastructure for independence. According to Tagore, it was an effort to make the village a self-reliant and self-respectful unit, with knowledge of its culture and history and to enable the people to make use of modern resources for their full upliftment - physical, social, economic and intellectual. Gandhi viewed rural development as aiming to make every village a 'Republic', in which no person would be unemployed, and everyone would enjoy sufficient nutritious food, houses with adequate hygiene and sanitation, and enough khadi for their clothing. Thus, rural development was not seen only in its micro-dimension, but as a new philosophy for society, which was to bring social consciousness or a revolution among the rural people. Tagore's Shriniketan and Gandhi's Village Construction Programmes were the forerunners of rural development that was to be taken up by the government after independence. The Community Development Programme undertaken by the Government of India drew heavily from the Gandhian concept.

The application of Gandhian ideas to the field of women's development had been done by the Kasturba Memorial Trust after the death of Kasturba Gandhi, which had been given a concrete form in the objectives and activities of the Kasturba Memorial Trust. This Trust was born with the objective of serving rural women by providing: (i) education for women and children; (ii) medical and health services; and (iii) socio-economic programmes in the form of khadi and village industries to relieve economic distress.

The Trust trained a number of gramsevikas and mid-wives and the training centres were specially conceived to train and mobilize village women, specially widows and deserted wives. The health programmes aimed at prevention of diseases as well as promotion of positive health through maternal and child welfare programmes.

When the Central Social Welfare Board decided to launch the Welfare Extension Projects in 1954, this threefold approach was adopted as the basic framework for provision of services. The activities included Balwadis, maternity services and general medical aid, social education and craft training for women. The original Welfare Extension Projects (WEP) were to serve a unit of 25-40 contiguous villages, with a population of 25-30 thousand through five centres. At the end of the Second Plan, there were 420 such projects with 2004 centres. Eight of these projects, with 40 centres, continue to be operated by the Central Social Welfare Board, while others have either been closed or handed over to Mahila Mandals and voluntary organizations which receive 75 per cent financial assistance.

Since the general objectives and methodology of this programme were similar to those of the larger programmes of community development initiated by the government during the First Plan in 1952, and to eliminate duplication of work, it was decided that Welfare Extension Projects should be started in Community Development Blocks on a coordinated basis. All original Welfare Extension Projects were converted into this pattern as soon as the area was covered by a C.D. Block. These projects covered a block of 100 villages with a population of about 60,000 through 10 centres. The work and the functionaries were supervised by a Project Implementing Committee which consisted of representatives of block officials and local voluntary workers. For the first year the budget was shared by the Central Social Welfare Board, the State Government and Community Development Block in the ratio of 12:65 and at the end of 5 years the total expenditure was shared in the ratio of 24:12:5. Later, there were 264 projects with 2,800 centres.

Since greater importance was increasingly attached to the role of voluntary organizations in the continuance of welfare programmes, 1,629 centres of the Welfare Extension Projects (original and coordinated pattern) were handed over to Mahila Mandals. 442 Mahila Mandals, who have taken over one or more activities of this project were given a grant of Rs. 25.69 lakh.

On the recommendations of the Central Social Welfare Board and an Evaluation Committee of Social Welfare on the Welfare Extension Projects, it was decided to revise services existing in rural areas in different patterns aiming to develop a countrywide programme of integrated welfare services for children. Thus the Family and Child Welfare (F&CW) scheme was initiated, whereas extension projects provided services for women and children, the Family and Child Welfare Projects aimed at integrated development of the pre-school child, training to young mothers and all services that were necessary for the proper growth and development of the child and rural family.

The family and child welfare projects were funded by the Central and the State Governments in a 75:25 ratio and aided by UNICEF with equipment, stipends and training facilities. They have progressively taken over the functions of the earlier projects of the Central Social Welfare Board and the Ministry of Community Development. The services provided are; (a) Integrated services to rural children; specially preschool; (b) Basic training to women and young girls in home management, health education, nutrition education, child care. General health and maternity services for women were also to be provided with the aid of the Primary Health Centres. Similar collaboration was also envisaged for nutrition. (c) Assistance to women through Mahila Mandals, specially established centres and existing welfare agencies, for getting supplementary work to augment their income. (d) Cultural, educational and recreational activities for women and children.

Initially, there were 221 projects in existence and later, 20 coordinated welfare extension projects were added to this scheme, bringing the total to 240. On 31st March, 1973, 281 projects were functioning.

Maternity and Child Welfare Services: With the integration of the First Plan, Maternity and Child Welfare Services were taken up by the Ministry of Health as part of the overall development programme in health. These services were augmented by WHO and UNICEF. A number of Maternity and Child Welfare Bureaus were established in States, staffed by qualified women medical officers. At the same time, the then Community Projects administration also undertook these services in the Community Development and National Extension Service Blocks. Other Ministries like Railways, Defence and Labour also promoted Maternity and Child Welfare Programmes through the Ministry of Health. The number of Maternity and Child Welfare Centres increased and these services were given an important place in rural development programmes. The Union Government assisted the States in establishment of primary health centres and sub-centres covering a C.D. Block. At present 5,195 centres are functioning in the country. Maternity and Child Welfare Services are also undertaken by the Ministries of Railways, Labour (under Labour Welfare and the various Acts in this section) and public sector undertakings.

Mahila Mandals: Practically from the beginning it was realized that the objectives of these rural development programmes could not be achieved without the active participation and leadership of the local community. Government functionaries, however, efficient and dedicated, can only provide some stimulus and act as catalytic agents to train and release efforts for self-help of the people. This was particularly true of women who had been paralysed by generations of social oppression, and denial of basic rights. Both the Central Social Welfare Board and the department of Community development concluded that the proper agency for the success of this programme would be a committee of local women. The organization of Mahila Mandals thus became one of the objectives of these rural development programmes.

The declared objective of community development is to enable rural women to organize themselves at the village level to assemble on a regular basis to learn from each other and from workers appointed by the Government. The basic idea is to create opportunities for rural women to improve their status as housewives and to take part in public affairs. The department therefore organizes Mahila Mandals, imparts training facilities to their members and provides incentive awards for performance.

Mahila Mandals, were organized in villages and blocks for promoting women's programmes. Nutrition, education, health, mother and child care, home improvement, adult literacy, recreation and cultural activities and training and house and family planning were part of their programmes. There were about 53,000 Mahila. Mandals with a total membership of 14,00,000 averaging 11 Mahila Mandals per block. Under the Applied Nutrition Programme, additional facilities are being provided for the promotion of economic activities of Mahila Mandals towards, development and management of kitchen and school gardens, organization of fishery units, etc. During the Fourth Plan 7,500 awards in various categories were given to Mahila Mandals.

The Central Social Welfare Board and the State Social Welfare Advisory Boards also realized the importance of Mahila Mandals and now they are being given grants up to 75 per cent for running some programmes of the Board. Subsequently, 442 Mahila Mandals received a grant of about Rs 25.69 lakh. They are also running some Welfare Extension Projects of the Board.

Voluntary-agencies like the Bhartiya Grameen Mahila Sangh have also established a large number of Mahila Mandals. The representatives of the Village Mahila Mandals form the District Mahila Samities and the representatives of the District Mahila Samities constitute the State panel or State branches. According to the Bhartiya Grameen Mahila Sangh, its branches in the 17 States now cover 7,000 villages.

Training Scheme for Workers: The various functionaries required for these rural development schemes are trained at centres located in different parts of the country. The training is organized by some government agencies like the Directorate of Extension of the Ministry of Agriculture and various schools of social work, non-governmental organizations like the Kasturba Memorial Trust, Visva Bharati, Jamia Millia with assistance from the Central Social Welfare Board.

The Department of Community Development in the Ministry of Agriculture has a programme for training associate women workers to enable members of Mahila Mandals to come forward to become organized. The members of Mahila Mandals get to know about the organization of Balwadis, health and nutrition, education, nursery, kitchen gardening, etc. About 20,000 women received training in the Third and Fourth Plans and a sum of Rs 11.17 lakh was spent during the Fourth Plan.

The Directorate of Extension of the Ministry of Agriculture also provides training for village level workers of Community Development Block at 25 centres. The emphasis is on the protection of Agricultural production and nutrition education. In service, training facilities are provided after 2-3 years service and two week refresher courses are given to Mukhya Sevikas. Refresher courses are also given to Instructresses for Gram Sevika and Mukhya Sevika training centres for six weeks. Associate workers such as Gram Lakshmis or Gram Kakis are also given one month's training. Under the nutrition education scheme, training was given to associate women workers.

Farm Women's Training Courses for one week are organized at about 100 training centres for farm women. This farmers' training was started in a few districts and is now being implemented in almost all districts. The emphasis is on agricultural production, reproduction patterns of high yielding variety cereals, stock managements, nutrition, etc. Radio broadcasting is also used for educating the farm women and organizing discussion groups.

The Bhartiya Grameen Mahila Sangh also holds various training camps for rural women. Among these are leadership training camps sanctioned by the Department of Social Welfare in border areas. Similar programmes have also been sponsored by the CSWB. The increased agricultural production programme is a seven-day camp sanctioned by the Ministry of Food and Agriculture for training in improved agricultural methods and covered 650 villages. The Ministry of Health has sanctioned the family planning orientation programme to train village women in methods of family planning.

Urban Areas

The structure of welfare programmes in urban areas varies from region to region. The municipalities and local administration are responsible for providing basic formal education and health facilities like schools, hospitals, dispensaries, etc. Welfare programmes as such have already been left to voluntary organizations, which in some cases receive grants through the Central Social Welfare Board or the State Governments.

In 1958 the Central Social Welfare Board started Welfare Extension Projects in the urban areas to meet the needs of people living in the slums, particularly in new industrial areas. These projects provided balwadis, creches, arts and craft classes and family planning and maternity advice for women; they also do placement of destitutes. 65 such projects were in existence at the end of the Plan. They were reduced to 33. Later, Welfare Extension Projects received Rs 2.78 lakh benefiting approximately 70,000 families.

Working Women's Hostels: An increasing number of women are leaving their homes and entering employment. The problem of accommodation in metropolitan areas, particularly impelled the Central Social Welfare Board to provide grants for hostels for working women as one of its services. The Board viewed this service as a preventive measure against the possibility of young girls in urban areas being exposed to undesirable and anti-social influences.

The scheme was started during the Second Plan and the Board sanctioned grants to voluntary welfare institutions willing to provide healthy accommodation at reasonable rates for working women of lower income groups. At the end of the Plan, 101 grants amounting to Rs 9.76 lakh had been sanctioned. Later, 29 hostels received a grant of Rs 66,000 from the Board. The Department of Social Welfare initiated a scheme for financial assistance to voluntary institutions for the construction of hostel buildings in capital cities and cities with a population of over ten lakh. The pattern of assistance is under review at present and in the current Plan a sum of Rs 15 crore has been set aside for hostels for working women.

Other Programmes

Condensed Courses of Education for Adult Women: The very high percentage of illiteracy amongst women as well as various difficulties in imparting education to them gave rise to the condensed courses of education for adult women which are being implemented by various governmental and non-governmental agencies. The programme was initiated by the Central Social Welfare Board with the dual objective of opening new vistas of employment for needy women and to create a band of trained workers for various projects in the rural areas.

Under the scheme, adult women between the ages of 18 and 30, who have some schooling, are prepared for middle schools, matriculation or equivalent examination within a period of two years. Grants up to Rs 35,000 per course for two years are given for maintenance, stipends, salaries to teachers and educational equipment. Women who complete these courses can go in for vocational training as nurse, mid-wife, gramsevikas, etc. In the Second Plan Rs 58.82 lakh were-sanctioned for 271 courses, though only Rs 28.88 lakh was released. In the Third Plan, a provision of Rs 150 lakh was made for 500 courses. Up to the end of February 1973, 1,386 courses had been started and Rs 3 crore were spent. Of 33,000 women enrolled about 25,000 completed their studies. The programme has been extended to wives of Jawans killed or disabled in action. The Community Development Department also has established adult literacy centres in blocks which cover women.

Socio-Economic Programmes: It was realized at an early stage of the welfare programmes that they would not have the desired impact unless the women were imparted some craft or technical training. This was a part of the three pronged approach of the earliest programmes. While health received some attention and resources from the Ministry of Health, and Family Planning, as well as welfare agencies, the economic schemes did not receive corresponding attention from the concerned governmental agencies. On a very minor scale, some socio-economic schemes were initiated by the Central Social Welfare Board and its grants-in-aid schemes and also organized on a small scale by the Department of Community Development and some voluntary organization. Initially started by the Ministry of Rehabilitation for refugee women, it was taken up by the Central Social Welfare Board, to provide leisure time employment to women in lower income groups and help them supplement their income. This was undertaken in cooperation with the Ministry of Commerce and Industry which provides them necessary assistance in technical training, finance and marketing. The scheme was working in co-operation with State Governments and State Social Welfare Advisory Boards. 95 demonstration-cum-training centres, set up on 26 pilot projects for industries in the Community Development Project areas have benefited women.

At present the socio-economic programme of the CSWB provides financial assistance to voluntary welfare institutions and Co-operative Societies for setting up small production units where needy women or handicapped persons are given initial training and subsequently provided with employment. In the implementation of this programme, the Board as well as voluntary institutions and Cooperative Societies obtain technical assistance from the National-Small Industries Organization and regional offices of the All-India Handicrafts Board and All-India Handloom Board. The categories of the scheme that are being implemented under this programme are: (1) Production units of small-scale industries, such as manufacture of toys and articles, printing books, binding, fruit preservation and canning, bakery, confectionary, ready-made garments, etc. (2) Handicrafts training-cum-procurement and production units; for example, cane and bamboo articles, mat-weaving, traditional embroidery, etc. (3) Handloom training-cum-production units; (4) Units ancillary to large industries; and (5) Industrial co-operative societies set up under the voluntary welfare programmes started by the Board.

Up to the end of March 1972, the Board had approved grants to 130 institutions for setting up production units with an employment potential of about 4,000 under various categories of schemes. An amount of Rs 54.60 lakh had been sanctioned for 140 approved units with an employment potential of 4,235.

The Annual Report of the Central Social Welfare Board mentions that the attention of the State Governments have been drawn to the need for extending some sort of protection or patronage to socio-economic units run by voluntary institutions buying their products. The problem of marketing remains unsolved and unless this is overcome, the objective of a number of socio-economic programmes will remain unfulfilled. A number of Ministries such as Railways, Ministry of Labour, apart from the Ministry of Agriculture and Community Development have small schemes for providing craft training to women. The Mahila Samities of the Ministry of Railways have handicraft centres to help women in learning some trade to enable them to supplement the family income. Some public sector undertakings have Mahila Mandals which also provide such training. While the emphasis on these programmes to improve women's earning power indicates awareness of the dimension of women's problems, it is doubtful whether these programmes are having the desired impact, since most of these women are unable to obtain the raw-material or market the finished goods. It is also remarkable that the governmental agencies responsible for promoting industrial development have completely ignored the reality of the problem that they are trying to solve.

Nutrition Programmes: The Plan emphasized nutrition as a major problem particularly in rural areas, and among the lower income groups. The Department of Social Welfare and the Central Social Welfare Board, the Ministry of Health and Family Planning, the Department of Community Development of the Ministry of Agriculture and the Ministry of Education are all operating various nutrition schemes for women and children.

The Special Nutrition Programme of the Government of India was introduced in 1970-71 to provide supplementary nutrition to children in tribal areas and urban slums, by the Department of Social Welfare. This scheme covers a number of pre-school children in 0-6 age groups and nursing the expectant mothers. Over 19,600 feeding centres have been set up in the tribal areas and about 7,500 in urban areas. The Department of Social Welfare also implements a nutrition programme for children in the age group 3-5, through the Balwadis and day-care centres run by the CSWB, the Indian Council of Child Welfare, the Harijan Sevak Sangh, and the Adimjati Sevak Sangh, covering 2,00,640 children and 5,577 instructions. The Balwadis of the Family and Child Welfare Projects were generally excluded from this Programme because provision for nutrition was already provided in the scheme. The Board, however, feels that it has not been possible to build up adequate machinery for implementation and supervision of this programme at the State and Central levels and it requires greater provision by the Government.

The Directorate of Extension of the Ministry of Agriculture has been running a Composite Nutrition Programme since 1969-70, to provide nutrition education in areas not covered under the Applied Nutrition Programme. It includes nutrition education, through Mahila Mandals, strengthening the supervisory machinery for women's programmes, encouragement of economic activities of Mahila Mandals, training of associate women workers and demonstration feeding. The Applied Nutrition Programme of the Department of Community Development was introduced in collaboration with UNICEF, FAO and WHO. It was intended to educate the rural people in improved nutrition by promoting the production and consumption of protective foods like fruits, vegetables, fish and poultry. From 1966-67, steps were taken to coordinate the operation of the Applied Nutrition Programmes with other schemes like the Mid-Day Meal Programme of the Ministry of Education, and Family and Child Welfare Projects of the Department of Social Welfare. The ANP covered 221 blocks and it covered, 1,101 projects and spent Rs 1.46 crore for this purpose. Under this programme, demonstration, in cooking and feeding is held, particularly designed to give- direction on nutrition through the Mahila Mandals, and to train women workers.

The Ministry of Health has increasingly emphasized nutrition particularly for pregnant women, lactating mothers and pre-school children of the weaker sections, through an integrated programme of supplementary feeding, health care, immunization as well as nutrition education. Now, concentrated attention will be given to these vulnerable sections in rural areas, urban slums, tribal development blocks and school going children of the weaker sections. Within the resources allocated, it should be possible to cover about 11 million additional beneficiaries in the Plan. This programme is under the budgetary control of the Department of Social Welfare.

The Fourth Plan Special Nutrition Programme for pre-school children and expectant and nursing mothers has been redesignated and included in the Integrated Child Development Programme in the current Plan. The services include supplementary nutrition feeding, immunization, health check-up and referral services, health and nutrition education. The entire expenditure for the ICDP during the Fifth Plan will be made by the Centre and implemented through the State Governments and Union Territories. It is proposed to cover about 7,000 nursing and expectant mothers in each project. Women between 15-44 years numbering approximately 23,000 will be provided nutrition and health education. In the tribal areas 2,450 nursing and expectant mothers and 7,000 women in the 15-44 age groups are the target population for each project. The ICDP depends on interdepartmental coordination between the Ministry of Health, State Health Departments,

Community Development Department and the Department of Social Welfare. The existing 33,000 feeding centres of the Special Nutrition Programme and Balwadi nutrition programmes are in operation in organized slums, tribal areas and other rural areas. They will initially be included into ICDP centres in the project areas.

Social Defence Programmes: Among the services available in the country for the correction and reformation of persons who come into conflict with the law are the following which apply directly to women: (a) Suppression of Immoral Traffic; (b) After care services; and (c) Welfare Services in Prisons.

These services are provided by the Department of Social Welfare and Rehabilitation Directorate at Central level.

The Suppression of Immoral Traffic in Women and Girls Act of 1956 provides for protective homes and reception centres. There are at present 33 protective homes and 68 reception centres and district shelters in the country. A scheme for short stay homes for rehabilitation of women and girls facing moral danger was approved in 1969-70 and two pilot projects - one in West Bengal and the other in Madhya Pradesh were provided grants of Rs 1.10 lakh in 1972-73. During the Second Plan, programmes were drawn up under Social and Moral Hygiene and After Care Programmes not only for those under the SIT Act, but also those discharged from Correctional and non-Correctional Institutions. The State Governments were assisted to set up special homes such as protective homes.

We visited some of these protective homes. In the Protective Home in Lucknow and in the Nari Niketan in Delhi, efforts are made to rehabilitate the inmates by providing training in sewing and embroidery. There is no formal procedure for marketing of these products, nor are the inmates given any training either to organize production or marketing. We were informed that sewing machines are presented to the inmates when they are discharged to help them to become self-employed. This practice was reported to be prevalent in many States. According to reports by social workers in different parts of the country, most of these young women find it difficult to earn an adequate livelihood from this occupation. Quite a number are compelled to dispose of the machines, and revert to their original profession. We were rather distressed to find that these homes house women rescued from immoral traffic as well as young girls sent under the Children's Act. Even insane women are housed in these homes. We consider this to be a very unhealthy and undesirable situation. We also feel that the training provided for rehabilitation in these homes is not adequate and requires much greater attention and planning as well as resources. We were informed that in some of the homes, efforts are made to return these young women to their families wherever possible, or to arrange marriages for them.

There has been considerable discussion on these programmes for rehabilitation of victims of immoral traffic. During a recent Judicial Seminar on Correctional Services, the speakers, who included representatives of the Association for Social Health, the Director of Social Welfare, Delhi Administration and members of the staff of the Delhi School of Social Work, pointed out the inadequacy of the arrangements for the employment of these young women. Without economic rehabilitation, much of the efforts made for their rescue is wasted. Some social workers have suggested to us that the best way for rehabilitation would be to set up production-cum-marketing centres along with these homes. It is also necessary to diversify the types of training provided to the inmates, since over-dependence on tailoring and embroidery has led to considerable waste. Economic independence is the only way to protect these women from the clutches of persons who have a vested interest in this traffic.

Homes are also provided for the aged and destitute women in various States though the total number of such homes is inadequate in terms of the population to be covered. A scheme for the welfare of destitute women between the ages of 18-44 and 45-65 providing for basic amenities of food, shelter, clothing, besides education and training in craft to enable the younger group to become self-reliant, as also services for dependent children up to 7 years was finalized in 1970-71. For the first group, residential institutions to accommodate 200 persons were to be provided. The scheme was to be implemented by giving grants-in-aid to voluntary organizations up to 75 per cent of the expenditure. The total Fourth Plan provision was Rs 100 lakh. We regret to note that the scheme remains unimplemented.

Grants-in-aid: Grants-in-aid are extended to registered voluntary institutions working for welfare of women, children and handicapped persons. Under the grants-in-aid for women's welfare during the First and the Second Plans, assistance was provided for expansion, development and improvement of activities of voluntary organizations. On the basis of the recommendations of the grants-in-aid Committee, the Board decided to limit the assistance during the Third Plan to consolidate and improve the activities initiated during the First and the Second Plans. Generally all grants except those given for developing special schemes were given on a matching basis.

The amounts allocated to these schemes during the four Plans indicate that while the First and Second Plans brought in a number of voluntary institutions within the network for administration of welfare services, Government's dependence on these bodies has registered a decline during the Third and Fourth Plans.

Voluntary Organizations

Voluntary welfare services in India have always been an integral part of the cultural and social tradition. The bulk of the social services were provided by the voluntary sector prior to independence. Social welfare services have always been present in some form or the other for the well-being of the weaker sections of society who, because of various handicaps, social, economic, physical, etc., could not make use of, or were traditionally denied, normal facilities. The weaker sections included women, children, the aged, infirm and handicapped, Scheduled Castes and Scheduled Tribes.

Voluntary organizations may opt for several alternative roles according to their objectives and composition. They may be innovational and experimental activities in fields where government has not entered. They may co-exist with the public sector and the private sector for social development because they may have some advantages over the former or they can provide the government with a supportive base, i.e. they can work like agents of the government at local levels and operate programmes of the government as their own.

Soon after independence, on the basis of a survey made by the Planning Commission, it was estimated that there were about 10,000 voluntary organizations in the field of social welfare. In order to strengthen and encourage these agencies the Central Social Welfare Board was established in 1953, with a nationwide programme for grants-in-aid. It was realized that the voluntary organizations, with the qualities of flexibility, of experimentation, human touch, nearness to the clientele, sensitiveness to the new problems and capacity to discover new ideas could be of great assistance, since it was impossible for any government to take care of all the welfare needs of the people. The voluntary agencies could also mobilize resources from within the community for social welfare.

The relative importance of the role of the State and the role of the voluntary agencies has been engaging the attention of policy makers, planners, social thinkers, administrators and voluntary workers. In 1959, a Study team on Social Welfare and Backward Classes, appointed by the Planning Commission, recommended that whereas all programmes of social welfare arising out of the statutory responsibility of the State should be sponsored by State departments of Social Welfare, other social welfare services to meet local needs, should be implemented through voluntary organizations. A seminar on Social Administration in Developing Countries held in New Delhi in March, 1964, felt that the cooperation of the State and voluntary agencies in meeting social needs would always bring out better results in promoting welfare services on a larger scale.

We met representatives of some national voluntary organizations working for women's welfare and the welfare of socially deprived groups. We also met representatives of voluntary welfare organizations in every State during our tours. Most of the women's voluntary organizations have been confined to the urban areas, with its membership drawn mainly from educated urban middle-class women. Their main activities are conducting literacy classes, adult education centres, Balwadis, promoting women's cooperatives, small savings, handicrafts, etc. Some of these organizations have also taken up family planning programmes. In times of emergency, such organizations have organized canteens, blood banks and other services. These organizations seek to raise the status of women in the social, economic, political and educational fields. They have passed numerous resolutions for the uplift of Indian women, but their constructive activities have suffered from limitations of resources, personnel, and failure to reach rural areas.

Only a few organizations have endeavoured to work amongst rural women, to improve their living conditions, promote leadership and assist them to take part in developmental activities. The government has given grants for some voluntary welfare activities. In some cases, the grant has been for administration and maintenance while in other cases it has been allotted for programmes only.

Apart from the Central Social Welfare Board's grants-in-aid programme, there is no machinery to coordinate and distribute the services provided by these bodies, to ensure greater efficiency and even distribution. Nor are the resources of the majority of these organizations adequate to maintain trained workers for their complex types of work. Initially, the important organizations were able to act as pressure groups in directing the attention of the government to social problems, and to mobilize support for social legislation. Our investigation has shown that these laws still remain unknown to the large mass of Indian women, who have not been able to take advantage of them. Most of these organizations operate independent of each other and as such have not been able to fully benefit the community.

Governmental Administration of Welfare Programmes

Expenditure for welfare programmes, including programmes meant for women is low in comparison to other sectors, since it has been viewed as a non-productive item in comparison to the economic sectors. In times of stringencies, financial cuts are made first in this sector, since returns from investments are not immediate. A break-up of allocations indicates that a major part of the expenditure is on maintenance and establishment charges, leaving only a small percentage for actual services. The administrative tradition in India has tended to emphasize maintenance of law and order, and economic development, and departments dealing with welfare programmes generally occupy a relatively less important position in the governmental structure. The training imparted to the administrators also emphasizes the same aspects. It has now been realized that administration must also be welfare oriented and recently a working group has been set up to frame a syllabus for social administration for the training of service probationers at the National Academy of Administration and other State level training institutes.

The administration and handling of welfare programmes has become increasingly technical. Administrators have to acquire technical orientation for successful implementation of social welfare programmes. The lack of emphasis on the required technical competence and the limitation of resources have had an adverse impact on the quality and success of welfare programmes.

Certain factors impede realization of a high degree of rationality in organization and flexibility in operation. The federal nature of our policy vests responsibility for implementing social policy and programmes with State and local authorities, but resources and agencies for planning are at the Centre. The weakness of local authorities further complicates the problems. There is dire need for greater coordination between voluntary agencies and organizations built up by Government, between activities of States and the Central Government and of the district or local level organizations and the States.

State Level: At present the majority of the States have a Minister-in-charge of Social Welfare, though this portfolio might include other subjects. State governments give still lower priority to social welfare programmes, and are reluctant to allocate sufficient resources. It has also been found that in the operation of the democratic process, the interests of the weaker sections are sometimes neglected, as they are relatively less vocal and less powerful than the dominant section of the population. Due to existing social prejudice and attitudes towards women, any policy regarding their welfare and development is limited either to education or welfare of special groups like handicapped or destitute women. Therefore, though social welfare is a State subject, the major share of the State's allocations go towards the maintenance of the existing social welfare activities initiated generally by the Centre.

As an illustration, it may be mentioned that during Shri Charan Singh's tenure as Chief Minister in UP, all women's welfare programmes of the Government were summarily discontinued. The State Social Welfare (Advisory) Board was however allowed to continue because of strong representation from the State Finance Department that its abolition would result in stoppage of Central assistance. The closure provoked a protest from the women functionaries whose services were held up as a model to other States, because of their success. The result of the closure has left only skeletal services for women in the States.

Most State governments do not have any machinery for collection of data or planning of welfare services. The State Social Welfare (Advisory) Boards, which might have fulfilled this role, serve mainly as a link organization to supervise, implement and report on the working of aided voluntary organizations in the State as an agency of the Central Social Welfare Board. The relationship between Central and State Governments, the Central Social Welfare Board and the State governments are also not clearly defined and the status of the State Boards differ from State to State.

Local administrations have shown even less interest in women's welfare programmes in general and local bodies authorized to allocate resources have given very low priority to them. Everywhere we were told that the Mahila Mandals were being starved of funds and not being provided even with accommodation. The process of co-opting women into the Panchayats has also not been very successful as their small numbers have prevented them from being more effective in emphasizing the needs of women. As a rule, they have not had an effective voice in policy making or the allocation of resources. The male members of the rural elite, are by and large not favourably disposed towards improving and changing the position of women and consequently women's programmes are prone to be neglected.

Increase in Role of Centre

The neglect and indifference to welfare activities by the local and State Governments has led to an increase in the role of central agencies in this field. Within the federal framework the Central government's role should normally be planning, monitoring progress of activities, stimulating particular activities to ensure a national minimum standard, and guiding States through policy directions, giving advice and providing technical and financial help. The reasons for this increase in the role of the Centre can, therefore, be summed up as follows: (a)Limitation of resources of State Governments; (b)Indifference and low priorities for welfare programmes on the part of most State Governments; (c)Absence of proper welfare agencies in most of the States.

The experience of the Central Social Welfare Board suggests that the Coordination Committees as envisaged at the local level of some of the projects of the Board were not very useful since local administrations were not willing to take up women's welfare programmes. The State Boards were not in a position to function autonomously and the State Governments were disinterested in women's welfare programmes.

Under the system of financial relations between the Central and the State Governments, the Centre provides assistance for development programmes during a Plan period either on sharing or on full basis. At the end of the Plan period full responsibility for continuing the programmes devolves on the States. In the case of the women's programmes initiated by Central agencies, State Governments have not always been willing to accept the responsibility for continuation. In such cases, these programmes have had to be discontinued or re-designated as a new programme so that Central assistance could be continued.

Standardization of Programmes

The concept of a local need-based approach to social welfare has gradually been overshadowed as a direct consequence of this centralizing trend. Programmes and policies are initiated at the Centre, and there is increasing distance between the level of policy making and the levels of implementation. National programmes are framed without adequate reference to local variations and needs and this defeats the very purpose of social welfare. It particularly affects the initiative of the local community and the voluntary sector, and leads to increasing bureaucratization. It has also prevented the State Governments from admitting their responsibility in the field of welfare.

Because of this bureaucratization and centralization, the authority and initiative of the field staff is considerably impaired. As an example, the field staff at the State level are not taken into confidence nor are their suggestions considered at the level of policy and planning. For a number of schemes of the Central Social Welfare Board, the State Boards have little authority for initiating and reviewing the programmes.

The delays inherent in routine procedure and functioning of the Government hampers the progress of the programmes. Government organizations and procedures, with rigid rules governing sanctions and expenditure by their very nature, are not suited to the essentially informal and personal approach required for welfare work. Generally the approach of the voluntary workers and organizations is more flexible and personal. Once funds have been allotted for a particular project, they cannot be diverted for any other purpose and these agencies have to function within the rigid framework of the government sanction.

Lack of Coordination

An examination of welfare and development activities undertaken in the country so far indicates that there is a multiplicity of programmes, agencies and functionaries. A large number of these programmes have very similar objectives and functions.

These programmes are run by different departments, have separate allocations, and the field staff belongs to different agencies. Areas of implementation in many cases are not rationally demarcated. Since most of these are Central programmes, planning and policy making is carried out by separate Ministries and Departments at the Centre. There is very little or no coordination between these Ministries and Departments, except where a coordinated programme has been envisaged (as in the case of Integrated Child Development Programme). This leads to a waste of funds in the duplication of administrative machinery, leaving a relatively small amount for the actual implementation of the programmes.

There is very little coordination at the State level also. Even though the State Social Welfare Advisory Boards have some government officials as members, this has failed to ensure any substantial coordination of governmental effort in the welfare of women. At the project level, the functional committees and implementation committees are constituted with representatives of the State Governments and State Boards. They have to work in collaboration with the Panchayats or other local organization. The experience of these committees has not been always happy. Besides, their scope of activities is limited, only to the programmes of the Board.

There is little justification for the vast number of agencies for implementing welfare programmes with almost similar objectives. A division in administrative agencies can be justified on one of the three following grounds: (a) territorial distinction, i.e., each agency functioning in clearly demarcated territory; (b) methodological distinction, i.e., if the method of work has to be different; (c) functional distinction, i.e., if the objectives of the agency are such as to warrant a separate organization.

The present allocation of work amongst various agencies has followed no such principle of clear distinctions.

Central Social Welfare Board

As one of the most important agencies for the implementation of social welfare activities, the status of the Social Welfare Boards is currently under consideration. Though in practice the Board has enjoyed some autonomy, legally it has no independent existence. It was given the status of a charitable company in 1969 to meet audit objections in the way of giving grants. This has not solved its problems and its relationship with the Department of Social Welfare in regard to policy, planning and approval of programmes and financial allocations clearly indicates its status as a subordinate agency of the Department.

The justification for creating an agency outside the ministerial framework of the Government lay in the peculiar nature of welfare work, which required a flexible, personalized and committed approach, not easily possible within a government department because of procedural rules and regulations. The intention of the government was thus undoubtedly to create a specialized agency with its membership drawn from the ranks of social workers, with direct experience of voluntary welfare activities. Some other specialized agencies created by the government have been given statutory autonomous status. The unfortunate vagueness of the status of the Central Social Welfare Board, created administrative difficulties and led to its registration as a company in 1969. This arrangement has been admittedly unsatisfactory, and there is an increasing demand for a more autonomous status.

It may also be noted that at the time of the creation of the Central Social Welfare Board, the Government of India had no central department responsible for social welfare. With the establishment of the Department in 1966, and its increasing role in planning and execution of various welfare programmes, the Central Social Welfare Board's position has become still more anomalous. Uncertainty regarding its ultimate status and consequently of the State Boards has had a very adverse effect on their functioning.

At a Conference of State Ministers of Social Welfare held in July, 1992, recommendations were made for the reorganizations of the Central Board. This reorganization was dependent upon the adoption of a general enabling enactment. The State Governments, who had been advised to implement recommendations of this Conference with regard to the State Welfare Boards, were asked to defer action until the reorganization of the Central Social Welfare Board.

At a second Conference of the Social Welfare Ministers and Secretaries held in January 1974, discussion covered four major points. In regard to functions of the Central Social Welfare Board, it was decided that in addition to its executive functions, the Central Social Welfare Board should be responsible for the following: (a) To advise the government on the problems and provision of measures for the welfare of women, children and handicapped; (b) To promote investigation into the study of problems in specific areas, particularly those affecting women and children; (c) To arrange training for social workers at all levels for promoting the involvement of women in national activities; and (d) To provide technical guidance to voluntary organizations for effectively rendering welfare services.

In regard to the composition of the Central Social Welfare Board, the Conference urged that all the Governments of States and Union Territories by rotation, should be represented on the executive committee and the General Council of the Central Social

Welfare Board. In conformity with their demand for greater control over the State Boards, the States and Union Territories wanted a greater voice in the nomination of State Board members. With regard to relationship between the Central and State Social Welfare Boards, some States wanted them to be set up by State Governments, while others wished to register them as independent societies.

Difficulties Faced by Field Agencies: Because of the present variations in status and functions of these multiple agencies for welfare and development activity, the field staff experiences many difficulties. The procedure for the release of grants to a voluntary agency often takes about six months and a great deal of hardship is faced by the voluntary agencies whose meagre resources often do not permit continuation of the programme. The uncertainty felt by the staff seriously hampers their work. Many voluntary agencies informed us that they do not have trained workers to manage the accounts in the manner required by the government.

The ad hoc nature of the programmes, their frequent conversion under the various Plans, and the reluctance of State Governments to take over maintenance have also caused a great deal of uncertainty among the field staff. For example, in the case of the Family and Child Welfare Projects, at the end of the Fourth Plan period, 13 States and 3 Union Territories have agreed to accept the responsibility. Six States have not agreed and the continuation of 74 projects are now uncertain. It is proposed to absorb them in the Integrated Child Development Programme. The feeling of the Board in this matter is clear. "With more time, more projects could have been started in consultation with State Governments. The proposed change in the nomenclature and contents of the programme and transfer of all the programmes from the Board to the State Governments, without ensuring continuity by allowing sufficient time for the existing schemes to achieve their objectives, only tend to confuse the rural population."

The staff of the Central Social Welfare Board and the State

Boards are not considered on par with government employees and do not enjoy the same facilities and benefits. Their status at the field level is also temporary and dependent on the allocation for the year or the life of the projects. They have a feeling of uncertainty because of the temporary nature of their appointment which is dependent on the continuance of the scheme. They face a number of difficulties, particularly accommodation problems.

We met a large number of these field workers in various States. In our experience, the workers from voluntary organizations and the Board's staff have, on the whole, established better relationship with the village community, since they are better motivated and dedicated to welfare work, as compared to government functionaries who are more concerned with their service conditions, promotion, etc. The Board's cadre are more knowledgeable about the programmes in their areas and can give a better idea about the difficulties with regard to their implementation.

In recognition of this problem, the Department of Social Welfare has, recently examined the service conditions of the staff of the Board, and some of recommendations of the Third Pay Commission have been made applicable to employees of the CSWB. An officer on special duty was appointed by the CSWB in 1973 for drafting service regulations for its employees. The draft is now under examination by the Department of Social Welfare and is expected to be finalized in the near future.

Deficiencies of the Programme: While most programmes for women have emphasized acquisition of knowledge and skills to improve their efficiency as housewives and mothers, and to improve their earning power, they have neglected the dissemination of information, particularly regarding their rights and duties, which could increase their awareness and improve their participation as citizens. The objective of improving their earning power has also not been adequately fulfilled.

Role of Voluntary Agencies: Though it would be difficult to demarcate territories, the relationship of the voluntary and the Government sector should be all along complementary and mutually supportive. The present relationship between these two have not been very satisfactory and a number of complaints have been voiced on both the sides. Ideally the Voluntary Sector should provide services for implementation of welfare programmes, while the financial contribution should come from the Government. Further, the voluntary agencies have a surveillance role to play to see to what extent social legislation and the Government have contributed and can contribute to social welfare.

Voluntary organizations complain of lack of involvement with Government programmes since they are not consulted at the planning stage. Being totally outside the decision-making process, they have been reduced to the level of grant receiving agencies. Due to paucity of funds many voluntary agencies have come to rely heavily on the Government and in this process, the initiative and humanitarian impulse of voluntary welfare work has been considerably reduced. The basic concept of social work is that it should arise out of the local community needs. Voluntary agencies have repeatedly stressed that they should be equal partners with the Governments in the fields of welfare and accountable only for rendering proper accounts for grants. At the policy planning level, voluntary agencies desire that their experience and advice should be taken into account.

The voluntary agencies also express difficulties faced by them because of lack of training of their workers. Training facilities should be provided by the Government, if possible. Without technical and organizational competence, they are unable to utilize resources in the most productive manner. One of the representatives of a voluntary organization needed to review their organizational structure with a view to improving the managerial and professional competence of their workers.

The rising cost of living has reduced funds from private sources. It has also affected the ability of women to devote the same time and resources to voluntary work. Consequently, the area of constructive work of most of these voluntary agencies is limited to their neighbourhood.

The Conference of State Ministers and Secretaries of Social Welfare held in January 1974, earmarked the following programmes as of interest to voluntary organizations: (1) Socio-economic programmes organized broadly on a cooperative basis; (2) Condensed courses of education for adult women; (3) Functional literacy for women; and (4) Integrated Child Development Service Programme.

It was also agreed that the procedures and rules for making grants should be liberalized, and new ways found for raising and training voluntary workers, to ensure greater coordination amongst them and to improve the dialogue between governmental and non-governmental sectors at all levels, particularly at the district level. This can succeed only with a change in the approach to the voluntary sector.

SEVEN

By Way of Planning

Education for women and their development began mainly as a welfare oriented programme in the First Five-Year Plan (1951-56). The Central Social Welfare Board (CSWB), set up in 1953, undertook a number of welfare measures through the voluntary sector. The Second Five Year Plan (1956-61) organized women into Mahila Mandals to act as focal points at the grassroot levels for development of women. The Third, Fourth and other Interim Plans (1961-74) accorded high priority to education of women and introduced measures to improve maternal and child health services, including supplementary feeding for children and nursing mothers, etc.

The Fifth Plan (1974-78), saw a shift in the approach for women's development from 'welfare' to 'development' to cope up with several problems of the family and the role of women. The new approach aimed at an integration of welfare with development services.

The Sixth Five-Year Plan (1980-85), marked a landmark in the history of women's development by including a separate chapter and adopting a multidisciplinary approach with a three pronged thrust on health, education and employment.

In the Seventh Plan (1985-90), the development programmes for women continued with the major objective of raising their economic and social status to bring them into the mainstream of national development. A significant step in this direction was to identify/promote the 'beneficiary-oriented programmes' for women in different developmental sectors which extend direct benefits to women.

The Eighth Five-Year Plan (1992-97), which was launched in 1992, marked 'a shift from development to empowerment in approach to women development schemes. It promised to "ensure that the benefits of development from different sectors do not bypass women" and women must be enabled to function as equal partners and participants in the development process.

In the Approach Paper of Ninth Five-Year Plan (1997-2002), two major, steps towards gender justice have been taken for the first time in the history of planning. Their first is the listing of empowerment of women as a major plan objective. The other is to propose inclusion of a Women's Component Plan in the Plan of all Central Ministries/Departments and State Governments/Union Territory Administrations.

Policies Advocating Concerns

In addition to the women-specific and women-related policies enunciated in various Plan documents, the government has been creating an enabling environment in which women's concern can be reflected, articulated and redressed by the governments, the voluntary sector and the corporate world. As part of this effort, many policy instruments have been brought forth over the years, leading to Action Plans and programmes in several spheres. Some of the important policy-guiding documents include The National Plan of Action for Women, adopted in 1976, which became a guiding document for development of women till 1988, when a National Perspective Plan for Women was formulated. The National Perspective Plan for Women (1988-2000) drafted by a core-group of experts is more or less a long-term policy document advocating a holistic approach for development of women. Shram Shakti - the Report of the National Commission on Self-employed Women and Women in Informal Sector (1988) examines the entire gamut of issues facing women in unorganized sector and makes a number of recommendations for the betterment of women in the informal sector relating to employment, occupational hazards, legislative protection, training and skill development, entrepreneurship development, marketing and credit, etc. The National Expert Committee on Women Prisoners (1986) examined the condition of women prisoners in the criminal correctional justice system and made a series of recommendations relating to necessary legislative reforms, prison reforms and reforms of other custodial institutions and rehabilitation of prisoners insofar as women prisoners are concerned. The National Policy for Children adopted in 1974 considers children as country's supreme assets. Therefore, the State accepts their nurture as its own responsibility. Further, it also recognizes child development as an important step in building up human resources which are pivotal to the economic and social progress of the country. The National Nutritional Policy articulates nutritional consideration in all important policy instruments of Government and identifies short-term and long term measures necessary to improve the nutritional status of women, children and the country as a whole. The National Plan of Action for the Girl Child (1991-2000) is an integrated multi-sectoral decadal Plan of Action for ensuring survival, protection and development of children with a special gender sensitivity built for girl children and adolescent girls. In addition to these women specific policies, there are many more women-related policies, like National Health Policy (1983), National Policy on Education (1986), National Population Policy (1993), which have been influencing the welfare and development of women and children in the country. The National Policy for the Empowerment of Women has been drafted after nationwide consultations to enhance the status of women in all walks of life on a par with men and to actualize the constitutional guarantee of equality without discrimination on grounds of sex.

Impact of Plan, Policies and Programmes

The various developmental plans and programmes over four developmental decades (1951-1991) have brought about perceptible improvement in the socio-economic status of women in the country. Important achievements have been made in major thrust areas.

In the field of health, significant gains in respect of women's health status have been achieved. Expectancy of life for females at birth which was 31.6 years in 1951, was estimated to rise 59.7 years in 1989-93. The infant mortality rate for females declined from 131 in 1951 to 75 in 1993. Similarly, the sex differential, which was quite high in the 70s has now been bridged. However, the 0-4 age specific mortality rate, even though it has significantly declined from 55.1 in 1970 to 24.8 in 1993, continue to show higher female mortality. The maternal mortality rate in rural India still continues to be uncomfortably high at 324 per 1,00,000 live births although it showed a declining trend from 468 in 1980 to 324 in 1989 (Source: RG's Office, 1991).

Similarly, in the field of education, a number of steps were taken up for promoting women's education and equality in line with the National Policy of Education, 1986. The main strategy for education was a distinct orientation in favour of women's equality and empowerment. There is considerable improvement in female literacy as it came up to the present rate of 39.19 per cent from 8.9 per cent in 1951. The enrolment rate of girls in primary schools has also improved from 24.8 per cent in 1950-51 to 92.6 per cent in 1994-95. The drop-out rates amongst girls at primary level showed a continuous decline from 62.5 per cent in 1980-81 to 37.8 per cent in 1994-95. However, the higher decadal growth rate of female literacy (66 per cent) as compared to male literacy (43 per cent) provides some consolation.

In the field of employment, the female work participation (total workers) has grown from 19.7 per cent in 1981 to 22.3 per cent in 1991. This could be to some extent, due to the special efforts made by the nodal department of women and child development to capture women's work in the informal sector and, thus, remove their present invisibility. Similarly, number of women in the organized sector has also risen from 12.2 per cent (27.9 lakh) in 1981 to 15.4 per cent (42.3 lakh) in 1995, recording an increase of 51.6 per cent. Of the total 42.3 lakh women in the organized sector, public sector accounts for 61.5 per cent while the private sector accounts for 38.5 per cent.

Further, employment of women in the Central Government has also been rising steadily from year to year. Women's share has grown from 3.64 per cent in 1981 to 7.58 per cent in 1991 reflecting a change in women's participation in the government. At the senior and middle management levels, though limited at present, their participation has increased marginally from 875 in 1985 (based on the data related to 12 selected all India and their allied services) to 1,511 in 1995-96 (8.4 per cent). Women's participation in decision making in the government (taking the IAS, IPS and IFS services into account) has also increased from 379 in 1985 to 631 in 1996 showing an increase of 66 per cent over a period of 11 years.

Empowering Strategies and Governmental Interventions

Creation of Separate Nodal Agency-Department of Women and Child Development: The first step initiated by the government to strengthen the national mechanism and focus on women's development was the setting up of an exclusive Department of Women and Child Development (DWCD) under the Ministry of Human Resource Development in 1985 and designating the same as the national machinery for the advancement of women in India. The support structures of the national mechanism, as instituted over a period of time include the Central Social Welfare Board (CSWB), a charitable company registered under Section 25 of the Indian Companies Act, 1956 assisting both in promoting voluntary action and implementing programmes fully funded by the Department; the National Institute of Public Cooperation and Child Development (NIPCCD), a society registered under the Societies Registration Act, 1860 extending both research and manpower development services to the Department; the National Commission for Women (NCW), a statutory body set up in 1992 for safeguarding the rights of women; the Rashtriya Mahila Kosh (RMK), set up in March 1993 to extend credit to poor and assetless women through the intermediation of NGOs; the National Children's Fund to support projects of NGOs for Child Development/Welfare and the National Creche Fund to extend assistance to NGOs to open new creches.

In March 1997, Joint Committee of Parliament on Empowerment of Women has been set up with the functions of examining measures for women's equality and considering the reports of NCW, among others.

The Department, in its nodal capacity, formulates policies and programmes, enacts/amends legislations affecting women and coordinates the efforts of both governmental and NGOs working to improve the lot of women in the country. The programmes of the Department, which are women specific, include - employment and income generation, welfare and support services and gender sensitization and awareness generation programmes. These programmes play the role of being both supplementary and complementary to the other women related development programmes in the sectors of health, education, labour and employment, rural and urban development, etc., being implemented by different sectors. Some of the important on-going interventions of the Government of India are detailed below.

Women Development Corporations (WDCs)

In order to give the necessary thrust to development of women in the states, Women's Development Corporations (WDCs) were set up in 1986-87. The major objective of the scheme is to play the role of catalytic agents to create sustained income generating activities for women to provide better employment avenues for women so that they can become economically independent and self-reliant.

The functions of WDCs are to identify women entrepreneurs; to prepare a shelf of viable projects and provide technical consultancy services, to facilitate availability of credit through banks and other financial institutions (through the scheme of marginal money assistance); to promote and strengthen women's cooperatives and other organizations; and to arrange training of beneficiaries in concerned trades, project formulations, financial management, etc., through existing institutions, such as women's polytechnic and ITIs.

So far, such WDCs have been set up in Andhra Pradesh, Goa, Gujarat, Haryana, Himachal Pradesh, Jammu & Kashmir, Karnataka, Meghalaya, Orissa, Punjab, Tamil Nadu, Uttar Pradesh, West Bengal and Union Territory of Chandigarh. As per the decision of the National Development Council, in its meeting held in December 1991, the scheme stands transferred to the State sector in April 1992.

Rashtriya Mahila Kosh (RMK)

Rashtriya Mahila Kosh was set up as a registered society under the Registration of Societies Act, 1860 in March 1993 to meet credit needs of poor women, particularly in the informal sector, who have little or no access to formal credit institutions.

The policies and procedures for lending to women borrowers through the intermediation of NGOs and other women organizations like cooperative societies, WDCs, etc., for which suitable eligibility criteria, such as lending/credit management experience, sound financial management, etc., have been prescribed by the governing board of the RMK.

An amount of Rs 31 crore was released to the Kosh during 1992-93 as the corpus fund. Short-term loans and long-term loans per borrower are extended through the medium of NGOs, and other eligible organizations. Since inception, total sanctions of Rs 3,355-99 lakh have been issued to benefit 1,88,146 women through 154 agencies as on March 14,1997.

Mahila Samriddhi Yojana (MSY)

In pursuance of government's policy to empower women by raising their socio-economic status, an innovative MSY was launched on October 2,1993. The scheme aims at promoting self-reliance and a measure of economic independence among rural women by encouraging thrift.

The DWCD implements the scheme through 1.32 lakh rural post offices working under the department of posts.

MSY has received a very enthusiastic response from both rural and tribal women, including those living in the remote areas of the country. Since inception of the scheme, 2.46 crore women have opened accounts with a total deposit of Rs 265.10 crore, till March 1997.

Indira Mahila Yojana (IMY)

In order to coordinate programmes and facilitate their convergence to empower women IMY was launched as a strategy on August 20,1995. It proposes to bring out a mechanism by which there could be a systematic coordination and a meaningful integration of various programmes of different sectors to meet women's needs and to ensure that women's interests are taken care of and provided for under each scheme. This mechanism will be operated at the district level as a 'sub-plan' for women to percolate down to the village level appropriately through the Indira Mahila Kendras (IMKs) at village level and Indira Mahila Block Kendras (IMBKs) at Block level to be established as a registered society and supported by mechanisms at both State and Central levels. The ultimate objective of IMY is to empower women by ensuring their direct access to resources through a sustained process of mobilization and convergence of all the on going sectoral programmes. The IMY will be operated as a Centrally sponsored scheme.

The major objectives of IMY include: (1) to ensure convergence of sectoral service at the local, Block and district levels through active involvement of women and sectoral departments; (2) to optimise utilization of scarce resources in speeding up of process of mainstreaming of women in development; (3) to create awareness in women through provision of information on different developmental programmes and issues of specific concern to women; (4) to initiate a process of awareness generation/education to enable them to understand, and analyse their problems and find solutions through their collective interaction; and (5) to help women become self-reliant and independent by their economic empowerment through income generation activities and active participation in decision-making at various stages.

The IMY has three basic constituents, namely, convergence of inter-sectoral services; income generation activities; and sustained process of awareness generation/education. Under the proposed convergence of inter-sectoral services, IMY will provide the umbrella cover and all sectoral programmes aimed at women's welfare, including non-formal education, training, formal primary education, skill development, health, family welfare programmes and other minimum needs programmes like drinking water, sanitation, housing, roads, electrification, etc., would converge at the village level as per the needs, demands and requirements articulated by the IMK. Income generation activities include creation of employment opportunities through group dynamics and participation in a broad range of economic activities suited to the local requirements and use of thrift and credit services to expand the income-generating activities. Under a sustained process of awareness generation/education, IMY seeks to create a general awareness among women through ensuring information specific to equality of social status, legal rights, like those to property and inheritance, constitutional safeguards and on different development, programmes/ issues of concern to women.

In addition to amount of Rs 5,000 given by the Government of India to the corpus fund of the IMK, each member of the IMK shall contribute Rs five as membership fee and will continue to contribute Re one per month to the Kendra. Such nominal contribution by each member will create a corpus of fund and ensure their effective and continuous participation in the group activities. The corpus so formed will be used as a revolving fund for small credit requirements of the individual members and send money wherever necessary, and for expenditure on holding of awareness generation camps and any other activity resulting in furtherance of the cause of IMY.

The IMY has been taken up in 200 Blocks of the country, on a pilot basis and will be extended in the subsequent years. Selection of these Blocks will be decided by the States keeping in mind the need to ensure maximum convergence of services; care will be taken to ensure that the Blocks are compact and not dispersed over, a number of districts. The IMY will initially be sanctioned for a period of seven years starting from 1995-96. The number of IMBs registered is 113 and the functional Indira Mahila Group (IMG) is 13,717, till March, 1997.

Special Thrust on Employment and Training

In line with the Eighth Plan strategy, the nodal DWCD has reset its priorities to accord special emphasis on employment and income-generation activities for women. The ultimate objective in all these efforts is to make women economically empowered and self-reliant. For this purpose, the Department implements some programmes directly through voluntary organizations and interacts with other departments/ministries to ensure flow of benefits to women through their programmes.

Support to Training and Employment Programme (STEP)

The STEP scheme launched in 1987, aims to upgrade the skills of poor and assetless women, mobilize, conscientize, provide training, and subsequently employment on a sustainable basis in the traditional sectors of agriculture, animal husbandry, fisheries, handlooms, handicrafts, sericulture, social forestry, wasteland development, etc., in addition to the training and employment support, the programme advocates gender sensitization, women in development (WID) inputs and provision of support services.

Since inception of the programme 61 projects benefiting 3.32 lakh women, have been launched in various states. Dairying, handlooms, handicrafts and sericulture have been some important areas, since inception of the scheme till March 1997, it has provided employment opportunities for 3.32 lakh women with a total expenditure of Rs 94.13 crore. In 1996-97, 12 projects to benefit

76,875 women were sanctioned with a total expenditure of Rs.17.00 crore.

Training-cum-Employment-cum-Production Centres

The second major programme of Training and Employment, which is commonly known as 'NORAD assisted Training Programme for Women', extends financial assistance to public sector undertakings/corporations/autonomous bodies/voluntary organizations to train women in non-traditional trades, like electronics, electricals, watch assembly and manufacturing, computer programming, printing and binding, handlooms, garment making, weaving and spinning, hotel management, fashion technology and beauty culture, tourism, bakeries/confectionery and office management, etc.

During the Eighth Plan, an expenditure of Rs 38.28 crore has been incurred benefiting 79,797 women. Since inception in 1983, 1,10,002 women benefited with training for employment. In 1996-97, 275 projects to benefit 50,000 women/girls were sanctioned with a total expenditure of Rs 19 crore.

In the recent past, there was a progressive shift and increased attention on the most upcoming modern trades, like computer operation, electrical appliances, bakery and confectioneries, fashion technology, beauty culture, ANM training, canteen and hotel management, tourism, etc. This programme not only plays a preventive role in keeping the young and adolescent girls away from early marriages but also keeps them gainfully engaged with economic independence and self-reliance.

Condensed Courses of Education and Vocational Training (CCE&VT)

The CCE&VT scheme, in operation since 1968, has been revised from time to time to provide educational qualifications and relevant skills to needy women so that they become eligible for identifiable remunerative work opportunities.

Under these programmes, voluntary organizations are given grants to conduct courses of two to three years duration for women of the age-group of 15 and above for passing primary/middle/ matric and secondary level examinations. Under the Vocational Training Programme, grants are given to impart training to needy women of 15 years age-group in different vocations leading to wage/self-employment. Under these programmes, 5823 courses have been sanctioned during the Eighth Five-Year. Plan and a sum of Rs, 39.07 crore was sanctioned to benefit about one lakh women. In 1996-97, 598 courses were sanctioned with the total expenditure of Rs five crore.

Socio-economic programme, Welfare and Support Services

The Central Social Welfare Board had started the socio-economic programme (SEP) in 1958. Under this programme, financial assistance is extended to voluntary organizations to undertake a wide variety of income-generating activities providing opportunities of 'Work and Wage' to needy women, like widows, destitutes, disabled, etc., particularly those coming from economically backward and underdeveloped areas for setting up industrial units, handlooms and handicraft units, dairy units, and other allied economic activities like piggery, sheep and goat rearing, poultry, etc.

During the Eighth Five-Year Plan (1992-97), an amount of Rs 30.33 crore has been released to 2,457 units to benefit about 20,100 women in 1996-97, 13 units have been sanctioned with the total expenditure of Rs six crore.

The national machinery has spread a wide network for women and large number of welfare and support services for women and children belonging to lower economic strata through voluntary organizations. These support services represent an important plank for empowerment of women as they reduce the burden of child care and employment related problems, as detailed below.

Support Services

Hostels for Working Women: In order to promote greater mobility for women in the employment market, the Department launched a scheme of hostels for working women in 1973 to provide 'safe and cheap' accommodation to single working women who come to the cities/towns for the sake of employment. Under this scheme, financial assistance is provided to the extent of 50 per cent of the cost of land and 75 per cent of the cost of construction of the hostel building to voluntary organizations. Assistance is also extended towards purchase of ready-built buildings. Besides, voluntary organizations, public trusts, local bodies, women development corporations, universities, schools/colleges of social work also are eligible for financial assistance programme. Working women, whose consolidated income does not exceed Rs 5,000 per month, are eligible for accommodation. A resident is allowed to stay in the hostel for a maximum period of five years. Till now 805 hostels with attached day-care centres have been sanctioned to be constructed all over the country to benefit about 56,195 working women and their dependent children numbering about 7,558. In 1996-97, 28 hostels were sanctioned to benefit 3,122 women/girls with the expenditure of Rs 8.25 crore.

Creches for Working/Ailing Mother's Children: The Central Scheme of creches for working/ailing mother's children is under implementation since 1975-76. The scheme is implemented through voluntary organizations. The scheme envisages day-care services for children of the age group of 0-5 years. Service includes health care, supplementary nutrition, sleeping facilities, immunization and play and recreation for the children. The creche workers are employed to look after the children. The scheme of running of creches is being implemented by the Central Social Welfare Board through voluntary social welfare organizations and by two other national level voluntary organizations, viz., Indian Council for Child Welfare and Bhartiya Adimjati Sevak Sangh, all over the country. There are 12,470 creches in action all over the country benefiting 3.12 lakh children. Because of paucity of funds, the scheme has not been expanding and is stagnating at this number since 1988-89. In 1996-97, a total amount of Rs.19.75 crore has been sanctioned. In view of the increasing number of working women even in small towns and rural areas, there is a need for mobilizing the community to provide services of creches on a self-sustaining basis without financial burden on governments, etc.

Short Stay Homes for Women and Girls (SSH): The SSH scheme for women and girls, launched in 1969, extends temporary shelter and rehabilitation to those women and girls who are in social and moral danger due to family problems, mental strains, social ostracism, exploitation or other causes. The services extended in these homes include medical care, psychiatric treatment, case-work services, occupational therapy, educational-cum-vocational training, recreational facilities, etc. Under the scheme, grants are given to voluntary organizations to run short stay homes in various parts of the country. As per the approved schematic budget, each SSH receives an annual grant of Re 1,87,300 towards recurring expenses and Rs 25,000 as one time grant to meet the non-recurring expenditure.

National Creche Fund (NCF): The NCF was set up on March 21,1994 with a corpus fund of Rs 19.90 crore made available out of the Social Safety Net Adjustment Credit of World Bank to meet the growing requirement of opening more creche centres. The scheme envisages that 75 per cent of the centres to be assisted by the Creche Fund would be general creches and 25 per cent centres would be Anganwadi-cum-creche centres. The general creches assisted by the Fund would be on the pattern of the Creche Scheme of the Department of Women and Child Development and would provide children below five years, services which would include day-care facilities, supplementary nutrition, immunization, medical and health care and recreation. Children of parents whose monthly income does not exceed Rs 1,800 are eligible for enrolment. The voluntary organizations/ Mahila Mandals selected for opening the creches are required to open creches in schools or in places close to schools, in rural areas and urban slum areas dominated by SCs/STs. The creches have a maximum of 25 children and normally work for eight hours a day. The voluntary organizations/Mahila

Mandals are encouraged to involve the community in the implementation of the scheme so that the creches become self-supporting.

Gender Sensitization and Awareness Generation

Great deal of importance is attached to efforts which, trigger changes in societal attitudes towards women. An integrated media campaign projecting a positive image of both women and the girl child through media and film is the most important component of the governments communication strategy. A large number of TV spots, quickies, documentary films, radio programmes with positive messages about the girl child and women, have been produced by the department to undertake publicity and coverage.

Gender Sensitization: The Women's Development Division (WDD) of the NIPCCD, New Delhi organizes training programmes with a focus on gender issues under the DANIDA Bridging Arrangement as well as its regular activities. These training programmes were organized at national, regional and state levels. Some of the important programmes include para legal training; training of elected women representative of Panchayats; leadership of organization, training of voluntary agencies reaching women; awareness and gender sensitization programmes; incorporation of gender issues in development programmes, etc. The participants of these programmes include government officials, representatives of voluntary agencies, academic and technical institutions.

Under legal literacy, para legal training programmes were organized by the WDD in collaboration with these agencies working for women's emancipation. The major objective of these training programmes were to sensitize the participants about the constitutional, political and legal provisions relating to rights of women; to inform participants about legal structure and procedures; to create awareness about existing support schemes of government and non-governmental agencies and to conscientize them about the scope of rights, their potential to act as pressure groups, to access the entitlements of women. These programmes were organized in West Bengal, Delhi, Himachal Pradesh, Bihar and Haryana.

In the field of training for Panchayat members, training programmes were organized for women elected representatives of Panchayats in Orissa, Karnataka and Madhya Pradesh. About 300 elected women members were trained. The main objectives of these training programmes were to sensitize the leadership qualities among elected women members, to enable them to understand the structure, function and responsibilities of Panchayats and make them aware about various development programmes implemented at the grass roots level.

Besides, the WDD also organized training programmes on leadership and organization of grass roots level women, incorporating gender concerns in Prime Minister's Rozgar Yojana, courses for superintendents of remand homes/jails on custodial justice to women and children sensitization programmes for law enforcement machinery, media campaign on pilot project on gender issues in credit and support services, orientation training programmes for police personnel on atrocities against women, issues and interventions, consultation on women in human settlement development, awareness generation on constitutional and legal rights for women, consultation on violence against women, etc.

Awareness, Generation Projects for Rural and Poor: The programmes of Awareness Generation Projects was introduced in 1987-88. It aims at identifying the needs of rural and poor women and generating awareness among them of their status in the family and society and to activate them to work for achieving their rights and to deal with social issues, like community health and hygiene, technology application and environment, etc. The camps organized under the programme provide a platform for rural poor women to come together, exchange their views and ideas and in the process develop an understanding of their problems and come out with ways to tackle them.

Prevention of Atrocities

The programme of Education Work for Prevention of Atrocities Against Women, started in 1982, extends financial assistance to research and academic institutions like universities, colleges/ women's study centres and institutions of higher learning etc., and voluntary organizations for various items of education work, propaganda, publicity and research work such as production of publicity materials, research studies on particular aspects of violence/ atrocities against women; awards for best films, short stories, poems and other creative efforts, etc. Dissemination of information/publicity materials in regional languages is also envisaged under this programme. The focus is on those women who are subjected to deprivation, brutality, extortion and exploitation.

Integrated Child Development Services (ICDS)

The ICDS - gift to millions of children and mothers living in the most backward rural, tribal areas and urban slums all over the country - aims at improving nutritional and health status of preschool children, expectant and nursing mothers and adolescent girls through a package of services, viz., supplementary nutrition, immunization, health checkup, referral services, treatment of minor illnesses, pre-school education and nutrition and health education. Started in 1975-76, with 33 projects, the scheme has expanded gradually and reached, by June 30, 1997 to 5,614 ICDS projects by covering 3,663 Community Development Blocks and 260 major urban slums. Of the 5,614 projects, 3,397 are under Central sector projects and the rest of the 510 projects (including 316 TINP projects) are in the state sector. These projects benefit around 198.44 lakh (19.84 million) children and 35.37 lakh (3.54 million) mothers/ women.

Of the total 5,614 ICDS projects, around 1000 projects located in Andhra Pradesh, Bihar, Madhya Pradesh and Orissa are receiving assistance from World Bank to enrich the services with innovative activities.

It is proposed to universalize ICDS at the earliest to cover all Child Development Blocks/urban slums. Of these, 500 Blocks/slums are being taken during the current year, while the balance of over 1400 Child Development Blocks/slums are proposed to be covered during 1996-97 or in future years depending on the resource position and capacity of the States to operationalize the new Blocks.

Scheme for Adolescent Girls

For the first time in India, a special intervention has been devised for adolescent girls using the ICDS infrastructure. The scheme of adolescent girls focuses on school drop-out girls in the age group of 11-18 years and attempts to meet the special needs of nutrition, education, literacy, recreational and skill development of adolescent girls. It attempts to make the adolescent girl a better future mother and tap her potential as a social animator. The scheme for adolescent girls has been sanctioned in 507 Child Development Blocks and, when fully operationalised, would benefit about 4.50 lakh girls.

Special Initiatives

National Commission for Women: In January, 1991, the government constituted a statutory body called National Commission for Women (NCW) with a specific mandate to study and monitor all matters relating to the constitutional and legal safeguards provided for women; review the existing legislation to suggest amendments wherever necessary; and to look into complaints involving deprivation of the rights of women. Similar Commissions have also been set up in nine States. The NCW has taken up a number of activities which include (a) Setting up of 11 expert committees to tender advice on various women's issues; (b) conducting Pariwarik Lok Adalats, to which nearly 35,000 cases were referred; (c) Complaints and Pre-litigation Cell; (d) Legal awareness; (e) Welfare of women prisoners under trials; and (f) Action on issues of women and children.

Legal Literacy Manuals: Ten legal literacy manuals were brought out in 1992 to educate women about the laws concerning their basic rights. These manuals have been written in a simple and illustrated format so that even semi-literates and neoliterates are able to comprehend them. They cover a wide range of subjects, namely, laws relating to working women, child labour, contract labour, adoption and maintenance, Hindu, Muslim and Christian Marriage Laws, including right to property, dowry, rape, kidnapping and police procedure. The manuals have been distributed to State governments and NGOs for wider dissemination and are being translated into many of the Indian languages.

The National Plan of Action of Children (1992) and The National Plan of Action for the Girl Child (1991-2000 AD): The two Plans of Action are both integrated and multi-sectoral in their approach to ensure survival, protection and development, of children with an ultimate objective of building up a better future for children. While the Girl Child - being an integral part of the total target group of children - is expected to derive full benefits from the general Plan of Action, her gender-specific needs will be taken care of by the Plan of Action for the Girl Child with a focus on the adolescent girls.

National Resource Centre for Women: Government is also finalizing a proposal to set-up the National Resource Centre for Women and three State Resource Centres for Women which will act as an apex body for promoting and incorporating gender perspectives in policies and programmes of the government. A pilot project to test the concepts and methodologies underlying the National Resource Centre has been successfully implemented.

For the first time in the history of demographic records, an attempt was made to capture women's work in the informal sector in 1991 census. The provisional data of 1991 census on 'Workers and their Distribution', has shown that there was a substantial increase in the female work participation during 1991 census compared to that of 1981.

Reservation for Benefits for Women Under Poverty Alleviation Programme: Under various poverty alleviation programmes of rural development sector, 40 per cent of benefits have been reserved for women belonging to the below poverty line groups (families whose annual income is about Rs 6,000 to Rs 11,000).

Reservation for Women in Grassroots Democracy: The (73rd and 74th) Constitutional Amendment Bills passed in 1992 by the Parliament marks a holistic event in the lives of Indian women as amendments ensure one-third of total seats (33.3 per cent for women in all elected offices in local bodies whether in rural or urban areas). As a result of this, women have been brought to the centre-stage in the nation's efforts to strengthen democratic institutions at the grassroots level. About 0.8 million have emerged as leaders/decision makers at grassroots levels and entered into public life through the existing 0.23 million all over the country. Of these, about 76,200 are at the village, Block and district levels.

Training in Leadership Development: A massive country-wide training programme was launched in 1993 to extend leadership training for eight lakh women Panchayat members/chairpersons, emerging as a result of the elections to Panchayats and urban local bodies since 1993 when the 73rd and 74th Constitutional Amendment Acts came into force.

Voluntary Action: India has a rich tradition of selfless voluntary action. While the governmental interventions in this sector are operationalized largely through NGOs, the initiatives that the latter have themselves developed are rich and diverse. These efforts have often demonstrated success of alternative models of empowerment and development. Whether it is in the field of credit of poor women or women's health or women's awareness generation or women's literacy, or participatory rural appraisal involving women or organizing women's self-employment groups in traditional and non-traditional sectors of the economy. The Central Social Welfare Board, which is an apex agency of voluntary organizations at national level promotes voluntary action and community participation through its country-wide network of more than 12,000 Voluntary organizations at the grassroots level. Besides these, there are many more voluntary organizations working at block/ district/ state levels in the field of women and child development.

Future Approach

Holistic Development: The major approach for the future will be to bring in holistic approach for women's development. This underscores harmonization of various efforts in different fronts - social, economic, legal, political and cultural. This calls for consolidation of various programmes and efforts in different sectors of the Government and their integration in a logical fashion to converge various services and facilities required by women. A Sub-Plan approach to package all relevant resources and benefits for women's development will be laid down to ensure their systematic focus on women.

The over-arching strategy component for women's development in the Ninth Plan will comprise mobilization and convergence orchestrated by women's groups and supported by Panchayati Raj institutions. The organization of women will by itself empower them and provide them a forum for articulating their needs and contributing their perspectives to development. This will also give them experience in participatory decision making, thereby building up a cadre of grass root leaders, capable of effective participation in institutions of local government.

This capacity building has to start in the womb, without any deprivation, for the mother of the child, particularly the girl child. Her survival, protection and development as identified in the National Plan of Action for the Girl Child (1992) has to echo through all sectoral programmes. Access-to education, health, information and resources are, therefore, the vital areas of concern, that need to be effectively addressed in future to attain many of the goals for the next millennium.

The thrust in the future has to be on identifying traditional sectors of employment that are shrinking due to technology changes or market shifts, and retrain the women to take up jobs in the new and expanding areas of employment.

The provision of support services is another critical input that can greatly improve women's enhanced economic participation. Promoting women's labour market mobility through an expanding network of working women's hostels, the provision of toilet facilities for women in places of work and widespread provision of creches for working parents are essential if women are to derive maximum benefits from the economic liberalization process.

Areas of Priority

Keeping in view the aforementioned experiences, the following specific programmes could be considered for adoption in the future: (i) Expansion of education and training among women; (ii) EDP training; (iii) Provision of child-care support facilities for men and women workers so that either parent can avail of this facility at the work-place and not make it a cost on women's employment; (iv) Provision of hostel and residential facilities to enable women take up employment away from home; (v) Special employment and placement services which should seek to promote employment of women in non-conventional sectors through dissemination of information, counselling, etc.; (vi) Legal protection and legal aid services, (vii) Promotion of women workers organizations through voluntary effort; (viii Protection against flexibility. Considering the new trend towards economic liberalization such protection cannot be ensured through statutory means and should, therefore, be attempted, through negotiations and collective effort. The State, the employers as well as the workers must have separate layers of protection against loss of employment, (ix) Introduction of flexitime, multi-entry, conducive personnel policy on leave, transfer and promotion and training opportunities, to help women retain their jobs or move to new and higher areas of work, (x) Conducive credit policy to access credit to women through appropriate organizational and institutional mechanisms including self-help groups, and (xi) Improvement of the bargaining strength of women workers by encouraging their participation in trade-unions.

Separate Mahila Plan Component

The DWCD has recently launched the IMY which is intended primarily to mobilize the women around an integrated delivery system. IMY is a major step towards participation of women in the planning and development processes of their areas. It is also a mechanism that can establish a system of coordination and integration of the sectoral activities. In order to put the need perceptions and the sequential priorities of these women into the Sub-Plans, women would be organized into groups and empowered to participate in the planning process. A sub-plan, consisting of the women's components, would emerge through an interactive process of discussions at the district, block and Panchayat/local levels.

Different developmental schemes and programmes already have quantified components of SCP and TSP. In a like manner, these schemes and programmes could also have a "Mahila Plan" component. It will therefore, be helpful if all Central Plan schemes/ programmes, Centrally sponsored schemes/programme, State plan schemes/ programmes and non-plan schemes/ programmes identify a Mahila Plan component, with both physical targets and financial outlays. For plan schemes/programmes, such a component should exist for both the Annual and Five-Year Plans.

The basic approach to women's development and empowerment should continue to be based on the theme of convergence, i.e. convergence of the development programmes of different departments of the government to target women through a single delivery system as well as convergence of the efforts of both the government functionaries and community or NGOs in achieving a common objective.

New Targets for Empowerment

This Women's Day there was reason to rejoice. The Ninth Plan draft document has said that 'empowerment of women' is one of its prime objectives. While this is significant, what is also important is the sub-Plan that was evolved in the run-up to the preparation of the Plan, the fact that a think tank of women was set up to evolve a document that spelt out the specific demands of women in the country. Way back in 1974, the report of the Commission on the Status of Women had called for a sub-Plan, one that would address gender inequities but it was not taken seriously. So while some attempts were made in subsequent Plans to give women a place in the developmental process, it tended to be sectoral and haphazard.

The think tank, comprising academicians, activists and researchers held consultations with the Planning Commission, the Department of Women and Child Development, various ministries and women all over the country. The focus was on building consensus with a view to understanding what women wanted and what is perhaps even more important on what was working and what was not.

The concerns voiced were varied, but the key ones were the right to information about changes, opportunities, options, schemes, services and technologies, the gender sensitization of government functionaries particularly the police and the local administration in the areas of health, agriculture and animal husbandry, and the right to work and employment guarantee schemes.

Liberalization, it was pointed out, is here to stay but women were losing out and will continue to lose out because they have neither the skills nor the legal safeguards to be included.

Other important demands were gender analysis and gender audit of all plans, policies and programmes, the elimination of violence against women and girls through the strengthening of institutional capacity and legal provisions and the decentralization of democracy so that decisions can be taken at levels that are ipso facto more accessible to women.

Happily, if one is to go by the Ninth Plan draft, there is a veritable sea change in Plan perspectives. Until now women's development, to quote the document, was primarily 'welfare oriented'. The focus was always on health, nutrition, education and in the early nineties, on training for employment. Demands that they be recognized as participants in development made little headway. The approach was patronizing and chauvinistic.

The draft is therefore significant promising, as it does, "to create an enabling environment where women can freely exercise their rights within and outside homes as equal partners along with men". It goes on to add that "this will be realized through the early finalization of the 'National Policy for the Empowerment of Women, which lays down definite goals for targets and policy prescriptions along with a well-defined Gender Development index to monitor the impact of its implementation in raising the status of women from time to time. Also significant is the fact that the Ninth Plan directs both the Centre and the States to adopt the 'women's component plan' through which no less than 30 'per cent of funds and benefits are earmarked to the women related sector.

To quote Madhu Dandavate, Deputy Chairperson of the Planning Commission "Women have moved from 'footnote' to an 'objective' in the Ninth Plan" but a lot more will have to be done to ensure that policies are evolved along the lines of the Plan initiatives. Perhaps, as Anita Anand, a member of the think tank suggests, an autonomous body on the lines of the National Organisation of Women in the USA should be set up. Bandhs and dharnas will no longer suffice and a much more sophisticated approach is required in which people with expertise in policy analysis and advocacy will lobby for change. In fact, it must work in tandem with the Planning Commission to ensure the economic and political empowerment of women and gender sensitizing of issues.

The tendency all along has been to direct jobs, resources, political positions, credit et. al., to men especially in the macro sector. The assumption was that the benefits would percolate down to the women and children but, in actual fact, it has only further marginalized them. Panchayati Raj will of course go a long way in remedying these aberrations. Since the passing of the 72nd and 73rd amendments four years ago, almost a million women have come into local politics and in Haryana and Kerala there are all women Panchayats. But, the issues raised by them at the grass roots level will have little success if women's representation in the upper echelons of democracy remains low. Studies conducted in the US on disparities between the blacks and whites have shown how important it is to have a 33 per cent reservation. Anything below this has proved to be ineffective. This is why it is absolutely imperative that the 81st Amendment Bill providing for 33 per cent reservation for women is reintroduced and passed in near future.

EIGHT

Education after Independence

In addition to education, modern methods of production, marketing and planning call for a higher level of knowledge and those skills that are required by a traditional economy. The increasing complexity and interrelationship among production, investment and the process of competitive selection, increases the importance of education and dissemination of information.

Though educational opportunities did expand in the post-Independence period, it was relatively slower among women, particularly at the primary and secondary levels. The rate of expansion was much faster at the level of higher education, and was the virtual monopoly of the middle-class. In the case of women, both secondary and higher education was practically confined to the urban middle-class. On the other hand, the number of illiterates, who remained outside the reach of the educational system also increased the women outnumbering the men. This pattern of educational development, coupled with the changes in the economy, has, inevitably affected the economic opportunities of women.

The work participation rate by educational level shows that while employment opportunities for educated women have increased, there has been a negative trend in the participation rate of illiterate and semi-literate women, whose share in employment has declined.

During 1981-91 the participation rate for illiterate women had declined substantially from 71.1 per cent to 55.3 per cent in urban areas, but showed marginal variations in rural areas. As pointed out in section II B and III A, the employment of women has declined significantly both in unorganized nonagricultural occupations and in organized industry. Our review indicates that there is a large-scale displacement of illiterate and semiliterate women workers from organized industry and non-agricultural occupations in the unorganised sector. This is also evident from the fact that the drop has been more marked in the urban areas. A superficial conclusion that could be drawn from this data, is that the decline in the numbers of illiterate or semi-literate women workers, indicates a rising level of education.

The pattern of women's educational development in the years since independence, however, indicates that it has failed to penetrate, in any significant manner, the large mass of illiterate adult women, whose numbers have increased over the years. Since they also come from the poorest section of the population, where employment is a dire necessity, this change in the composition of the women workforce has to be regarded as, an indicator of the displacement of this section of women from the workforce, a consequence of the changing levels of technology, and methods of business organization. The increase in the participation rate of the technical diploma holders from 0.6 per cent to 2.3 per cent, indicates the growing demand for modern technical skills in new industries like electronics, pharmaceuticals, electricals, etc., and in new services for technical personnel. The distribution of degree holders and technical female personnel by labour-force status and level of education indicates that the majority of them were employees and only 2.1 per cent being self-employed.

Among the educated women, the worker rates for women who have received a technical degree and diploma (mainly in teaching and medicine) were substantially higher than those who had received non-technical degree or diplomas or had studied up to the Higher Secondary level. The differential according to fields of specialization of technical degree and diploma holders are smaller among males than among females. The distribution of women degree holders and technical personnel by sector of employment show that 58 per cent are employed in the public sector, 36.6 per cent in the private sector and 5.4 per cent are selfemployed.

The extent to which persons of different educational levels undertake productive roles in the economy is an indicator of the nature of utilization of the investment in their education. Women with degree or diploma in medicine and teaching generally pursue a career. The differential participation rate between such women and their male counterparts in not more than 20 per cent.

The rising participation rate of educated women is also witnessed by the Employment Exchange statistics. Since 1963 the number of female job seekers with matriculation as well as higher education on the live Register has increased more rapidly than for males. Between 1964-68 the number of female job seekers registered with Employment Exchange increased by about 81 per cent while that of male job seekers increased by only 14 per cent. For matriculates and higher educated job seekers the corresponding increases were 72 per cent and 116 per cent for males and females respectively (Visaria, 1971). In 1973 the percentage increase of women work seekers over the previous year was 25.7 per cent for those with qualification below middle school, 39 per cent for matriculates and undergraduates and 95.4 per cent for graduates and postgraduates. This phenomenon assumes importance in view of the relatively rapid spread of women's education in urban India and the paucity of employment opportunities. Taking different subject fields together, the average duration of unemployment is higher for women than for men.

According to the Census of 2001, the average waiting period for a male graduate before getting employment was 9.9 months as against 11.6 months for a woman graduate. The only exception to this is the field of medicine and nursing where the average waiting period for men with postgraduate qualification and with doctorate is higher than for women. This sometimes acts as a strong deterrent for many a woman without specialization from seeking employment.

The total stock of degree holders and technical personnel by subject field, level of education and sex, and the distribution of degree holders and technical personnel who were found unemployed, was obtained by CSIR on individual enumeration slip in 2001. The study revealed that out of 7 lakh women degree holders only two and a half lakh were employed which is only 5 per cent of the total working women in the country. Of these employed women, 52 per cent earned less than Rs. 1000 and 20 per cent earned between Rs. 1000 and Rs. 2000. Of total number of unemployed women graduates only 160,000 women were seeking jobs and the largest number of this component were holding degree -in Arts and Humanities and the next were those holding degrees in Science. Of the women who were not seeking employment, 65 per cent had degrees in Arts and humanities, 60 per cent in Science, 20 per cent in technical or engineering and 10 per cent in vocational courses.

Dilemma of Idleness among Educated Women

The paradox of women's employment is that while illiteracy drives many out of employment, education does not necessarily lead to their employment.

> That participation ratios are not higher has at least as much to do with considerations of status and prestige as with the absence of jobs for those who seek but cannot find them. It is of course conceivable that a more progressive and expanding society could elevate the position of women and change attitudes towards female work. But an economy whose capacity to absorb men of working age is strained, does not encourage the elimination of traditional forms of discriminations against economic activity by women. G. Myrdal (Asian Drama).

Idleness can both be voluntary and involuntary. Since our labour market does not provide full, productive and freely chosen employment and jobs are at a premium, many women prefer to avoid the competitive pressures. Utilization of labour in any society depends to a certain extent on social institutions, taboos and inhibitions related to status and work which affect women more than men. These attitudes are reflected in social institutions, and the relationship between institutions and attitudes is mutually reinforcing.

The development of education has been mainly confined to middle-class families, among whom the attitude to women's employment outside the home had been most restrictive. This attitude however has been changing rapidly under economic pressure and the changing social scene. The real difficulty lies in the failure of the economy to absorb all its labour power and to appreciate the need for an institutionalized pattern of labour utilization that takes note of women's roles as housewives and mothers. So far, in spite of occasional lip service to the idealised image of women in these roles, little attempt has been made to assess its productive value. Still less attention has been given to providing the necessary infrastructure to remove women's disabilities in the labour market. Education alone cannot remove these disabilities.

Vocational and Technical Training

The need to relate education and particularly vocational training to actual employment opportunities has been repeatedly emphasized by various expert bodies like the ILO, the National Commission on Labour, the All-India Council for Technical Education, the Institute of Applied Manpower Research and the University Grants Commission, Committee on Coordination of University Education with Manpower Requirements.

In view of the current social prejudices against employment of women and their large-scale displacement from employment as a result of structural and technological changes taking place in the economy, vocational training for women requires special attention and priority. This has been emphasized by the International Labour Conference in 1965 and the UN Commission on the Status of Women in each of its reports. In India, the National Committee on

Women's Education, had pleaded strongly for better and more extensive facilities for vocational training for women particularly since the general educational system paid little regard to the needs of industry and commerce.

The inadequacy of vocational training opportunities for women, widens the productivity gap between men and women at all levels and makes them unwanted by the economy. Training facilities when they are provided, display the existing social bias regarding the suitability of particular occupations for women which leads to over concentration in a limited group of subjects.

Our examination of opportunities for vocational and technical education for women is based on the following: (a) on the job training; (b) pre-employment training—technical and professional; (c) training programmes undertaken by different Government Departments and Voluntary Organizations for developing skills and human resources. We have not included professional training at the university level because, as will be discussed in the next chapter, there is no real evidence of discrimination or any substantial wastage of training at this level.

On the Job Training

The major factor limiting women's contribution to the modern industrial sector is lack of adequate opportunities for on the job training. We have already pointed out that women have been greater victims of rationalization and modernization in industry. Some of the new industries like electronics, simple engineering, telecommunications, etc., provided in-service-training to women with comparatively higher educational qualifications. In spite of opportunities provided by these few industries, however, the disparity in opportunities available to men and women is glaring. Under the Apprentices Act, 1961, 161 trades with 87,000 places have been located for apprentices in 101 industries. 52,500 apprentices have actually been engaged against these places of which only 104 are women. The bias for confining women trainees to limited group of trades is clearly visible.

Representatives of trade unions informed us that the training provided to workers for handling new machinery in different industries, seldom extends to women except in the few specific industries like machine tools, telecommunications and electronics in which women's greater aptitude for particular operation has already been recognized.

Pre-employment Training

In the non-engineering trades where women constitute 64.6 per cent of the total number of trainees, the most popular, trades are cutting and tailoring, embroidery and needle work, knitting, and stenography. Of these, the first two are completely monopolized by women even in co-educational institutions. The situation is very different in the engineering trades where they form a mere 2.7 per cent of the total trainees. The most popular courses are for draftsman, instrument, mechanics, radio and T.V. mechanics, electronics, surveyors, carpenters and painters.

On the recommendation of the National Committee on Women's Education, the Ministry of Education took up a scheme to establish women polytechnics for post-matriculation training in various skills in industrial, commercial and public service occupations in accordance with developing needs of the national economy and to promote awareness of new opportunities and needs for women workers in such fields as social welfare, nursing, chemical and pharmaceutical industries, etc., in which women could be gainfully employed'. The total admission capacity of all these polytechnics is over 3000 for courses which require 2 to 3 years for completion. According to the Ministry of Education in commercial practice, stenography, catering and food technology, the admissions exceed the sanctioned capacity, while in other trades they fall short of the available number of seats. The out-turn for all the courses is considerably lower than the admissions. The total out-turn during 2000 amounted to only 1820 against an admission figure of 4500. This points to both wastage of available facilities as well as a failure in the realization of the objectives of this scheme. In the absence of inadequate assistance in placement, quite a few women on completion of these courses remain unemployed. The second reason for this is that the courses are not designed with any particular consideration for the employment potential of the locality. For example, during the Committee's tour of Andhra Pradesh we were informed by officials of the Industries Department that though there was an increasing demand for women in the telecommunication and electronic industries, none of the women's polytechnics in the State were providing training in these subjects. On our asking why nothing has been done, the officials replied that the control of polytechnics rested with the Department of Education and not industries. In Himachal Pradesh we received a number of requests from women's groups for training in food technology so that the products of their orchards are not wasted but no training facilities of this type exist in that State. Courses introduced are not always in relation to the demands of the region, e.g., dress and costume designing, a significant avenue for employment of women in bigger cities, hardly constitutes an important or a significant source of employment in the interior of the country. A heavy concentration on the same course, e.g., tailoring, also leads to minimization of job opportunities.

In 1968-69 the All India Council for Technical Education had reviewed the functioning of women's polytechnics and came to the conclusion:

1. A direct relationship should be established between course of training provided and employment opportunities available. For this purpose, for each polytechnic, there should be an advisory Committee including representative of employing organizations. Before any new course is started, close consultation should be held with the prospective employers to determine available job opportunities.

2. Each polytechnic should establish a production centre in the relevant field to provide practical training and improve standards and content of the courses. Such production centres might be started with the assistance of small-scale industries departments of the State concerned.

3. Polytechnics should offer short term job-oriented courses in selected fields where employment opportunities exist.

4. Start an employment advisory service for its students.

5. Service units should be established in these institutions to cater to the needs of the local public in such matters as providing practical, services blueprints, model estimates, etc.

Earlier 75 per cent of the non-recurring expenditure and 75 per cent of the recurring expenditure was borne by the Central Government. Since the commencement of the 4th Plan the Central Government stopped direct financial assistance for implementing specific development programme and now it is for the State Government to implement these recommendations.

Unfortunately while the Ministry of Education supplied information regarding the list of sanctioned courses and admission capacity in each of the 24 polytechnics, we were unable to obtain actual information regarding the teaching facilities available in the different institutions. Unofficially information received from different sources suggests that in many of the institutions some of the courses exist only on paper, particularly since the stoppage of central grants. Many of the State Governments find it difficult to provide adequate support to these institutions for their general maintenance. This could account for the very poor number of admissions against the courses for the country as whole. The second reason is the failure to implement the recommendations of the All India Council for Technical Education regarding the opening of production centres and provision of employment advisory service. Technical training for women is a relatively new field in India. In the absence of greater assistance in the placement of successful trainees, parents will be reluctant to send them to these institutions.

It is to be noted that some private institutions providing similar types of training to young women in the large cities, including a placement services, which connect training to the actual employment potential of the area, have proved to be highly successful. Mention may be made here of two institutions in Delhi. The Secretarial Training School, started by the Young Women's Christian Association some years ago has proved to be so successful as to justify its expansion to other types of vocational courses during the last few years. A similar unit started by St. Thomas Girls Higher Secondary School has also expanded rapidly, and is attracting students with even university degrees. Their success lies in their placement assistance and in the liaison that they maintain with employing agencies.

In the present socio-economic set up, self-employment of women requires much more than training in a particular productive trade. Without knowledge of the market mechanism, and capital resources, training alone cannot help women to face the competition. The production centres recommended by the All India Council for Technical Education as a part of polytechnic training have remained conspicuous by their absence. In our view, without supportive assistance in the way of training in organization of production and marketing and in procuring capital and raw materials, it will not be possible for the majority of these young trainees to utilize their training in self-employment.

The officials of the Industries Department in Andhra Pradesh informed us that in spite of the existence of a Government scheme to provide financial assistance for generating self-employment, the Department has been unable to assist many women to obtain the required help from banks. Even when such projects are sanctioned by Government, banks hesitate to provide the loans as they feel that the life of the projects may terminate when these young women get married.

Training Programmes Undertaken by Different Agencies in Charge of Development

Unlike the more formal programmes of pre-employment training, in the sphere of informal training programmes, a great deal of emphasis has been given to training women by various agencies in charge of development and welfare. All agencies specifically concerned with women's welfare and development, both government and voluntary, have always attached the highest priority to improving women's earning capacity.

Training Schemes to Improve the Earning Capacity of Women

Programmes have been developed to solve the economic needs of women hard pressed by the processes of social change and break-down of familiar obligations to support needy women widows, deserted and aged women as well as women from lower income groups.

(i) The Central Social Welfare Board is the most important agency providing assistance for these programmes operated by autonomous and voluntary organizations. It provides financial assistance for setting up production units in small-scale industries, handicrafts and ancillary units for larger industrial undertakings. In 1999-2000, 54 handicraft units were functioning with an employment potential of 2000. Apart from this, 31 handloom training-cum-production centres are being assisted by the Board. Some training centres have also been set up in association with the All-India Handicrafts Board. There are 30 institutions running production units for handlooms under this programme in various States with an employment potential of 1900. According to information available, a total of 240 units are in existence under this programme providing employment to 7500 workers.

(ii) Training of development cadres: Under the insistence of various developmental agencies, particularly the Central Social Welfare Board, training courses have been developed for village level workers (Gramsevikas, Gramlakshis, Mukhya Sevikas, Balsevikas, etc., by agencies like the Kasturba Memorial Trust, Visva Bharati, Jamia Milia and various schools of social work. They are mostly pre-service or in-service training for these cadres, fully financed by Government.

(iii) The programmes by the Kasturba Memorial Trust, Visva Bharati and Jamia Milia, have displayed considerable innovative acumen in developing new types of cadres for working in rural areas.

(iv) The Indian Council for Child Welfare also runs 45 centres in different parts of the country for pre-service and in-service training for Bal-sevikas. The training is financed by the Government.

(v) The Ministry of Health has training programmes for Health Visitors and auxiliary nurse midwife for developing health services in both rural and urban areas.

The Ministry of Food and Agriculture has also organized 43 community canning and food preservation centres. There are four institutes of catering technology and applied nutrition in the country. Though not exclusively for women, they train some women. Under the co-ordinated programme for community development, training is given in selected productive activities like kitchen-gardening, poultry keeping, dairy science, etc.

The Ministry of Home Affairs has a scheme for training of women and children of Central Government employees belonging to the low income groups. There are 80 centres under this scheme. Training is provided in cutting, tailoring and embroidery. Students are recommended as private candidates for the diploma courses of the Industrial Training Institutes. Some home employment is provided to these women through Government contracts.

Similar programmes have been initiated in few of the States by the Department of Welfare, Labour, Industry and Education for training mainly in sewing, embroidery, handicrafts and tailoring.

We visited a number of these training centres. In our view, much of these well-meant efforts end in futility, because they are not linked to production and marketing. The bias for traditional or home crafts limits their scope since the indigenous markets for these products are now on the decline, and marketing, both internal and for export, is mainly in the hands of intermediaries. Strangely even the Government Emporiums are also dealing through middlemen and do not buy directly through the production centres, even though the latter are financed by Government. Even without these handicaps, the scope of the programmes are so limited that they can only make a marginal impact on the employment needs of women. Another difficulty lies in the multiplicity of agencies engaged in this work, leading often to duplication and overconcentration in a few areas, leaving the large areas of the country completely untouched.

It is unfortunate that though the training programmes developed by welfare and other developing agencies have shown greater understanding of the employment needs of women, their efforts suffer from lack of adequate resources and coordination.

PART — FOUR

Prospects

NINE

Fruits of Education

In today's World, a modern educated women suffers from various tensions. If she is a housewife she feels stressed because her education has not incurred her any relief from domestic chores. If she is working woman she is stressed because of lack of co-ordination between her home and office life. This chapter identifies stresses typical to the modern educated woman and offers some suggestions for dealing with them.

The ambivalence that women feel as they take on dual roles of housewife and worker is quite tension producing. Undoubtedly, many women are able to combine both roles with smooth adjustments, particularly if the husband and the family members are co-operative and supportive. However, in many families, the conflict between both the roles has created estrangement between either the husband or the wife or the wife and the other members of the family.

We have in the previous chapters traced the psychology of the Indian women in terms of her desire for domination and her will for subordination. The large number of women who have traditional outlook are meeting with their tensions and stresses by overtly subordinating themselves to men and covertly trying to dominate them by their extreme devotion and sense of duty. The modern emancipated women are revolting against this duplicity. They are denying the superiority of the male and seeking an equality between the sexes overtly and covertly both. We have also advocated that through our educational system the women should learn to move towards equality of sexes without involving themselves in any duplicity in their behaviour pattern. But the danger in such a move is the enhancement of tensions and stresses in the individuals, in the families and also in the society.

Ambitious men of lower income group want their wives and daughters to work and earn to help raise the family's standard of living. At the same time these men cannot tolerate the idea of independence such as that they themselves have on the job. They are unable to free themselves from the myths of Sita and Savitri. They become agitated when their women become assertive and begin to express their personal views and opinions and their likes and dislikes. They feel that women are transgressing their freedom, which they have so generously bestowed on them. Their ego is hurt if their wife's income exceeds their own Income. But the women when they go out for work cannot be bound in the chains of orthodoxy. Hence the modern woman's tensions enhance as she has to cope with the demands of her job and the dictates of her male relations.

In a study by Mukta Mittal on "Educated Women Power," it was found that the need for supplementing the family income was the chief motivating factor for encouraging the respondents belonging to "lowly educated" and "moderately educated" groups to become job seekers and get themselves registered at the Employment Exchange Bureaus. But in the case of "highly educated" respondents, the prime motivating factor behind encouraging them in their becoming registrants for job was "desire to be free from dependence on family members and relatives".

Many a Conflict

Many conflicts arise when both husband and wife are working. The husband desires that the wife should take up job but disapproves the complete involvement of the wife in the job. For him the job of the wife is only a secondary commitment. Her primary duty he feels is towards him and his family. He wants his wife to work and also to take up full time duties of looking after the household. When the wife is unable to cope with this situation the seeds of conflict and estrangement between the husband and wife begin to germinate. After returning from her work the wife is tired but she receives no sympathy or help from her husband or in-laws. When the tensions so created become unbearable the wife has no option but to resign from the job. But this is also not liked by the husband who resents the loss of income and blames the wife for not being able to reconcile between her job outside and her duties to her family.

The tension reduction in such cases is possible when all the family members recognise that the household work is to be shared and is a joint responsibility of all the members of the family. In those families in which the joint responsibility is recognised the tensions are suitably dealt with.

Till nearly three decades earlier the women were giving utmost importance to the role of the housewife. In a study by Cora Vreede Stuer in 1970 it was reported that quite a substantial number of girls "consider the role of the housewife as the most suitable." But when they were asked that if they had to go outside the home to work, most of them said they would prefer to teach or do social work. One girl in Cora's study remarked: "I would be willing to work in my field, but if my husband opposed it, I would submit to his wishes." Similar views were expressed by 18 of 15 educated women in Rama Mehta's study of the Western Educated Hindu women in 1970. One woman in her study expressed this view: 'Working was not important enough for me to go against my husband's wishes. After marriage, one cannot do as one wants, working is not an important enough issue to create tensions". It may be noted that till seventies or may be later also the working women, generally, perceived their main role as that of wife or mother. By such an attitude they were meeting with their tensions created by their becoming working women. But the situation at the end of the twentieth century is not as simple as that. The aspirations and the motivations of the women have increased manifolds and so also there is increase in their stresses and tensions.

Society now has a more favourable attitude towards the employment of women in the middle income groups. It has become an economic need. Promilla Kapur in her study in seventies took a sample of 300 working women from three major occupations — teachers, office workers and doctors. She observed that because of society's change of attitude, as well as change in attitudes of the educated married women towards their own employment, their number has multiplied to the extent that they now constitute a class by themselves. This class is facing the greatest change and, challenge ever offered anywhere in the world to the feminine population.

The number of women seeking jobs has increased manifolds now from that of seventies. The challenges before them have also become quite serious. The educated women have first to face the spectre of unemployment. The job market is very tight. It is difficult for men to get the jobs and when women also compete with them the number of the job seekers becomes quite high. With the limited job opportunities the women also suffer from the various types of restrictions which are put on them by the society. They still search the jobs, which are considered feminine in nature like the teaching, or nursing or office work, etc. They also want a job in the town or place to which they belong. They do not opt for the jobs in the villages or remote areas. It is not only due to the intention of the women that they do not want to work at the distant places from their homes but also due to the living conditions. It is difficult for a single working woman to find a decent living place in most of the towns or big cities. The security environment in the country is also not such as the women may move very freely. The cases of eve teasing are on the increase and the single working woman becomes an easy prey of unscrupulous males.

The women's problems are three-fold with regard to getting employment. First of all, they have to compete in an overcrowded job market. Secondly, their families and society do not allow them to serve in those professions, which are branded as predominantly masculine in nature, even though there may be no restriction from the side of the employing authorities. Thirdly, they have the problem of finding suitable living accommodation if they get a job away from their homes or native place and added to this is the problem of security for a single working woman. All these problems are stress producing in the educated women. But it may be said that the stresses of the women can be reduced if they themselves and the society approach towards the solution of the problems with some dedication. There is no doubt in it that the number of jobs has to be increased. More efforts should be made to educate the women to generate self-employment. They may also be given vocational training. A change is to be brought in their own attitudes and the attitudes of the society and the family that it is a myth that the women are incapable of taking up some jobs which are masculine in nature. The women are capable of taking up all those jobs, which are considered masculine. In previous pages we have forcefully built the case of sexual equality on the basis of the physiology of the male and the female. Lastly, the government and the society must come forward to build "Working Women's Homes." In some towns they have been built. The need is to have a chain of such homes in each town and township.

There is another type of conflict with which the working women suffer. This is in relation to their work environment. The working women rightly demand that they should be accepted and respected as equally capable and efficient workers as males. The conflict occurs when they simultaneously demand special privileges and advantages because they are the women and the weaker sex. For example, they take up jobs that require night duties but after taking the job they may claim that since they are ladies they may be exempted from working in the night. They may press the employer to transfer them to some daytime job and transfer some male to this job. This becomes a conflict-producing situation. Some women also shirk work claiming that they are women and so entitled for light work. To avoid such conflicts the women need to develop professional attitude. There are many examples of successful women.

There is another side of the picture as well. The men resent the working women in their midst. In an office in which men and women both work the men do not feel as free with the women as with their men colleagues. If male becomes too intimate gossips are unleashed. If he ignores them he is branded as the chauvinistic male. There seems to be a need to develop a code of ethics for interpersonal relationships in those situations in which the males and females have to work in close co-ordination.

A Serious Situation

A very serious situation is developing in some places of work where the boss is male and he tries to sexually exploit his female employees. The women organizations, the government and even the courts are seized with this problem. Some women take the courage to make complaints about this behaviour of their officers or male colleague but there are lots of women who silently suffer at the hands of office sharks. Sometimes men also become victims of women's manipulations. They make false complaints about their exploitation so that the persons concerned are defamed. It is because of this danger that the complaints of women regarding exploitation are being scrutinized cautiously. Such situations can be avoided in case men and women both are made to realise that there shall be no discrimination in the work situations on the basis of sex. Both men and women must view each other as equal partners in work performance and must expect that recognition shall depend on their efficiency and quality of work and not on their sex.

As has already been pointed out that greatest danger resulting from a woman being career oriented is disharmony within her family. In Kapur's study of much marital maladjustment, the husband expected the wife to work as well as serve him and the household. The husbands generally believed in absolute supremacy over their wives and desire complete surrender and devotion from them. Those women who asserted their individuality were severely punished and ruthlessly treated, In cases where women could not tolerate the brutalities, they were separated from their spouses.

If the husband demands that his wife quit work and she refuses, it creates much tension in the family. In those cases in which the husband is transferred and the wife refuses to quit her job and go with him, legal problems arise. The husband may sue his wife for the restoration of conjugal rights. In such cases the attitude of the Indian courts has not been very decisive. Kusum (1976) cited many cases in which the wife was asked to leave her job and join her husband. In one case (Gaya Prasad Vs. Smt. Bhagwati) in Madhya Pradesh, the wife worked as Gram Sevika due to financial circumstances. The husband petitioned for the restitution of conjugal rights. The observations of the court while delivering the judgement were: "Merely on the ground that the husband has a small income, and the wife if allowed to serve at a place away from the marital home, can substantially augment the family, cannot be held to be a sufficient reason to deny the wife's society to the husband".

The above judgement was given in the sixties. From seventies onwards the change in the attitudes of the courts is noticeable, as judgements have become much less traditional. The judges concede that in case of genuine economic necessity, the wife has a right to maintain her job. But the main problem here is not only the economic necessity but also a woman's freedom to take her own decisions. The woman's personal satisfaction, sense of confidence and security and her intellectual needs must be the guiding factors in making a decision about her quitting the job or remaining in service while living away from her husband or family. Whatever may be the decisions of the courts the stressful life between the husband or and wife will continue to be lived till there is the recognition that wife also has aspirations, ambitions and a will of her own. The idea that the women should work only to supplement their husbands income is to give them much inferior position in the family than that of husbands and of considering them as only the instruments for augmenting the family incomes. The women should not be viewed as the objects or instruments, but as entities unto themselves.

Narrow and conservative concepts of in-laws are also tension producing. The in-laws, in many cases want that their daughters-in-law take up jobs but at the same time are extremely critical if she is late in returning from her place of work or is not able to do the household work as efficiently as they expect her to do.

Some studies indicate that women seek work equal to the level of their husband's prestige. In case a wife is not equally educated or trained she may prefer to stay at home rather than accept work below her husband's level. In such a case if she is forced to undertake inferior status work, she remains tense and suffers from inferiority complex. The woman herself can take steps to come out of such situation by undertaking courses or training to improve her qualifications.

There is another side of the picture also. If the wife is employed in a job which has higher prestige and emoluments than the husband's job, the husband feels jealous and threatened. In many cases the tension between the husband and wife becomes so intense that living under the same roof becomes a torture leading to divorce or separation or to perpetual quarrels between them. There can develop proper amity and understanding between them if the wife tries to understand the sentiments of the husband and the husband realises that his wife deserves what she is getting. Truly well adjusted couples are those who respect each others individuality. A husband and wife can achieve harmony through mutual support and self-esteem. When both work role differentiation should not exist. The husband should give full emotional support to the wife and the wife should be considerate to the needs of the husband, may they be either psychological, physical, sexual or economical.

Matching Problem

The girls including those who are educated find it very difficult to get a husband who does not demand dowry. In fact now the eligible bachelors and their families are demanding that the girls be educated so that they can earn money and also a dowry to meet the initial expenses of setting the home. Dowry demands are increasing day by day with the rising ambitions for equipping the houses with the modern gadgets. The educated girls whose parents search bridegrooms who are well-employed and highly educated face demands of exorbitant amounts as dowries. Such demands many parents are not able to meet with. The sensitive girls feel themselves as the cause of their parent's woes and blame themselves for being born as girls. Sometimes their tensions increase so much that they even commit suicide.

The statistics relating to dowry are very grim. Sometime back it was announced in the Lok Sabha that as many as 878 cases of dowry murders and 1,479 cases of dowry suicides were registered in the country in 1990. The educated girls who resent their husband and in-laws demands of dowry are brutally killed or forced to commit suicide. In order to stop these great human tragedies and combat horrible social evils, it would be necessary to bring about radical transformation, in the old rigid social structure. The parents of the educated girls rear them up in such a rigid environment that they themselves are incapable of finding their own life partners. They have to depend on the traditional system of marriage. The educated girls may be saved from much stress if they are left free to make a choice of their own mates. The rigid social structure can be changed only when a brave new philosophy of life steeped in socio-economic and moral values of equality of all castes and both the sexes is evolved out and adopted. Such a philosohpy will enable the male as well as the female child to spontaneously internalise the principle of equality of man, woman of all castes and creeds.

Marching Ahead

The Indian women are marching ahead in each and every field of work and activity. They are in the forefront of all the movements for progress and development. But unfortunately the area of social reforms, which touches them directly, is as yet a neglected area. The movement for women emancipation and empowerment are ridiculed and made fun of by the traditionally oriented males. The women have little say in the Parliament or state legislatures because their number is extremely limited in these bodies. The Bill for 30 per cent reservation of seats for women in the Parliament is opposed on one flimsy ground or another. Our Parliament and legislatures are responsible for the governance and the administration of the country. On them are needed such persons who are highly motivated towards efficient management, adequately educated, well-informed and possess a zeal for social service. The country at present has quite a substantial number of such women who can adorn the seats of the Parliament. There are, however, some leaders who want those women in the Parliament who are mere appendages of their husbands or male relatives. The ridiculous thing is that they want to do it in the name of social justice.

The stresses and the tensions of the modern educated Indian women can be minimised if they involve themselves in a strong movement of women emancipation and empowerment. In the Indian context it means the deliverance from the myths which have been woven around them and the false pedestal at which they have been put since long.

In 1963 Frieden wrote the Feminine Mystique which attempted to explode many myths about women. Her thesis is applicable to both East and West. She writes- 'the Victorian culture did not permit women to accept or gratify their basic sexual needs, our culture does not permit women to accept or gratify their basic need to grow and fulfill their potentialities as human beings, a need which is not solely defined by their sexual role". Just as the Indian women have been led to believe that their fulfillment lies in motherhood and wifely duties, so Friedan observes about American women: "In the feminine mystique, there is no other way she can even dream about herself, except as her children's mother, her husband's wife."

Simone de Beauvoir considers that the myth of feminine 'mystery' has several advantages for the male. He can dismiss inexplicable moods, behaviours, and feelings by saying:"Oh Women! Who can understand them any way?" Rohrbaugh

Joanna adds: "Since woman cannot be understood, man cannot be expected to build an authentic relationship with her. He is free to relate to her in terms of his own perceptions, fantasies and desires".

Williams referring to the myth of woman as mystery says : "By defining her as mysterious other, man spares himself the necessity of analysing her behaviours and understanding it as a consequence of her position vis-a-vis him. To do that would require acknowledgement of her oppression, and a possible shift in their power relationship? The price would be very high".

In such a 'mystique' or lifestyle, a woman's intelligence has no meaning and her capability is negated. By following a monotonous daily routine, she loses all interest in the outside world, draws herself into a shell and spends her time in gossips. She is little more than an instrument, which keeps a constant supply of members through her powers of reproduction.

Friedan emphasises that one's individuality when becoming a wife and mother should not be given up, but strengthened. She says: "Maslow found that the individuality is strengthened, that the ego is in one sense merged with another, but yet in another sense remains separate, and strong as always. The two, tendencies, to transcend individuality and to sharpen and strengthen it, must be seen as partners and not as contradictory". Self-actualised educated women should serve their society and contribute their best to humanity, just as men have the opportunity to do so. The world has suffered enough because half of humanity has remained dependent on the other half.

Indian women are often viewed as passive, prudish and fragile. Many of them feel that a mere lustful glance or touch by a non-relative male leads to the loss of their chastity. The women's movements should actively try to alter such a nonsensical perception. It may be remembered that the women in general and the educated women in particular are in danger of becoming not only household slaves but also work place slaves if they do not learn to become individualistic and assertive.

An Indian woman with lustre with a brilliance of her won, with a dynamic attitude towards life and with the charm of a sturdy woman going about her business is always in danger of being branded as aggressive, too outgoing and, perhaps, flirtatious, This type of woman is incongruent with the image of the ideal that has been imprinted on the minds of the Indians for the centuries. The women's movements should be in the direction of relieving intelligent, modern women from the clutches of orthodoxy. The real women's movement which India need and towards which the Indian feminists seem to be fully conscious is that of removal of orthodoxy, blind faith, poverty, helplessness, dependence and complete subjugation of woman's will. The reformers should try to bring the changes in the attitudes of both male and female regarding marriage and the family. The must attack fanatical religious rites, ill conceived notions of virginity, wrong notions of chastity, custom of giving or taking dowry, wastage in the marriage ceremonies and similar other outdated customs and traditions.

We may agree with Carden when he says that : "The new feminism is not about the elimination of differences between the sexes, nor even simply the achievement of equal opportunity; it concerns with the individual's right to find out the kind of person he or she is."

TEN

New Trends

A developing country, which India is, it depends very much on its vast potential of human resources, if these resources are properly tapped the country is bound to progress efficiently, effectively and rapidly. Women form the most important part of the human resources of the nation and they may contribute very substantially in building a strong, powerful and affluent nation. They can, however, make their best contribution when they are properly educated and are able to explode the myths, which have kept them in a state of backwardness and neglect. In the present chapter we are trying to project the type of education which is needed in future for Indian women in view of their socio-phychological make up.

Today too much theory based on little reality exists. Men talk of morality while all the time degrading their women. The reformists talk of abstinence to reduce population while they themselves might have fathered more, than half a dozen children. The harmony in family life is preached while subjugating the women in the name of old ideal of Pativrata. The quarrels between the husband and wife may involve much cruelty yet the divorce may be very much condemned. There is an urgent need to cry a half to this type of duplicity in talks and action. For example, when there is genuine discord between husband and wife or there is much cruelty involved in their relationship then divorce is the only viable solution. It will injure the ego of the children much less than their upbringing in a daily quarrelsome situation. But this point of no return in the relationship between husband and wife will not come up if both respect each other's individuality and live together with mutual trust, faith, desire and love. In a stable marriage alliance consideration of each other's viewpoint is desirable and Indian men and women have the capability of developing such consideration.

There is enough scientific evidence available, which shows that since birth onwards girl child receives rejection; unequal, indifferent and discriminatory treatment as compared to male children. Access to food and other household assets allocation of domestic duties, participation in community and neighbourhood activities, school education, etc. reflect serious gender based differences and inequalities.

Modern scientific techniques like amniocentesis and ultrasound have been widely misused as "sex determination test" for selective elimination of the female foetuses. Between 1978 and 1983, 78,000 female were aborted in India, following sex determination tests. A Mumbai-based survey in 1984 revealed that out of the 8,000 foetuses aborted following such tests 7,999 were female. Many State Governments have framed or are framing legislation against this practice. But still there is a danger that secretly such tests will continue to be conducted and female foetuses aborted. The tradition of having a male child is so deep-rooted that the women themselves do not hesitate in destroying their pregnancies if the tests reveal that the baby to be born is a female. Proper education is needed to discourage this tendency. It has been noticed that many educated women also indulge in the practice of destroying foetuses hence our emphasis is on proper education by which we mean an education, which frees the woman from gender biases.

Conservative cultural values, coupled with assumption of domestic responsibilities dictate the girl child's withdrawal from formal education in our country the female literacy rates are very low. These are 39.4 per cent according to the 1991 census. The drop out rate for girls in the school is estimated at 55.5 per cent at the primary stage and 77.7 per cent at the middle school stage. There is thus great need for having a crash programme for women education.

In Spite of Education

It is unfortunate that in spite of Indian women getting all those legal rights which are being demanded by the women of some developed nations they are having quite difficult time in keeping themselves from the old fossilised traditions. The mother cult may be one of the reasons for their remaining tradition oriented. Though that which is motherly is represented as noble, it has its drawbacks as well in those situations in which the women cannot think of any other thing except being mothers. The motherhood syndrome is incompatible with modern woman's development and exists because of cultural conditioning. According to Evelyn Reed: "The subordination of the women is not the result of a predetermined biological handicap i.e. child bearing." She considers that attribution of inferior status of women to her faulty biology is a false preposition.

Self-reliance, self-esteem and a reality-oriented approach to life must be the goal of Indian women. Some people may take exception to this suggestion because of the fear of loss of domestic harmony but unless the women are able to assert their will the family and the social life will remain in a state of disharmony.

Planning for Education

After independence India framed planning, strategies and techniques to steer the nation's economic development towards attaining a socialist pattern of society. The first five-year plan was launched in 1950-51 and thereafter nine more five-year plans besides some yearly plans have already been adopted. In each of these plans women's development issues, especially their economic, educational and health issues, have received considerable attention and various welfare measures were taken to ameliorate their conditions. The result of all these measures is that the status and position of the Indian women have much improved. But as we have repeated again and again in this book there is much, which has still to be done.

The Draft of the National Policy on Empowerment of Women released by the Ministry of Human Resource Development seeks to eliminate all forms of violence against women as also to abolish discrimination against the girl child. It commits the government to ensure that women are not denied of their human rights and fundamental freedom. This policy also seeks to provide equal opportunities for power sharing and decision-making to women at all levels and processes in public and private sectors. All these are highly desirable goals. But these alone would not be sufficient unless the government policies and its mechanism are supplemented by a social will, a wave and a movement by women themselves for achieving these goals and for promoting rational attitudinal changes.

National Policy on Education

The National Policy on Education (NPE) 1986 has given very important recommendations for women education. It has paid attention to the basic issues of women's equality. In the section titled 'Education for Women's Equality' the Policy states:

> "Education will be used as an agent of basic change in the status of women. In order to neutralise the accumulated distortions of the past, there will be a well-conceived edge in favour of women. The national education system will pay a positive role in the empowerment of women. It will foster the development of new values through redesigned curricula textbooks, training and orientation of teachers, decision makers and administrators, and the active involvement of educational institutions--- women's studies will be promoted as a part of various courses and educational institutions encouraged to take up active programmes to further women's development.

The removal of women's illiteracy and obstacles inhibiting their access to, and retention in, elementary education will receive overriding priority, through provision of special support services, setting of time targets and effective monitoring. Major emphasis will be laid on women's participation in vocational, technical and professional education at different levels. The policy of nondiscrimination will be pursued vigorously to eliminate sex stereotyping in vocational and professional courses and to promote women's participation in non-traditional occupation, as well as in existing and exerged technologies".

The above recommendations have given very important guidelines for the futuristic education of the women. The government definitely took interest in implementing the policy framework and so there were developed "Programme of Action" in 1986 and 1992. Also a National Perspective Plan for Women's Education 1997-98 to 2000 AD was drawn. The National Perspective Plan formulated some important specific objectives for women education so that women may also participate actively in the social cultural, economic and political areas. These important objectives were to be obtained by 2000 AD. These objectives included elimination of illiteracy and universalisation of elementary education, substantial vocalisation and diversification of courses at secondary level, making education as an effective means for women equality, making necessary intervention in the content and processes of education to inculcate positive and egalitarian attitudes, providing non-formal and part-time courses to women to enable them to acquire knowledge and skills for their social, cultural and economic advancement, and to provide impetus to women to enroll themselves in various professional degree courses so as to increase their number in medicine, teaching, engineering and other fields substantially. To achieve the above mentioned and some other objectives the National Perspective Plan made important recommendations that awareness needs to be generated among the masses regarding the necessity of educating girls so as to prepare them to effectively contribute to the socio-economic development of the country, to strengthen their role in society and to realise their own capacities for improving and minimising drop-outs and wastage of girl students.

The Revised Plan of Action (1992) has laid down suitable strategies for implementing the above mentioned targets.

In spite of all endeavours made so far for promoting women education, we still find that for every 100 boys there are only 62 girls in primary schools, 43 girls in middle schools, 36 girls in secondary schools and 31 girls at different stages of higher education. According to the 1991 census female literacy is 39.4 per cent compared to 63.8 per cent for males, the total number of female illiterates is 197 millions which is more than male counterparts by 70 millions, even though the female population is less than the male population by 32 millions. There are rural urban disparities, and among rural women, literacy is about half of the urban female literacy.

The above figures lead us to conclude that more intensive efforts are needed to educate our women specially those who are living in the rural areas or the slum areas in the towns. Since most of these women who are illiterate and do not go to the school the programmes for educating them may be accompanied with the programmes of improving their financial conditions. The programmes for the poverty alleviation should be intensified. It may be emphasised that the success of any scheme of education depends to a great extent on it being productive both in the material as well as social sense. Actually education should lead to social, economic and moral development. An educated person must be able to earn more than an uneducated one. The national education system will play a positive, interventionist role in the empowerment of women. It will foster the development of new values through redesigned curricula, textbooks, training and orientation of teachers, decision-makers and administrators, and the active involvement of educational institutions. Women's studies will be promoted as a part of various courses and educational institutions encouraged taking up active programmes to further women's development.

Removal of Illiteracy

The removal of women's illiteracy and obstacles inhibiting

their access to, and retention in, elementary education will receive overriding priority, through provision of special support services, setting of time targets and effective monitoring. Major emphasis will be laid on women's participation in vocational, technical and professional education at different levels. The policy of nondiscrimination will be pursued vigorously to eliminate sex stereo-typing in vocational and professional courses and to promote women's contribution effectively towards bringing desirable social change and be honest, sincere and affectionate individual. For our women such education is required which may help them in getting gainful employment and in improving their financial position.

From the above discussion it may be evident that the government is very much aware of the need of providing education to the women of the country. In the recent decades it has made some genuine efforts to bring the women on the national scene by giving them incentives, providing for their education schools and colleges, giving free education to the girls up to a particular stage, developing centres of women studies, opening various avenues of employment to them, providing non-formal centres for their vocational training. It is very much desirable that no discrimination is made on the basis of jobs meant exclusively for males or for females. The interest of the student should be the main consideration. From the lower classes onwards the attention of the students should be directed towards creating social awareness and motivating them for higher achievements in all the areas of concern to them. India needs good housewives as well as efficient women workers. Education for women must be organised around these two powerful needs.

It is to be noted that the outlook of the women has changed considerably during the last four decades. Much of it is due to the expansion of education that has taken place in the country. The young women of today are neither afraid of moving out of their homes nor are as dependent on their parents or husbands as were their mothers and grand mothers. The woman wants to be economically independent. She has realised the importance of education and is quite conscious of the need of raising the standard of living of the family through her engagement in the world of work. The educated women are prepared to fight for their rights and to assert their individuality. Hence web may say that the educational efforts made so far have yielded positive results. These efforts are now required to be intensified. Certain changes in the educational system are also needed so that the women learn to be self-reliant, are able to develop self-esteem and become caring, loving and the source of amity and goodwill in the family. The following are some suggestions regarding the changes to be brought about in the educational system:

1. All out efforts should be made to implement the constitutional directives of compulsory elementary education up to 14 years of age. Education should be free up to this age for both boys and girls.

2. The girls should be taught the same subjects as are being taught to the boys, which means that if home craft is taught to the girls it should also be taught to the boys. The physical education should be given to both boys and girls. At the onset of puberty the girl's menses begin. At this age some training in personal hygiene may be given exclusively to the girls.

3. From the lower classes onwards the attention of the students should be directed towards social evils and in them social awareness should be created. They should also be motivated for higher achievements in all the areas of concern to them. As said earlier India needs good housewives as well as efficient women workers. Education for women must be organised around these two powerful needs.

4. The girls should be encouraged to join technical, managerial, professional institutions of higher learning so that they can compete with boys in the job market.

5. The methods of teaching should be so planned that they

inculcate the habits of thinking freely and expressing their views freely.

6. The curricula of all the subjects, which are taught to the school children, should be free from sex bias.

7. The education of the school children must include co-curricular activities in which both boys and girls should participate and learn to take independent decisions.

8. In our educational institutions the courses in the maintenance of inter-personal relationships be introduced. Some of these courses must be compulsory for both boys and girls.

9. Some special courses for girls in mother craft, in the home economics and household affairs should be introduced. Some of such courses may also be open for boys.

10. Non-formal system of education must be strengthened. It should be available to all those girls who are unable to join the formal system of education. Education from the elementary to postgraduate levels must be available through this system.

11. A network of adult literacy centres must be established throughout the country. In these centres the education for social change must be stressed. The women must specially be prepared to fight against social evils and to rise above their mythical existence.

12. A network of counselling centres must be set up. These centres must be equipped with to give educational, vocational and personal counselling. Special emphasis should also be placed to marital and family consellling. Each big school must have adequately trained counsellors. Counselling is very much needed at the adolescent stage to both the boys and girls. Our educational system must be able to fulfil this need.

13. Precaution should be taken in teaching those topics, which involve the status and position of women. It will all depend on the teachers how they present an episode where the women are depicted as serving their husbands. It may be taught in terms of inferior position of the women or it may be taught as an ideal example of love and affection. The teachers training colleges or colleges of education should pay special attention towards the teaching of such lessons by their teacher trainees so that the myths regarding women perpetuated in our society for centuries are exploded and the modern outlook is inculcated.

14. The educational institutions must also provide placement services so that the boys and girls are not only prepared for jobs but are also able to be placed in jobs.

15. The emphasis on the education of the girls must be specifically on making them strong so that they are able to reverse their image of being delicate and unfit for jobs requiring tough exterior.

The above are some of the suggestions which have emerged out of the discussions made in the different chapters of the present book. Many useful and worthwhile suggestions have been made by various commissions and committees, plans and policies. We have refrained ourselves form repeating them, as they are available in the from of reports in full details. In planning or the futuristic education they may all be taken into consideration.

In conclusion we may say that the Indian women have always been quite strong. They have always been in the forefront of the struggle for the betterment of the mankind. They have been great support to their male counterpart. It is their power of resilience that in spite of the persistent efforts of the male to enmesh them in the web of myth they have never lost their composure and cool and today they are bravely facing the challenges of their subjugation. Education is the only answer.

ELEVEN

Career and Profession

In post-independence period, unlike, the situation in non-agricultural occupations and organized industry, the services and profession have provided greater opportunities to women. Earlier, both in the public and private sectors, women's participation was practically confined to health and education, though the Second World War period ushered in a small but significant entry of women into clerical and secretarial occupations. Other services and professionals were the monopolies of the urban educated middle class, whose views about women's employment were extremely restrictive.

While the range of jobs open to educated women has widened in both public and private sectors, as has already been discussed in the preceding sections, the demand for unskilled women labour is shrinking.

Emergence of Women in Non-traditional Fields

The immediate factors responsible for the emergence of women in non-traditional fields of employment in the post-Independence period are:

(a) the Constitutional guarantee of non-discrimination and equality of opportunity in matter of employment;

(b) development of women's education and their entry into areas of education and employment hitherto monopolized by men;

(c) an increasing tendency among the urban educated women to take up paid employment which reflected gradual ideological change in social values as well as the growing economic pressure on urban middle class families;

(d) expansion of employment opportunities in the tertiary sector, as a direct consequence of the increasing rate of development.

Emerging Factors

The Constitutional guarantee of 'equality of opportunity' and non-discrimination on grounds of sex in employment and office under the State and the specific directive 'to promote with special care the educational and economic interests of the weaker sections of the people' had a direct bearing on the employment aspirations of middle class women. The emphasis on women's equality, that emerged during the last phase of the freedom movement had influenced the attitudes of educated middle class women in a most marked manner.

The immediate expression of this in the period after independence could be found in three spheres. (i) in higher education; (ii) the employment market, particularly for jobs requiring higher education; and (iii) in politics. Women began to enter the competition for services under the Government from the very beginning, and the success of a few in these most prestigious occupations, which had hitherto been the monopoly of men, inspired others and helped them to shake off their traditional inhibitions and lack of confidence. By this they set in motion the attitudinal change of society, particularly of men in Government agencies to their unfamiliar presence in these occupations.

The rapid expansion of women's education that characterized the post-Independence period both contributed to, and gained further momentum from this process. Hitherto women's education had been seen more as a measure for promoting social justice and family welfare. The possibility of employment under Government provided the stimulus that women's education had lacked so far, particularly in the field of higher education. The demand for increasing opportunities led to increase in the number of institutions, while the demand for equality broke down the resistance of academic authorities, and opened to women training in engineering and other applied and vocational sciences which had been monopolies of men till then.

Apart from education the most important force behind this increasing entry of a new class of women in the field of wage employment, is sometimes, described as 'emancipation born out of necessity'. With a few exceptions in the higher strata of society, the majority of women take to work for economic reasons.

This has been confirmed by several studies on women's motivation for employment among the urban middle classes. An increasing number of these women now have to support their families, both before and after marriage. Rising prices and levels of unemployment, added to the increasing costs of education and housing, and absence of social security, have increased the degree of economic pressures on the major section of this class. At the same time, for at least an important segment of this group, aspirations for a higher standard of living have increased the necessity of having more than one earner in the family.

Reasons of Taking up Work

According to a study undertaken by the Sriram Centre of Industrial Relations in 1972 covering a total sample of 500 respondents drawn from middle class working women, the respondents attached highest important to "reducing the economic burden of their families". In terms of specific economic advantages arising from their employment, they attached primary importance to "augmenting the education and diet of the family members of children in particular." Next in order of importance was savings from future economic security of the family as compared to the expense on current consumption.

> In the scheme of thinking of the respondents, personal enjoyment, up-keep or comfort were rated very low as the end results of additional earnings from their own job. On the other hand, relatively much higher importance was attached to proper furnishing of the house and for being able to use gadget and conveniences for facilitating the performance of their own domestic chores.

Though some of these studies have referred to non-economic motives among women of this class in taking up employment, the recent studies indicate that the importance of such factors is relatively much less significant. The study cited above found one non-economic reason to be significant among trained women. This was to utilize their education and training.

The Committee's experience during its tours as well as the results of our survey confirms the reality of this trend. Wherever we went the most repeated demand from middle-class women in urban and rural areas was for increasing employment opportunities without which many families would be reduced to starvation. In West Bengal, a region where the taboos on women's work outside the home had been higher than in most other areas, we met with this demand from even elderly middle-class women. In their view, if their daughters and daughters-in-law did not obtain some employment, then the families, particularly the dependent, old and young would face destitution.

According to our survey, an overwhelming majority of the respondents, male and female, supported women's employment to augment the family's income. Almost half of the respondents agreed that a woman can do same work that a man can do, and 87 per cent observed that they should get the same wages as men for similar work. This response was in spite of the view of nearly half the respondents that general service conditions are unfavourable for women. Views on purpose of educating women revealed that fear of insecurity, resulting from loss of support from the breadwinners of the family caused by death or other reasons is still the most compelling force behind this change of attitude to women's employment.

The disintegration of joint families and the loss of their rural income has made many of these families totally dependent on their earnings from jobs. At the same time, the number of unmarried, widowed, divorced or separated women who can no longer expect to be fully supported by their families is on the increase.

An argument which is often raised in debates regarding women is that their employment deprives men of jobs that they need to support their families. It is assumed that all women who work are only supplementing the family income to ensure a higher standard of living. These theorists have never tried to investigate how many women who work are sole or main earners in the family. The majority of working women whom we met during our tours, were supporting either their parents and younger brothers and sisters or their own children. We came across some married women, who had continued to work after their marriage in order to support their aged parents and to educate their younger brothers and sisters. Such cases may be rare, but they are significant as they express a complete transformation in social attitudes. A few years ago, parents would have considered it highly improper to accept any support from married daughters. Even today though economic necessity has helped to erode this attitude, the women who take up such a responsibility require considerable courage, because it is generally disliked by their in-laws. The fear of loss of earnings of a daughter is becoming an important factor in deferring marriage of middle-class women in urban areas.

The last factor stems from the pattern in India's economic development in the post-Independence period and, the relatively higher rate of growth of the tertiary sector. This has opened up considerably more avenues for employment of women than in the past, both in the public and private sectors.

Occupational Distribution of Women Workers

The occupational distribution of women workers in public and private sectors and their proportion to total workers in each category indicated in Tables 5.1 and 5.2 yields some interesting information. In the public sector, while the number of women employees in the categories of professional, technical and related workers and primary and middle school teachers, has been continuously rising since 1960, their proportion to total employees has more or less remained constant with only minor fluctuations.

The number of women as administrative, executive and managerial workers increased from 0.10 lakh in 1960 to 0.12 lakh in 1966 but there was a downward trend in 1968. Their proportion to total workers, which was more or less constant at 3.3 per cent declined to 2.5 per cent in 1968. In the category of clerical and related workers, the number of women with the only exception of 1962, has gone up from 0.37 lakh in 1960 to 0.79 lakh in 1968. For the same period their proportion to total workers in this category has gone up from 4.2 per cent to 7.6 per cent. The number and proportion of women workers in transport and communication has remained steady, while in services, sports and recreations, their number has gone up from 0.05 lakh in 1960 to 0.13 lakh in 1968. It may be noted, however, that in this occupational division majority of women were working as maids, cooks, housekeepers, cleaners, sweepers and laundrers. The number of women as unskilled office workers declined from 0.25 lakh (4.5 per cent) in 1960 to 0.16 lakh (2.9 per cent) in 1968.

In the private sector, the categories where both the number and proportion of women to total workers has shown a steady increase are: clerical and related workers, service, sports and recreation workers and primary and middle school teachers. It may be interesting to note that there was a general slump in the employment of women in all categories in 1963 except for unskilled office workers. This decline was more marked in the administrative, executive and managerial workers and professional, technical and related workers.

Women employed in the management cadre belong generally to the upper-middle class, where no distinction is made in the education of boys and girls. These highly educated women hold degrees in specific disciplines relevant for business management. Some of the fields where they are usually employed are in public relations, advertising, market research and cottage industries. This situation derives from certain socio-psychological reasons regarding their special abilities in these fields. There is a trend to employ women more in areas where the market or clientele consists primarily of women or where the nature of the job calls for a woman manager. The expansion of the hotel industry, for example, has opened some new avenues for women in the field of marketing, personnel management, house keeping and public relations. Some illustrative examples of women in managerial positions are as follows: The India Hotels Private Limited has a woman as the Sales Manager and Marketing Manager. Hindustan Milk Foods has a woman as Product Manager. India Tobacco Company Limited has a woman Accountant heading its Tax Department and a woman as Head of the Personnel Department of its Research Section.

In some traditional industries, however, women have not yet been accepted at this level nor has industry yet developed the conditions suited to the life cycle and special requirements of women. It is for this reason that they find it more difficult to reach top level jobs. While some of the companies have opened their management cadre to women, it remains to be seen whether this will become an agent for change or whether it will terminate at an experimental stage.

The detailed statistical data needed to assess the major occupational trends, namely, the extent of women's entry into various professions and services and the levels of their employment in various collared jobs is unavailable over a period. It is, therefore, difficult to give a correctly statistical profile of the educated women workers. However, a review of the available data indicates that while a change is perceptible in the occupational pattern of women in this sector during the last two decades, two trends are clearly visible:

(a) the concentration of women in the profession of teaching and medicine; and

(b) recognition of certain low prestige jobs in the clerical services as particularly suitable for women and a consequent concentration of women in these occupations.

Women in Profession

According to an ILO study, made in 1970, only 17 per cent of the professional and technical workers were women of which three-fourths were teachers. The Directorate General of Employment and Training's data for selected professions in public and private sectors (organized) identifies teaching, medical and health, clerical and related workers and telephone operators as the four occupations, where there is the largest concentration of women workers.

The national classification of occupation adopted by the Census of India, 1971 indicates that the number of women teachers was 6 lakh, whereas their number in other professions was negligible — physicians and surgeons .2 lakhs, nursing and other medical and health technicians 2,500, lawyers 1,700 and architects, engineers and surveyors 700, accountants, etc., 2,700. Apart from persons serving as teachers, other qualified scientists, serving in professional capacity (physical scientists, life scientists, social scientists, mathematicians) add up to a total of 18,000. Of this last group, social scientists form the major section (16,000). It would thus appear that research, particularly in the field of social research and social work are emerging as new occupations where women are present in a significant number. In relation to men, their ratios in these selected occupations are given below:

Physicians and Surgeons	7.1%
Lawyers	1.2%
Teachers	30.3%
Nursing and other medical and health technicians	72.2%
Scientists	10.9%

Within teaching, primary school teaching account for about 71 per cent of the women teachers followed by secondary schools which accounts for 21 per cent.

Teachers

The heavier concentration of women professionals in teaching and medicine reflects both opportunities as well as preferences. Teaching as an occupation, particularly at the school stage, requires relatively little training beyond general education, in comparison to the professions of medicine, engineering, etc. In the prevailing social ethos, a long-term professional training for women is still accessible to a minority among the upper middle-class. The second reason for their preference is respectability attached to this profession in society in spite of its lower salary structure. Teaching has been always accorded a high status in Indian society, though its income potential has always been limited. Middle-class families prefer to see their women in this profession more than any other. One of the reason for this is perhaps because it gives a woman comparatively more time for her household duties, as there are more vacations and limited hours of work.

Another reason for the heavy concentration of women in teaching has been suggested by sociologists, who report that the percentage of women teachers in lower age-group is much higher than the men teachers at practically all levels of teaching. Women enter the profession in substantial number but their number declines beyond the age of 30 and drastically after 35.

This may be interpreted to suggest a substantial entry of women into this profession before marriage and a tendency for some of them to leave employment with increase in their family responsibilities. In the absence of studies based on the same cohort of teachers over a time period, it is impossible to accept this explanation. An alternative explanation; and in our opinion the more valid one, is the increasing rate of expansion of employment opportunities in this profession in recent years, and the greater degree of preference for women teachers in primary and middle schools which would account for a larger number of younger women in this profession. A third possibility, which required investigation, is the relatively lower salary structure in many private schools. It is an accepted fact that it is easier to obtain the services of women for such low rates than men since women constitute a higher proportion of the educated unemployed.

Doctors

According to the manpower Survey of 1967-68, the existing medical workforce comprised 12,000 women out of a total of 1,20,000 doctors. According to 1971 Census (1 per cent sample data) however, the ratio of women physicians and surgeons is only 6.1 per hundred men — 23.8 thousand women to 336.3 thousand men. The number of qualified women doctors is however about 25 per 100 men. This may indicate both under utilization due to women-doctors dropping out of the profession, or alternatively their migration to other countries for employment.

It may be noted that though medicine has been an accepted and respected profession for women for a considerable period the general tendency has been for women to concentrate in the practice of obstetrics and gynaecology. In recent years they have also entered paediatrics, surgery, medicine, pathology, radiology, anaesthesia, etc. Since the majority of their clientele continue to be women, as very few men would still consider it proper to consult a woman doctor, it is but natural that the majority of women doctors should take up specialization in women's and children's diseases. A new field for women doctors is administration in hospitals and public health. During the pre-Independence period, there was a considerable disparity between men and women medical officers in the management of hospitals. In some of the States, women doctors were not given the same status or pay scales as men. This disparity continued in Punjab until 1962, when women doctors were given the status of Civil Surgeons, after considerable struggle on their part.

One particular problem in employment of women doctors is their heavy concentration in urban areas, and the regional disparities in their utilization. Out of 23,000 employed doctors in 1971 as many as 19.5 thousand were serving in urban areas. According to the Ministry of Health and Family Planning, in large urban centres like Mumbai, Delhi and Chennai women doctors form 20-40 per cent of the total number of doctors. In relatively backward States like Assam and Madhya Pradesh they form only 2-4 per cent while they constitute about 16 per cent in Punjab and 20 per cent in Maharashtra. Since most women doctors come from urban middle-class families, they tend to stay in urban areas, while rural areas continue to suffer from a shortage of women doctors. It would be difficult to improve their representation in rural areas unless adequate arrangements for housing and other amenities, particularly the schooling of young children are provided.

We would like to note here that as compared to the rather indifferent reception of other women workers in the rural areas, the professions of teaching and medicine have come to receive a high degree of respect and acceptance from rural society. We were informed by women in different States, that these two groups of professionals now enjoy a great deal of respect in rural areas. It should, therefore, not be difficult, in our opinion, to elicit a greater degree of public cooperation to make their stay in these areas easier.

Nurses

Regarding the other categories of medical personnel, Table 5.4 indicates the increase in the number of nurses, mid-wives and health visitors during the last two decades. Nurses and midwives constitute the largest of these three groups. According to the Census of 1971, the total number in all categories of para-medical personnel amounted to 1.55 lakh, of which .9 lakh were concentrated in urban areas, their ratio to men being 72.7 per cent. While these professions do not carry the same status as that of the doctors, nor the same pay scales, there is no doubt that their status has increased in the post-Independence period. Before independence, nursing used to be a monopoly of a few communities like Anglo-Indians and Indian Christians, viz., communities which did not impose any taboo on their women taking up this profession.

These taboos have lessened to a very great extent in most States and better training opportunities for women in Nursing schools and colleges have helped to increase the status of this category of professional workers. The expansion of health services has increased employment opportunities. In spite of this, however, the arduous nature of the duties which includes night work and the relatively low scales of pay still constitute handicaps for women in this profession. It should be noted that there has been an increase in the migration of qualified nurses from the country in recent years. Unless this trend is arrested by providing better terms of service and facilities, this trend may form one of the important elements of the 'brain-drain' from the country.

While the principle of discrimination against married women in both these professions has been formally abandoned, elements of discrimination still remain. It was brought to our notice that in the Army Medical Service, which employs a large number of women doctors and nurses, until 1972, married women, had to leave the nursing service. Revision of the rules in that year has made it possible for them to continue in the service at their request, by grant of 2 years extended tenure at a time. Married women are still not recruited to the Military Nursing service, and if they marry during probation they have to leave the service. Married women may, however, be recruited on local basis on one year contract renewable annually. One glaring omission in the Army Service Regulations is the lack of provision for any paid maternity leave to both women doctors and nurses. This, in our opinion, constitutes a definite disability, and should be removed forthwith.

Lawyers

In the absence of any reliable data of case studies, it is difficult to make any observation regarding the status of women in other professions. We have, however, received complaints from women lawyers in many States regarding lack of opportunities extended to them for judicial appointment. While the number of practising lawyers has been on the increase, only one woman has, so far, been appointed a High Court judge. In our view, a change in this trend is necessary not only in the interest of women in this profession, but also for the large number of women who find a lack of understanding of their personal difficulties in family matters from the judicial profession. The Family Courts and the Special Tribunals that we have recommended elsewhere, if accepted, should provide increasing opportunities for women trained in law.

Social Workers

A new profession which is emerging mainly after independence is social work, a field where leadership was generally assumed by women on a voluntary basis in the years before independence. The majority of professionally trained social workers today work in institutions, departments and organizations engaged in social welfare, both public and voluntary. The first school of social work in India was established by a woman. These schools offered equal opportunities to men and women from the beginning.

According to a study undertaken by the Indian Council for Social Welfare in 1968, there were about 3153 social work graduates at that time. This number is estimated to have risen to about 6000 by 1971. Out of a sample of 1107 covered by the study, 30 per cent were women. In employment opportunities, however, women were found to have obtained their first jobs earlier than men. Out of 319 women, 40 per cent found employment within one month after training, while only 29 per cent of the 732 men succeeded in doing so. 80 per cent of the women could find employment within 6 months of training, while this was true of only 53 per cent of the men in the sample.

The reasons offered for the greater ease with which women get employment in this profession are: (a) personal inclination on the basis of aptitude which makes them less selective about the type of employment; and (b) the greater difficulty for social workers obtaining employment in industrial jobs. Since men tend to specialize more in labour and industrial relations, they find it more difficult to get jobs. According to Ramachandran and Padmanabhan (1969): "On the contrary, the women who normally tend to specialise in primary social work and community organization, have less difficulty in getting absorbed in the related settings."

19 per cent of the women, however, complained of poor services and working conditions as a discouraging trend in the employment of social workers. The salaries for this occupation in both voluntary as well as private sector generally ranges between Rs 200 and Rs 800. According to Sita Basu (1973):

> This is not true of the few who today hold high positions both in government departments as heads of educational institutions or other capacities, who draw a fairly large salary in keeping with the positions held, but they are a very small minority. Academic institutions such as schools of social work and industrial establishments offer better salaries, service and working conditions and opportunities for professional growth, than the primary social work fields.

Positions held by the majority of women in this profession are generally in the middle and the lower category with very few holding key posts. Only two schools of social work are headed by women and very few heads of departments dealing with social welfare or related subjects at the Central and State levels are professionally qualified women.

Concentration in Low Level Jobs

Registers of Employment Exchanges and the views expressed by various employers, both in public and private sectors, make it clear that jobs of receptionists, clerks, stenographers and typists are absorbing more and more educated women. Out of 9.18 lakh of women work seekers registered with the employment exchanges at the end of 1973, as many as 69,355 were seeking clerical and related jobs. The concentration in particular fields is indicated below:

Typists	50,448
Stenographers	7,080
Clerks	2,800
Key Punch Operators	2,592
Telephone Operators	1,392
Middle School teachers	27,525
Primary School teachers	26,100
Secondary School teachers	24,163
Manual Training teachers	6,885
Nursing attendants	5,926
Midwives	2,555
General Nurses	2,058

The demand for unskilled women labour is shrinking both in public and private sectors and the growth in the numbers of women in white collared jobs is definitely on the increase but predominantly in the low prestige occupations.

A sample survey of the pattern of graduate employment in the country undertaken by the Directorate General of Employment and Training towards the beginning of 1960 also found that the second highest percentage of employed women graduates were engaged in clerical and related work in the Central Government. About three-fourths of the employed women were earning below Rs. 300 per month and only 6% had a monthly income of Rs. 300 and above.

The Committee

The Committee obtained information from various Ministries and Agencies of the Central Government regarding the number of women employees at different levels. The data presented in the Table indicate that the largest numbers are concentrated in Class III, i.e., ministerial and related staff. The expansion at this level has been much faster than that at the other levels, increasing from 720 in 1961 to 4175 in 1971. As compared to this, the number of women in Class H services has increased from 231 to 269 and that in Class I from 42 to 251. The number of Class IV employees increased from 10 to 84. The percentage increase of employees in this limited group of Central Government agencies indicates a faster rate of growth of women employees than the total. A detailed analysis shows that the highest number of Women Class I officers is to be found in the Department of Atomic Energy (121). Other Ministries with a relatively higher number of women at this level are the Ministry of Education and Social Welfare, External Affairs and Tourism and Civil Aviation. Their numbers in the other Ministries are negligible. In Class II, the highest numbers are found in Tourism and Civil Aviation (626), Education and Social Welfare (65) and Atomic Energy (48). In Class III, the largest concentration is again in Atomic Energy (1092), Defence (652), Supply and Rehabilitation (637), Educational and Social Welfare (628), Tourism and Civil Aviation (206), Irrigation and Power (195), Commerce (148), Shipping and Transport (131). This indicates that only a few Ministries have shown themselves particularly friendly to receiving women on their staff. The new Department of Science and Technology would also come within this group — 11 women in Class I, 14 in Class II, 99 in Class III. While we regret our inability to make this study comprehensive, our failure to obtain similar information from the other Ministries confirms our belief based on unofficial information, that certain Ministries and agencies of the Government of India are practising a subtle form of discrimination by resting the posting of women on their staff. Another inference that may be drawn from this data is that the discrimination against women is considerably less in agencies which employ a larger proportion of scientists and other professionals. The case of Atomic Energy, Education ' and Social Welfare and Science and Technology provide distinct evidence of this. Since these are relatively lower staffed agencies, their impact on the total employment of women in Central Government agencies can be only marginal.

We tried to obtain similar data regarding the employment of women at different levels from various public and private undertakings. Information was obtained from 137 public undertakings and 72 private ones. The trend is clear regarding their concentration at the clerical level, both in public and private sectors.

The greater percentage of women employees is found in the production level with the exception of fertilizers, advertising and steel. In the public sector it is remarkable that their proportion in clerical work outstrips their proportion in the production level (Simple engineering, heavy electricals, fertilizers, textiles, steel and oil). At the level of executives only the advertising industry in the private sector seems to have accommodated a few women. In the public sector, while finance, banking and insurance, steel, heavy engineering and heavy electricals have a certain number of women their proportion is exceedingly small. The number of women at the managerial level is negligible except in fight electricals in the private sector.

The distribution of women clerical staff at the levels of supervisors, assistants and lower grade employees indicates the same pattern. The concentration is generally in the ranks of typists, stenographers and receptionists except in mining and steel, heavy electricals and tele-communication.

Data supplied by the Union Public Service Commission also indicates an increase in the number of women being recruited as stenographers and assistants in the Central Services. Their ratio to men has shown a steady improvement during the last decade.

The Central Services which threw open their ranks to open competitions, giving equal opportunities for women, since 1948 show a slow but steady increase in the number of candidates as well as successful entrants. In the IAS/IFS/IPS examination the ratio of women to men recommended for appointment has improved from 1: 65.6 in 1960 to 1: 7.6 in 1972. In the other services, however, e.g. the Indian Economic Service, the Statistical Service and the Engineering Service their proportion still remains low, though in the Electrical Engineering Service their position is relatively better as also in the ranks of Geologists. The Forest Service has received no women even though women have been appearing in these examinations, though in very small numbers. It should be noted that the Indian Police Service, which had refused to accept any woman earlier, withdrew its resistance after a representation from some women candidates.

While we regret that we did not get any response from the Ministry of Railways to our request for information, we have been unofficially informed that of the 10 Services under the Railways, women have been accepted at the Class I level only in two, viz., Accounts and Medical. Certain candidates who had sought admission to the Traffic Service, were denied the opportunity and persuaded to opt for Accounts. We have also been informed that the Railway Board has resisted the posting of Class I women officers on the staff of the Board.

The important issue concerning women in the Central Services that received considerable public attention recently was regarding the constitutional validity of Rule 5(3) of the IAS Recruitment Rules 1954. According to this Rule, when an unmarried woman officer married "the Central Government may, if the maintenance of the efficiency of the service so requires, can upon her to resign". This rule had been cited in a case which came up for consideration before the Supreme Court under the Industrial Disputes Act, 1967. In this case, the legality of a service rule adopted by the respondent concern, (International Franchise (Pvt.) Ltd.), by which the services of a woman worker were automatically terminated on marriage, was sought to be defended on the analogy of Rule 5(3) of the IAS Recruitment Rules. The Court, while striking down the said rule in the respondent concern in the interests of social justice, observed as follows:

> It will be seen that this rule for the Indian Administrative Service is not unqualified like the rule in force in the respondent concern. It only lays down that where an unmarried woman married subsequently, the Central Government may, if the maintenance of the efficiency of the Service so requires, call upon her to resign. Therefore, this rule does not compel unmarried women to resign on marriage as a matter of course, as is the case in the respondent concern. It is only when the Central Government considers that marriage has impaired the efficiency of the women concerned that the Central Government may call upon her to resign. The rule which

> is in force in the respondent concern however assumes that merely by marriage the efficiency of the women employee is impaired and such an assumption in our opinion is not justified.

Though Rule 5(3) was upheld by the Supreme Court, we are happy to note that it was deleted from the IAS Recruitment Rules in 1972 after an assurance given by the Prime Minister in Parliament, since it amounted to discrimination against married women.

Low Proportion

The low proportion of women in the higher ranks may be a reflection either of prejudices and discriminatory recruitment policies or lack of career orientation and career commitment on the part of women. Disparities in the proportion of men and women at different levels of responsibility are important indicators of the unequal employment status and opportunity for men and women which are the direct result of a combination of factors, i.e., the educational system, training, job orientation and culture conditioning. Many private concerns do not recruit women into their managerial cadre as a matter of policy as they believe that women cannot exercise supervision and control and they are weeded out in promotion. Such prejudices tend to persist and are difficult to break down. In response to our request for information regarding policy in regard to recruitment of women, one nationalized undertaking (A Unit of LIC India) observed:

> Our general policy has been to avoid, as far as possible, appointment of female employees in the organization. Lack of education among womenfolk, socio-economic backwardness of the State, have been largely responsible for creating an atmosphere which has been discouraging to women's employment. Amidst these conditions, while very few women candidates were coming forward for jobs in our organization, we were reluctant to appoint them lest it may create administrative problems. Besides, as a

> private business organization prior to nationalisation, we gave due consideration to efficiency discipline, administrative ability, hard work and in our opinion women candidates in general were not upto the mark.

The ILO report on "Women Workers in a Changing World" noted that "while formal discrimination in employment based on sex is tending to disappear, informal policies and practices are tending to persist. The residual forms of discrimination tend to operate, formally and informally at a higher level in the occupational pyramid, often blocking the advancement of women on the ground of their individual merit irrespective of sex."

'In spite of these limitations, an overview of the trends during the last five-six decades reveals that the contribution and achievement of women in this has been significant. The number of women working as lawyers, engineers, technologists, scientists, accountants, auditors, journalists, business managers and executives, may be small but they indicate a qualitative change.

While the overall increase in the number of women in these occupations indicate a relatively widening field for employment of educated women, this should not be given undue importance. We did not attempt any definition of the type of work or of the sections of workers employed in this sector since it was neither possible nor necessary. Broadly, the tertiary sector constitutes that sector of the economy in which no production of material goods take place.

In this sense, all work in the tertiary is unproductive. In an economy like ours, where an unusually high proportion of total capital is invested in trade and commerce or where because of social and political considerations, allocation of resources for defence, maintenance of law and order and certain social services like education and health are high, the tertiary sector is somewhat bigger in volume than in other developing countries. As a result of this, employment in the tertiary sector in general and in the public sector in particular has increased at an exceedingly fast rate. The expanded role of Government at all levels of the development process has been one of the greatest contributory factors towards this.

As compared to this, the actual production of goods has not increased at the same pace. It has been increasingly realized that a developing economy cannot bear the weight of this very heavy tertiary sector, with the increasing constraints on resources available for development and inflationary tendencies. The increasing financial crisis has already imposed severe constraints on public resources and calls for reduction in public expenditure and nonproductive expenditure in the economy as a whole. The major impact of these demands are bound to be on these sectors where we have noticed a concentration of a larger proportion of women's employment, viz., education, health and other social services. It is an established fact that this is the sector which receives the first impact of an economy drive, both in the public and in the private sector. We may, therefore, anticipate a slowing down, if not an actual reduction in the opportunities for women's employment in these services and professions.

The overriding inference from the existing trends in different sectors of the economy suggests that without increasing opportunity for women's employment in the productive sectors, it will not be possible to arrest the established trend of decline in women's economic participation that we have pointed out earlier. The marginal contribution that the tertiary sector can make to the employment situation as a whole is negligible, and in the interest of economic development of the country as a whole, attempts are bound to be made in the near future to reduce the present imbalance between the production and the tertiary sectors. This points to the imperative need to increase opportunities for women in the former.

Infrastructure for Participation in Economy

The sector wise examination of women's rights and opportunities for economic participation, indicates that the major forces affecting women's employment, stem from structural changes within the economy — in agriculture, industry, and the economy as a whole. The change from traditional to a modern market economy, from laissez-faire to deliberate planned development, from unorganized to organized production, from unregulated to regulated relations of production, from labour to capital intensive technology, and the intensification of socioeconomic inequalities, all have had an impact on the employment situation.

PART — FIVE

Protective Cover

TWELVE

Legislative Measures

As far as education is concerned, the existing legislations should be reviewed so that equality and social justice can be ensured to women of all communities and creeds. Where this involves amendments to existing personal laws of the minority group, initial efforts should be concentrated on arousing a desire for change from among the members of such minority groups. A vigorous campaign should be made to educate women about their rights, and to generate among all communities, a desire for a common civil code, to be achieved by the end of the UN Decade for Women in 1985.

Legal aid should be organized for women in need with the active assistance of the Bar Councils.

The setting up of family courts should be considered for speedy and effective adjudication in all cases concerning the family. Women, particularly in rural areas, should be protected against harassment.

The practice of dowry should be eradicated. The legislation should be strictly enforced. This is a social evil which requires sustained action not only on the part of government agencies, but also on the part of voluntary organizations and public leaders.

The provisions of the existing Child Marriage Restraint Act should be reviewed. Special attention should be given to streamlining the enforcement machinery and involving local authorities and voluntary organizations in the implementation of the Act. Active public support should be mobilized by governmental agencies, voluntary organizations and public leaders against child marriage, particularly in rural areas. Simultaneously, systematic programmes of education and training should be developed for girls till they marry.

Administrative Measures

Education: Education is the greatest known catalytic agent for social change. All out efforts should therefore be made to achieve the goal of universal primary education as early as possible. The ideas of equality between the sexes and participation by women in development should be woven into the fabric of the educational system.

The employment of women teachers should be actively promoted. The existing employment procedures, including those for part-time, employment, should be reviewed and, where necessary, relaxations in age, etc., made so that more women teachers, can be employed and husbands and wives are posted in the same schools or at the same station.

The content of education should be strengthened in terms of both life and work relevance. Attention should be given to vocationalization and diversification of courses which should not only be limited to traditional women's vocations but also give emphasis on the preparation of women for participation in modern sectors of industrial production. Polytechnics (including mini-polytechnics) should be started for girls in the smaller urban centres to provide training facilities in trades crafts which will prompt self-employment.

At the stage of higher education special incentives like, freeships, scholarships, hostel facilities, and book loans should be made available to girls from rural, backward and hilly areas, from backward classes and from poor families. A greater diversification in the courses offered should be made to enhance work opportunities in non-traditional vocations in modern sectors of industrial production.

Adoption of multiple entry in education, non-formal part-time education facilities, condensed courses for education, correspondence courses and courses for continuing education should be made available in a larger measure to women in semi-urban and rural areas, and to working women in urban and semi-urban areas. Adult education and functional literacy programmes should be vigorously pursued through both official and voluntary agencies.

Employment: Equal Remuneration Act, 1976, has been passed, providing for payment of equal remuneration to men and women workers and the prevention of discrimination on grounds of sex. Special steps should therefore be taken to review recruitment, promotion and other personnel practices in all public and private sector undertakings to ensure that there is no discrimination against women candidates. Women apprentices should be taken without discrimination in industries. Representatives of women's voluntary organizations, should be associated, in the machinery set up to ensure adequate participation of women in employment.

Village industries which provide scope for the employment of women should be further promoted-Special training services should be organized and credit, marketing facilities, etc., extended, specially in regard to crafts which can have a ready export market, through modernization of design, etc. Integrated pilot projects to cover training, production and marketing should be started.

The existing requirement procedures and employment conditions should be reviewed to encourage the re-entry of women into the workforce. For this purpose, the provisions relating to maximum age of entry into services should be reviewed. Part-time employment of women should be promoted wherever feasible. Refresher courses and training programmes should be organized for adult women to make them fit for re-employment.

Organizations entrusted by the government with the task of promoting self-employment opportunities should develop special women's entrepreneurial training motivation programmes and provide special assistance to women entrepreneurs and to women's co-operative in terms of credit, licensing, etc.

The existing legislation in regard to maternity benefits should be reviewed. It should simultaneously be ensured that there is no consequent adverse effect on the employment of women.

Health Care, Nutrition and Family Planning: Maternal and child health care facilities should be expanded, particularly in semi-urban and rural areas, and coverage provided to high risk pregnant women. Ante-natal and post-natal clinics should be started in every Primary Health Centre and district hospital.

Nutrition supplementation should be provided to high risk pregnant mothers. Simultaneously, nutrition and health education should be given to girls and to mothers through all available media and institutions (school, hospitals, PHCs, etc.).

Family welfare planning services should be expanded and measures intensified to educate and prepare couples to avail them, specifically in rural, backward and tribal areas. The facilities under the Medical Termination of Pregnancy Act, 1971 should be made available in semi-urban and rural areas and information regarding the provisions disseminated among women, immunization facilities should be gradually extended to all children.

Facilities of Working Women: The establishment of day care centres, creches, and balwadis should be promoted on a large scale in rural, semi-urban and urban areas to help working mothers and active women social workers discharge their duties, and enable the older children to attend school.

Hostel facilities for working women of the lower income groups should be expanded.

Care for the Socially Disadvantaged: Women without any means of support, and the physically handicapped should be provided services for education, training and rehabilitation so that they can become self-reliant. Old age homes should be opened for the aged and the infirm. Special programmes should be developed for unmarried mothers and their children.

The provision of the Suppression of Immoral Traffic Act (1956) should be reviewed to facilitate their more efficient implementation. Comprehensive rehabilitation programmes for victims of immoral traffic and their children should be developed. Special steps should be taken to prevent vulnerable young girls and women from becoming victims of this social evil.

Promotion of Voluntary Effort: The growth of voluntary organizations, especially in rural, backward and tribal areas and in urban slums should be promoted to mobilize public support for different programmes of welfare. Training facilities should be provided on a large scale to voluntary workers. Leadership training programmes, particularly for women from weaker sections, should be developed so that they can function effectively as agents of change. The establishment of Mahila Mandals should be promoted in every village so that they can function as field level agencies for social and economic transformation. Voluntary organizations have critical role in mobilizing public opinion in favour of equality among men and women and eradicating superstitions, social evils and waste.

A vigorous campaign of education and action should be launched in favour of community sanitation and hygiene. Public utility services for women should be expanded wherever called for.

Machinery for Implementation: In order to ensure that the Resolution unanimously passed by the two Houses of Parliament is acted upon and the implementation of the Plan of Action is ensured, it is proposed that:

(i) A Standing Advisory Committee should be set up at the national level which will review the progress every year so that a report is submitted to Parliament annually. The Committee may be called 'The National Committee on Women'.

(ii) To service the above Committee a special bureau should be set up in the Ministry of Education and Social Welfare (Department of Social Welfare). The Bureau will keep in touch with the implementation of the various programmes by the Central Ministries, State Governments and non-official agencies.

(iii) At the State level similar committees should be set up under the chairmanship of the Chief Minister. These Committees should also have adequate administrative support.

Education in General

In realization of the importance of education in general and the need for equality in opportunities for the intellectual development of men and women, successive Five-Year Plans have consistently placed special emphasis on the acceleration of women's education. The emphasis with regard to women's education has all along been to equip her for the multiple roles as citizens, housewives, mothers, contributors to family income and builders of the new society. Efforts have been made during the past two decades of planned development to enrol more girls in school; to encourage girls to stay in schools; to continue their education as long as possible; and to provide non-formal education opportunities for women. The Draft Fifth Five-Year Plan has declared that "the outlays for the education of girls will be stepped up.". The fulfilment of the constitutional directive in respect of providing free and compulsory education up to the age of 14 years has been included as one of the components of the Minimum Needs Programme.

These efforts have had a significant impact on the progress of women's education in India. For example, there is a primary school within easy, walking distance from the home of almost all the children. This has resulted in an increase in the enrolment of girls in classes I-V as a percentage of total enrolment in these classes from 28.1 in 1950-51 to 37.6 in 1973-74. In respect of classes

I-VIII, IX-XI/ XII and university education also there has been an appreciable increase in the percentage of girls' enrolment to total enrolment, between the years 1950-51 and 1973-74. In fact, girls' enrolment is observed to be growing at a faster rate than those of boys.

Despite these encouraging trends and marked progress made in respect of women's education, the educational status of women is still far from satisfactory for the following reasons:

(a) Literacy among women is generally lower than that among men. According to the 1971 Census data, only 13.4 per cent of women in this age group of 25+ are literate.

(b) Enrolment of girls in classes I to V is only 66.4 per cent of girls in the corresponding age group, i.e., from 6 to 11 years; while in respect of boys the relevant percentage is 100.2.

(c) Drop-out rate is also very high in classes I to V. A recent study has shown that the drop-out rate especially accentuated in the case of girls from rural areas and from the less privileged sections of society, is as heavy as 42.85 per cent between classes I and II.

(d) In classes VI to VIII, percentages of enrolment of girls and boys to the total girls and boys in the relevant age group (i.e., from 11 to 14 years) are 22.2 and 48.3, respectively.

(e) At the secondary stage, i.e.., from classes IX to XI the girls enrolled constitute only 12 per cent of girls in the relevant age group 14 to 17 years as against 31 per cent in respect of the enrolment of boys in this age group.

(f) Enrolment of girls in Post-Matric classes constitutes only 2.3 per cent of girls in the concerned age group 17 to 23 years, while the enrolment percentage of boys in this age group is 7.5.

Factors Retarding the Progress of Women's Education

Girls and women in India have thus not been able to take full advantage of the available opportunities/facilities for intellectual development. This is mainly because of several social and cultural factors in addition to various other reasons. Action plans and strategies for women's education should, therefore, aim at neutralizing the effects of the factors which have retarded the progress of women's education in India. With a view to facilitating the formulation of such a plan of action, in what follows, some of the major reasons which have operated against girls/women in taking full advantage of educational opportunities/facilities are listed below:

(a) General indifference to education of girls.

(b) Social resistance arising out of fears and misconceptions that education might alienate girls from traditions and social values and lead to mal-adjustments, conflicts and nonconformism.

(c) Early marriage and social inhibitions against girls pursuing education after marriage.

(d) Prevalence of child labour among girls belonging to weaker sections and the hard domestic chores which some of the unmarried girls - even in the middle-class families - are required to perform.

(e) The prevailing notion that the sole occupation of women is to bear children, look after her husband and children, and thus be restricted to domestic work.

(f) Discrimination effected by employers against women labour in both organized and unorganized sectors in matters of recruitment, training and promotion.

(g) Many girls and their parents find that the school curriculum do not conform adequately to their needs and interests.

(h) Unsuitable and inflexible school timings and inadequate facilities for girls in schools, particularly in the co-educational schools.

Major Objective of Women's Education

It should be recognized here that the general objective of any policy towards women's education cannot be different from those relating to men. However, in view of the social and cultural handicaps that have operated against women in general and in view of the multiple role that women are required to play, the need for a set of objectives specific to women's education is imperative. The following major objectives are, therefore, considered here:

(a) Prepare women to fully participate in socially productive work, fully aware of family planning needs with a view to achieving her full integration with the democratic and developmental efforts of the country.

(b) Help break down overt covert biases against women.

(c) Make women aware of the various legal, social and economic rights, provisions -and privileges available to them and the way they can take advantage of them, for their advancement.

(d) Enable women to be self-reliant to achieve economic independence.

(e) Impart the idea of equality between the sexes and participation by women in development through the educational system.

(f) And above all, to find full expression for her talent, ability and personality and for this purpose, enable her to adopt a discriminating attitude so that she can escape the bonds of superstition and obscurantism.

Action Plans: Action plans here are evolved within the general framework of major objectives mentioned above. In addition, the action plans have taken into consideration other objectives which are specific of educational categories like elementary education, middle stage education, secondary stage education, university education and non-formal education. For the sake of convenience, in what follows, action plans specific of each age group of girls, are all mentioned separately.

Elementary Education

Girls in this age group constitute the population of girls of primary school going age. Action plans for this age group will need to be in two directions:

(a) To universalize primary education for girls, and

(b) To strive for the retention of girls already enrolled.

Towards this end, the following action plans are suggested:

Administrative and Structural Measures

(i) State Governments should take note of the habitations without primary schools as indicated by the Third Educational Survey and make arrangements for providing primary school within a distance of 1.5 km of all habitations within next five years.

(ii) Mobile schools should be provided for children of all nomadic tribes, migrant labour and construction workers.

(iii) Girls in this age are often required to look after younger children and attend minor household duties, particularly in the rural areas and among weaker sections of the society. As this is one of the major reasons that holds such girls from attending school, special efforts should be made to enlarge the scope and coverage of pre-school education programmes like Balwadis and Anganwadis, where the older girls can be given practical work experience and child care.

(iv) These pre-school education programmes should, wherever possible, be attached to primary schools or at least located in the vicinity of primary schools, as that would help in cultivating a school going habit right from the childhood.

(v) Supervision and inspection of primary schools should give particular attention to the problem of enrolment of girls, their retention, involvement of the community, etc.

Promotional and Motivational Measures

(vi) Special and sustained persuasive and motivational campaign and organizational drives should be undertaken among regions/communities which have shown markedly a low achievement in girls enrolment. Voluntary organizations at local levels like Mahila Mandals and local bodies should be fully involved in this programme.

(vii) Promotion and support to girls' education should also be tackled through a multipronged programme of incentives - both for bringing girls to schools and for retaining them in schools. The incentives can be in the form of mid-day meals, free supply of books and reading materials, scholarships awards, etc. Active collaboration of voluntary organizations may be sought in this regard.

Pedagogical Measures

(viii) The primary teacher training course should undergo a major revision with a view to adequately preparing the teacher for the promotion of girls' education. Emphasis should be more on the use of such non-formal methods of imparting education that would interest and attract more and more girls to attend schools.

Education for Girls in the Age Group 11-14 years: Population of girls in this age group constitutes girls of middle school going age. This group can be divided into three sub-groups:

(a) Girls students attending middle schools;

(b) Girl drop-outs at various stages from classes I to V; and

(c) Girls who have not attended school.

The objectives of education and training are different for each of the sub-groups.

Action Plan: Action plans for education of girls in this age group should be concerned about:

(i) encouraging further enrolment of girls at this stage;

(ii) retention of girls already in middle schools; and

(iii) rendering the curriculum more relevant.

The following action plans are suggested:

Pedagogical Measures

(i) The content should be more oriented to the needs of girls in the village communities so that both the parents and the girls see relevance of this education for their own lives. The curriculum of the middle school stage needs to be given a strong work experience orientation, introducing girls to crafts and skills which will be of direct use to them in the family, community and farm, and help them in rural employment and self-employment. It should also introduce girls to scientific knowledge, principles of home-making, family life education, nutrition and diet, environment education and civic education.

(ii) Women Teachers: It is very important for the promotion of girls' education to employ women teachers in schools. Infact, the general view is that women are more suited to be teachers and larger number of teachers should be women, However, the problem may come up in different ways. More number of men may be qualified and trained women may not be in a position to accept employment as full time teachers due to personal problems; women also have difficulties in working in rural areas.. There has to be relaxation from age restrictions. The States may consider reserving a certain number of posts of teachers for women and where there are not adequate number of trained teachers, untrained persons may be recruited and deputed for training. The question of giving posting to husband and wife both of whom are teachers in the same place may be considered.

It may also be worthwhile in those areas which have schools without women teachers, to select educated women in that area and send them for training and appoint them in the schools in that area. Where educated women are not available for posting in a school, local women may be selected and posted as school matas (school mothers) to keep the girl students company and induce parents to send their girls and children to schools. The rules relating to age and qualification of recruitment and service may have to be relaxed in these cases and the deficiency made up through in-service training.

Women should not be discriminated against in matters of recruitment. Selection and recruitment should be made on merit. No qualified meritorious woman candidate should be overlooked. State Governments may contemplate providing for 50 per cent of teachers in schools being women and to look into this aspect while sanctioning grants to institutions.

In single teacher institutions (the exact position will be brought out by the Third Educational Survey), it may be desirable to ensure that where there are two teachers, one of them should be a woman. If locally educated women are available, they can be recruited. Husband wife teams can be posted.

(iii) The primary teacher training course needs to undergo a major revision to adequately prepare the trainees for their special responsibility for the promotion of girls' education in rural areas, especially in adapting the content to suit the needs and interests of girls, in adopting non-formal methodologies and in linking with community and developmental activities.

(iv) Supervision and inspection of schools should be given particular attention to the problem of enrolment of girls, their retention, factors contributing to wastage and stagnation, revision of curriculum, involvement of the community, working conditions of women teachers, etc.

Promotional and Motivational Measures

(v) School timings should be flexible, as many of the girls in this age group are required to help their mothers in routine domestic chores.

(vi) Adoption of multiple entry and part-time courses is recommended.

(vii) Incentives like mid-day meals, scholarships, free school uniforms, free books and study materials, stipend, awards, etc., should be extended to all girls in the rural areas and slums in the urban areas.

Middle School-Girl Drop-outs

Alternative Measures

(viii) For school drop-outs of girls, pre-vocational training programmes should be organized on an extensive scale to cover all girls in the rural areas and in the slums of urban areas. The objectives of such training should be to render them self-sufficient in home management, and help them to achieve economic independence. With this in view, such training programmes should include courses in sewing, knitting, cooking, nutrition, minor repairs of the house, motherhood, child care, etc.

Girls who never attended schools

(ix) For the non-student girls in this age group, the objective should be to provide adequate preparation in life through a combined three-year course in general education and vocational training. Vocational training should be on the lines of pre-vocational training mentioned above.

(x) Such training programmes should be extended to all girls in the rural areas. In the urban areas, preference should be given to girls in slum areas and destitute girls.

Education for Girls

Girls in this age group also can be classified into three groups:

(a) Girl students with motivation to attend secondary school;

(b) Girl drop-outs from classes VI to VIII; and

(c) Non-student girls, i.e., students who never attended schools.

Girl Students

The action plans under this category should emphasize more on:

(i) facilitating more girls to pursue education at the secondary stage, and

(ii) strengthening the content in terms of both life and work relevance.

The following action plans are suggested:

Administrative and Structural Measures

(i) Separate girls schools or separate sections should be started where the social/ cultural environment demands them.

(ii) In co-education schools special attention should be given to the provision of adequate toilet, rest and recreation facilities, separately for girls.

(iii) State Governments which have not yet made high school education free for girls should do so on a priority basis.

(iv) Multiple entry system and part-time education may be provided.

Promotional and Motivational Measures

(v) All courses of training in vocational and technical schools at the secondary stage should be open to both boys and girls. There should be no discrimination in this regard.

(vi) Liberal incentives in the form of book allowances, book-bank facilities, etc., should be extended to encourage more girls in rural and backward areas to pursue secondary education.

(vii) Separate hostel facilities should be provided particularly in rural areas and residential scholarships should be offered.

Pedagogical Measures

(viii) The curriculum should be more diversified taking into consideration the various occupational opportunities available to women and the interests and aptitudes of girls.

Girl Drop-outs

Alternative Measures

(ix) Condensed courses of education started in 1958 were found very useful. Under this scheme women in the age group 13-30 years who have had some schooling are prepared for middle school, matriculation or equivalent examinations within a period of 2 years' duration. The minimum age limit here should be reduced to 15 years. This scheme should be extended to cover all rural areas and weaker sections of the urban community.

(x) The condensed course should be organized for smaller groups, say 5 to 7 persons, using the community resources like girls' high schools and girls' colleges.

(xi) Apart from imparting general education, condensed course should also aim at imparting job-oriented training with the active co-operation of existing vocational training institutions.

(xii) Correspondence courses and self-study programmes may be introduced.

(xiii) Efforts should be made to cover at least about 215 lakh of girls in the age group 15-30 under the condensed courses programme during the Fifth Plan period.

Non-student Girls

(xiv) Fourth Plan introduced a programme of functional literacy with the objective of imparting elementary general education and vocational training-related to the functions performed to men and women in the rural areas who never attended schools. This programme should be expanded to cover all rural areas.

(xv) Apart from imparting general elementary education and knowledge about farming technologies, the curriculum for women should include courses of training in occupational skills like kitchen gardening, food processing, poultry keeping, animal husbandry; and household, arts like cooking nutritional values of foods locally available, sewing, knitting, etc., and motherhood, child care and family planning as also electronics and like fields.

(xvi) Similar programmes should also be designed for girls in this age group and under this category belonging to urban areas.

In the Age Group 17 Years and Above

Education for girls in this age group also can be divided into three groups, as in the case of other age groups:

(a) Education for girls at the higher education stage;

(b) Education for girl drop-outs from the educational system beyond the secondary stage; and

(c) Education for non-student girls - girls who never had any education.

In respect of the last category here, i.e., education for non-student girls, action plans are the same as those concerning non-student girls in the age group 14-17 years. Hence, this category is not dealt with separately here.

Education for Girls at the Higher Education Stage

Action plans in this area should aim at:

(a) Making higher education available to the less privileged sections of the society, particularly girls from the rural areas; and

(b) Making the curriculum more relevant and responsive to the cultural and occupational needs of women.

The following action plans may be taken up for consideration:

Administrative and Structural Measures

(i) The general policy here should be to discourage separate institutions for women and to promote co-educational institutions for women and to promote co-educational facilities. However, in areas where separate institutions are required to promote education of women, they may be permitted on the merits of such cases.

(ii) Vocational counselling and guidance services should be organized in a more meaningful way to help girls in colleges and universities opt for suitable courses relevant to their talent, interests and needs.

Promotional and Motivational Measures

(iii) Incentives like scholarships, freeships, etc., should be provided to enable girls from rural areas to pursue higher education.

(iv) For girls belonging to weaker sections, in addition to freeships and scholarships, bursaries should also be provided to meet their expenses on food and lodging.

(v) Provision of self-cooking facilities in hostels for girls should also be considered.

(vi) Girls pursuing higher education should be provided easy access to textbooks and other reference material through book-bank facilities.

(vii) Girls should be encouraged to enter professional courses. If necessary, reservation of seats for girls in professional courses may be considered.

Pedagogical Measures

(viii) Diversification of courses at the junior college level and undergraduate level should be undertaken on a priority basis with a view to preparing the girls for the various employment opportunities open to them.

Education for Girl Drop-outs

Girls in this age group drop-out of educational system for various reasons. Marriage is one of the reasons which force girls in this age group to discontinue further formal education. Economic hardship is another reason which forces some girls to drop-out and seek jobs, with a view to supporting their families. Social prejudices and cultural attitudes also force some of the girls to leave the formal educational system. For girls in this category, therefore, the policy should be to extend non-formal educational facilities on a large scale.

The following action plans are suggested:

(i) Facilities for part-time self-study and correspondence courses should be expanded on a large scale to enable working girls and non-working married and unmarried girls to enhance their educational qualifications.

(ii) In addition to course leading to degree/diploma, short courses in specific subjects through summer schools/sessions, ad hoc programmes like seminars, laboratory work, workshop experience, etc., should be organized for working girls, with a view to upgrading their professional skills and qualifications. Facilities for further education not necessarily leading to a degree but for upgradation of knowledge and skills could be provided.

(iii) While the initiative for organizing such programmes should be taken by the Central and State Governments, the employees should also be increasingly involved.

(iv) Pre-examination training facilities should be organized on a large scale for educated women from the rural areas and those belonging to weaker sections with the objective of equipping them to successfully compete in examinations for public jobs.

(v) Entrepreneurship development programmes should be organized separately for educated women in the age group 18-30 years with a minimum of matriculation level of education.

The objective of such training programmes should be:

(a) Make them aware of the various opportunities for self-employment;

(b) Motivate them to take up self-employment;

(c) Impart needed skills/training; and

(d) Promote achievement motivation among them.

Administrative Measures

To make the various action plans successful and to achieve a real breakthrough in women's education, there is an urgent need for a matching and effective administrative set up, both at the central and state levels. With this in view, the following suggestions are made:

(i) In the Union Ministry of Education and Social Welfare, a special unit/cell may be set up to be in charge of women's education to review and initiate follow-up action.

(ii) In each State education department, a senior officer should be placed in charge of girls' education in order that it may receive adequate emphasis, execution and co-ordination.

(iii) As the district is the operational unit for all educational programmes and as the needs of girls vary in extent and kind from area to area within a district, a separate cell for girls' educational — formal and non-formal may be created within the purview of the district educational officer at the district headquarters.

(iv) School supervisory system should be staffed with more women.

THIRTEEN

Benefits of Reservation

Education is a field, where female students benefit the most. In fact, women throughout the world have a low socioeconomic and political status. Even though democracy made great gains in 1989-1991, women members average only 11 per cent of world's legislatures. The presence of woman in formal democratic process is woefully inadequate at all levels, centre, state and local/grassroot level. They are on margin in political decision-making processes. This fact has evoked concern in recent years about the political status of women. It has been increasingly realised that unless empowered politically. the socioeconomic status of women cannot be improved. Thus, the movement for the political empowerment by women has steadily gained momentum today.

International Concern

A brief outline in international arena regarding the voices raised for political empowerment of women, becomes essential. Preparations were made by the United Nations Organization (UNO) for a convention, way back in 1952, about women political rights. Again in 1967, there was a Declaration on Elimination of Discrimination against women by the UN General Assembly. 1975 witnessed an international conference in Mexico, where a world plan of action was drafted. It emphasised that political participation comprised of women having voting power, their acting as pressure groups, their being elected as representatives and as governmental employees. Again in 1980, there was a conference in Copenhagen, which was named as 'Participation in the Political and other

Decision-making Processes and participation in Efforts to Promote International Coperation and Strengthen Peace.' The year 1985 witnessed a conference at Nairobi, where forward looking strategies for the advancement of women and the international blue print for action until year 2000 was planned.

In this context, the 1995 Beijing conference was a landmark, where the focus was on political empowerment of women, and consequently, on the issue of women's reservation. This received an international recognition. The Inter -parliamentary union meeting held in New Delhi on 1997 February 14-18, attended by about 240 representatives from 78 countries, focussed on the theme: 'Towards Partnership between Men and Women in Politics.' The final consensus was that establishment of quota for women's political participation was legitimate and practical. It was also felt that women need to be established in the political system as well in the membership and hierarchies of political parties, and with respect to candidates chosen by them to contest election.

Experiences have proved that despite the constitutional arrangements, women all over the world have not been given actual power. It was realised that democratic norms cannot be realised if marginalised sections, which include women, are not in the mainstream of political process. There will be no change in the political milieu of the country, particularly since most women both as voters and voteseekers are within the patriarchal structure. Not only a change within the existing political structure is required, but also within women's own perception of sensitive issues that directly concern their lives. Why we need the strategy for affirmative action or positive discrimination in favour of women is because the age-old traditions have kept women out of the periphery of political power. This calls for a debate, devising methods through law for their access to political power. This again brings us to the debate on quota system/ reservation for women as a strategy for their political empowerment.

With this backdrop, an attempt has been made to understand the extent and magnitude of women's political participation in free India.

Scene in India

True to the spirit of freedom struggle, and in recognition of the important role played by women in freedom struggle, and also the promises made by the leaders of the nation, the Constitution of India pledges itself to full equality among men and women. The Preamble to the Constitution of India resolved to secure to all its citizens: Justice, social, economic and political; liberty of thought, expression, belief, faith and worship; Equality of status and opportunity; and to promote among them all fraternity assuming the dignity of all individuals and the unity of the nation.

To action these national objectives, the Constitution guarantees certain fundamental rights and freedom such as freedom of speech, protection of life and personal liberty. While these may be termed as positive rights, the negative rights are the prohibition of discrimination on the basis of race, caste, religion, sex or denial of equal protection on such grounds. Indian women are the beneficiaries of these rights in the same manner as men. Article 14 ensures equality before law and Article 15 prohibits any "discrimination" interalia of sex. All these provisions ensure equal opportunity of political participation by women along with men, and that they needed to be represented within the system and the status quo. This false sense of complacency that women have been granted political right along with men on an equal footing by the Constitution, remained for quite some time. Thus, in the 1950s and the '60s there was no such open expression. However, with the '70s studies undertaken by the Committee on the Status of Women in India (CSWI), revealed shocking data (as per 1971 census). This was a watershed year which raised concern among lawyers, thinkers, planners, regarding the servitude position of women in India. Since then, the demand for improvement and the political empowerment of women started at the global level.

Why Reservation?

Before coming to the issue of the strategies, debates and resultants of the problem of women reservation, it becomes necessary to debate on the need for reservation. A very pertinent question arises as to why reservation is the only alternative for the victims of age-old oppression and exploitation? The remedy, if rationally thought upon, can only be either 'equal opportunity' or 'reservation'. For some time, equal opportunity will not work because of the top-dog/under-dog attitude that dies hard. Can there be equallity immediately in an unequal society? Reservation is a means of protecting the weaker sections of society, who have for centuries been socially, historically and politically exploited, giving them a chance to come on a par with the stronger sections and be prepared to take advantage of equal opportunity. Women are in this category a historically victimised group. Women are nowhere in the planning process after five decades of democratic politics. Economic independence cannot alone suffice. Power at political level would only change the status quo, Parliament is a sad spectacle. Reservation, thus, aims at giving not only panchayati women, but all women participation in public Life.

Beginning of Serious Concern

The Committee on the Status of Women in India (CSWI) though agreeing to the problems especially of rural women's life, only recommended the establishment of statutory women's panchayats. In case of state assemblies and Parliament, the committee failed to address the problem of under representation caused by institutionalised inequalities, which 25 years of democracy had failed to dislodge. But with an increase in grassroots organisation, the new groups of poor women demonstrated for greater dynamism and challenge. The issue of reservation was periodically raised by political activists as well as serving women legislators in various government-sponsored conferences.

The Rajiv Gandhi government in 1985, took the issue of women as a priority issue. Subsequently, women's division within social welfare became a Department for Women and Child Development within the Ministry of Human Resource Development. But this did not make much impact, as in 1988, the first draft of the National Perspective Plan (NPP) for women to the year 2000, which recommended 30 per cent reservation for women in all elective bodies - from Panchayats to Parliament, put in a proviso that in the initial years, this quota may be filled by nomination co-option. The final version of NPP, however, only recommended 30 per cent reservation in Panchayats and municipalities to be filled by election. During Rajiv Gandhi's regime, efforts were made to amend the Constitution so as to provide for 33 per cent reservation to women in local grassroots level Punchayat bodies. But the amendment (73rd) was made in 1992 under the next government providing for 1/3 reservation to women in the women panchayats with Schedule Castes and Tribes inbuilt quotas for women. The bill was released is April 1993.

The conferring of constitutional status on local self-government as an integral part of the Indian governance structure, and mandating 1/3rd reservation for women in all these bodies, with an in-built quota for Schedule Castes and Tribes women were quietly ratified in April 1993.

Between 1993 and 1996, women's organisations united for a joint demand for reservation in state assemblies and Parliament. The demand was accepted and featured in the manifestoes of the major parties:

Janata Dal (JD)	The reservation on 30 per cent elective post in local bodies for women has to be extended to union and state legislatures.
Congress	The Congress has already reserved seats for women in the gram panchayat and municipalities. It also proposes to provide reservation for women in state assemblies and Parliament.
CPI	Having made a beginning with panchayats, the next step should be to reserve 1/3rd seats for women in state assembly and Parliament.

CP1 (M)	1/3rd of the seats in legislature and Parliament be reserved for women.
BJP	In state assembly and Parliament and all elected position, 33 per cent reservation will ensure that at the dawn of the 21st century, Indian women will have true participation.
Samata Party	The party will initiate legislation for the reservation of constituencies for women candidates in rotation for one third of the seats in both the Lok Sabha and state assemblies.

But against these theoretical assurances, the major political parties are taking vogue positions on the issue of caste-based and religion-based women's reservation regarding four sub-categories within the women quota-backward castes, Muslims, Christians and Sikhs. In September 1996, when the reservation bill was brought before the house, the first obstacle was about the fixed quota women from the other backward castes (OBCs). The main votaries were Sharad Yadav, Ram Vilas Paswan), Mulayam Singh Yadav and other OBC MPs. The main argument advanced by them was that with a blanket reservation, the upper caste women would grab all the party tickets and get supremacy in Parliament.

The pressure was mounting by the women activists. It gained momentum after the ratification in 1993. In 1996 general elections, only 34 (that is, 6.3 out of 537 declared) seats went to Women. Mainstream national level parties which had a longer history of involving women such as congress, the janata Dal and the Communist Party did not do much better. Only 103 women out of 388, who contested the election to the 11th Lok Sabha were supported by the parties. Congress had 16 women in Parliament. BJP had 14 women and JD had only nine seats. Such induction reflects tokenism rather than power sharing. It could also be termed as the patriarchal frame of society, which has marginalised women in mainstream parliamentary politics.

The Bill being Tossed Around

Amidst, such a scenario of opposition, the double face of parties and MPs, the Constitution amendment (81st) Bill 1996 was introduced by the United Front Government. All hopes were dashed to the ground at the end of the discussion on an aggressive plea for proportional representation of seats for women belonging to OBC. The bill was then referred to a joint select committee of 32 parliamentarians under Gita Mukherji for amendments with a brief to see if the demand of having reservation for the OBCs from within the 33 per cent could be met. The committee in its final recommendation wanted the bill to be passed at the earliest and rejected the demand for an OBC quota. Both the houses witnessed clamorous scenes with members cutting across party lines.

1997 : Once again the government failed to put the bill before Parliament due to strong objections to the bill in its present form. It was deliberately attempted to keep the bill in cold storage by stating that the consensus needed to be evolved.

1998 : Although, Prime Minister Atal Behari Vajpayee assured representatives of the women's organisation that he would not only introduce the bill in the Budget session but also put it to vote and the Union Cabinet also approved the introduction of the bill, It was once again put under the lid on the issue that the quota should be slashed to 15 per cent for OBC women. The women's bill was stalled in the Lok Sabha and was finally deferred on July 17.

What does this show? Women's reservation bill is surrounded by shame and hyprocisy and more by male chauvinism. The shelving of the Women's reservation bill calls for a serious debate on the text of the Bill.

Women's Reservation Bill

The proposed bill is debated upon from many angles. It requires analysis and discussion. The bill envisaged reservation by rotation of the constituencies through lottery system so any constituency could be selected for the reserved category. The debate and doubt is on the issue of rotational principle.

The Debate

Senior advocate of Supreme Court Abhishek M Singhvi, has opined that though the rationale is unclear, it appears evidently to be actuated by a desire not to permanently shut men off. He reiterates that the constitutional mandate for rotation of constituencies reserved for women is impracticable and harmful. Madhu Kishwar, Women's activitist also contends that the bill has been drafted irresponsibly. She opines that the rotational principle means that neither male nor female aspirants will know which constituency they can stand from. The result, at least 1/3rd of male legislators will be routinely uprooted and denied seats from their chosen areas of work and Influence, and an equal number of women will be told at the last minute where they can fight an election from. This will further erode the incentive to serve a constituency because everyone will remain forever uncertain about whether or not they can actually get elected from their areas of influence.

To this problem, Madhu kishwar comes out with a suggestive measure. Instead of 33 per cent rotating lottery system of reservation, we provide for 50 per cent reservation by having double member constituencies. This would give women a share of seats in proportion to their population. That is to say, each constituency should be represented by two members, one of which has to be a woman. The other constituency would remain open and general, which means there would be nothing to prevent even two women be elected from it on the basis of winning the highest common vote and the other on the basis of acquiring the highest vote among women candidate. This system will encourage team work among men and women in parties. It will also create a healthy competition between them to serve the constituency. Doubling the figure of MPs will also lighten the load of work and remove the possibility of 'biwi-beti brigade'.

If the rotational principle is not to be eliminated, it may be provided that in case reservation for women in legislatures is to continue beyond the presently mandated duration of 15 years, the next round of reservation after 15 years may commence with new and rotated constituencies.

The delay and debate on the issue of absence of reservation for OBC women, impartially seen has no actual link to the issue of women's reservation in general. It has already marred the process of the actual proposed bill. Reservation for backward classes generally never existed in Indian legislatures. Reservation for Schedule Castes and Scheduled Tribes on the contrary, was a subject of debate in the constituent assembly and found specific inclusion in a specific set of constitutional provisions. Ever since 1992, women reservation in Panchayati Raj institution operated without any linkage with the lack of reservation for OBC women in these institution. Even as CP Bhambhri rieterates that the logic that women should participate in the decision making process gets diluted if participation is on the basis of their religion or caste because they are reduced to the level of sectorial leaders and not women leaders. Veena Nayyar too on the issue contends that the talk of quota within quota is a blatant attempt to divide the women. That they forget about OBC & when it came to the 73rd Amendment because it concerned only governance at the village level and there was no need for considering a system of proportional representation whereby the legitimate political aspirations of each group can be satisfied without breaking down the whole system with competing quotas.

Therefore, quota or no quota only the most deserving should get the benefits. Why not pass the bill as it is first and later decide about the quota within a quota. Women have to begin somewhere. As Kannabiran and Kannabiran contend that women are fighting for the principle of reps mentatim. Women's representation in politics will some how improve the status of all women including the Dalits, OBCS, etc.

Another argument put forth disfavouring the bill in its present form, is the concern for creating a zenana dabba argument. The objection seeks to encapsulate the apprehension that men will limit women to only 33 per cent which might become a maxima or an upper limit for women's presence in legislatures. But then assuming without conceding that in the first phase women's reservation will result in an upper ceiling of only 33 per cent. It is for stronger presence than the present 6-7 per cent. With the time pace, this would reflect a sufficiently strong voice to result in allotment of ever increasing number of seats.

The one more objection on proxy control and the 'biwi brigade' deserves to be considered. The proposed reservation will be cornered by elite women, by wives, daughters conflict of personal interest between them and the women at that level.

Basically, the OBC politicians used a clever tactic to stall women's reservation. Caste and communal card was used to confuse the whole issue. The OBC leaders too, were not sincere about either the backward caste women or the Muslim women's share. Supporting the quota for OBC, several women leaders too have come out with their expressions like Salija, Meera Kumar (CWC member) and Uma Bharti (BJP) Uma Bharti's comment "I'm for 'Mandal and Kamandar" is indeed surprising. Because what is essential today is the general involvement of women at all levels of power structure to ensure a true society, without any quota within quota for political leverage. Mamta Banerjee rightly affirms: "What percentage of OBC and Muslim women candidates Laloo Yadav and Mulayam Singh Yadav had put up in the last election ?" As Brinda Karat opines, there is no reservation for OBC in any state assembly or in Parliament and nor has any such demand ever been raised by OBC. Therefore, to raise the demand, OBC women now is nothing but a pretext to shelve the bill, as it protects the interests of OBC men. The last Parliament had about 200 OBC male MPs. Why are OBC women not there if OBC women's representation is their real concern? Their talk of quotas within quota is a blatant, attempt to divide the women. Madhu Kishwar maintains that mothers and mistresses of powerful men will be used by them as agents or nominees of proxy control. When party tickets are given to the wife of a Kamal Nath as a means of keeping him in power through her, or when wives of local politicians are given panchayat and Zila parishad seats simply because a certain number of women have to be compulsorily fielded in the elections, it makes a mockery of women's participation of politics. Some of the women candidates may be representatives of the parivar syndrome, but it is not a permanent phenomenon 'Biwi brigede' would be easily overshadowed once women realise their power in a democracy; more and more women would come forward to participate in elections, and would be elected on their own merit. Evaluation reports have suggested that women leaders in panchayats have given a greater thrust to the developmental activities in their respective areas. Moreover, the parivar syndrome is not restricted to women alone, this malaise affects men too. Could Laloo Prasad Yadav be stopped from bringing his wife? In any case would Prakash Singh Badal or Farooq Abdullah or Karunanidhi be stopped from fielding their sons? Just because they are men, no one points finger at them. So why question women? This very culture of male-female segregation prevalent in our society adds to the disabilities suffered by women in the political world.

Amongst the various objections to the proposed bill the suggestion for constituencies may be clubbed into one and represented by one male and female member (as also suggested by Madhu Kishwar, discussed earlier in this chapter) - is actuated by an apprehension that simple reservation for women would result in ghettoisation of women and pit women against women. But this does not have much Innovation. This kind of suggestion does not operate in any legal stem or legislatures in the world. Moreover multi-member constituency would not fit in with our existing constitutional alteration of several provisions and chapters of our Constitution based on representational democracy. It would also raise several other issues regarding the total strength of our Parliament (whether it would remain 550 or become 1, 100), the potential enhanced expenditure involved in maintaining double the member of MPs, the Issue as to which of the two members would speak for the constituency.

Though probe and thought on all these issues still requires more open debate and discussion, one can impartially admit that through reservation the state intervenes to admit the imbalance in an effort to at least rectify it. Abraham Lincoln's (Lincolra's) concept of democracy is an ideal, unachieved in the world. Democracy falls short when women of whatever colour or ethnic group cannot vote or cast an effective vote cannot expect success in electing representatives of their choice or being elected to the legislative bodies, and have little hope for enactment of laws they believe are critically needed.

Arguments For and Against

The arguments pro and against the issue of reservation of women in Parliament, have been quite conflicting and mixed from various comers even after the debate and discussion of the basic text. The politicians, women activists and thinkers are divided on the issue of women's reservation.

Argument against the issue has come up from Shatkari Mahila Aghadi that experience of reservation in panchayat in Maharashtra has not been favourable. The relatives of established male leaders are fielded, with no impact on inefficiency and corruption. Yogendra Makwana calls the bill as an inflated one. What is needed is more women candidates in elections, rather that providing statutory reservation for them in Parliament. Nearly 50 per cent of the voters in our country are women. Should they not exercise their voting strength to get more tickets instead of begging for statutory reservation? He reiterates that in a country where a women ruled for 17 years as Prime Minister in EUP and Congress Vijaya Raje Sindhia and Sonia Gandhi have respectively reached the top position, Najma Haptullah is elected deputy chairperson of Rajya Sabha for the third term and earlier. Margret Alwa was also elected to this position thrice - it seems paradoxical to talk of women reservation in Parliament. Vishwa Hindu Parishad Lobby among EUP MPs does not want women reservation. Ram Was Vedanti - a VHP block Lok Sabha MP from Pratapgarh along with Uma Bharti and Ganga Charan Rajput agitates on women s quota business: "Women should not be given any reservation." The Congress Party was no better off than BJP on the women's bill. It forced even its women president Sonia Gandhi to buckle under party MPs' pressure. Rajesh Pilot and P Shiv Shankar led the revolt within the Congress. They demanded 27 per cent OBC quota within the overall 33 per cent women reservation. They questioned why shouldn't BC women get a share when the very concept of women reservation is based on the backwardness criteria. Madhu Kishwar counters the demand for reservation of seats in Parliament and the state assemblies for women with the contention that it would stultify the political process and prevent the emergence of outstanding women who practice better politics of renewal and change.

For : On the other hand, Promila Dandavate, an avid crusader of women's rights, is in the forefront of the struggle for reservation and a chunk in the power structure for the women of the country. She opines that the quality of parliamentary debate will definitely improve with at least 180 women MPs. Former Union Minister, Margaret too is playing a leading role in mobilising women MPs and other organisations, and is quite disgusted by the way the bill has been treated. Veena Nayyar also favours the bill suggesting there can be no empowerment without power. With the amendment what women are seeking is not reservation but de-reservation that is, male representation be scaled down to 67 per cent from 95 per cent is only when women will acquire an 'effective voice' and become a legislative force will agenda's for women in terms of education, health, shelter, access and control to set targets for their empowerment can be implemented. Margaret

Alva has showed her concern for the 5 per cent of meagre representation of women of the total contestants. Of these who get elected constitute a still smaller percentage. Therefore the big task before us today Is to ensure justice.. to reduce the disparities in the opportunities and facilities available to women and make them equal partners in development.

However it would be dangerous to conflate the two discrete spheres of political activity, namely that of Panchayati Raj institution and that of legislatures and Parliament. At the level of Panchayati Raj institution, what matters is the nature and strength of familial and social patriarchy no matter what caste the women may belong to. On the other hand, the women who make it to the legislature and Parliament have usually attained a class status that enables their movement out of the household, and thus, It is the patriarchal power arrangement of the party that matters more. All parties have thus found it convenient to deploy women only strategically, resulting in the emergence of 'biwi brigade'. But today reservation has become an. imperative not an option. The policy of 'tokenism' by having a few women in the legislature and executive wings of government offers serious obstacles to their acting as spokeperson for women's rights and opportunities. If this process continues, women would loose their faith in political process to change their condition. Reservation would provide an impetus to both the women and political parties to give a fairer deal to nearly half the population in the various units of government. The system would generate greater freedom to articulate their views, increase women legislators sense of responsibility and concern for the problems affecting women. Instill socioeconomic change and broadening the political elite structure.

Moreover, women reservation cannot lead to their becoming isolated pockets in the nation because women are not marginal to society as a minority group. It might be a transitional measure to break through the existing structure of Inequalities. This will not be retrogression 'from the doctrine of equality of' sexes and the principle of democratic representation' as felt by representatives of political parties and most women legislators, but it may serve a long-term objective of equality and democracy in a better manner. Women need to represent their own interests. Statistics and social Indicators show that women's interest have not been served.

The argument that women should come into Parliament only on their merit, against the 'parivar syndrome' is true, but then their representation isnegligible in a merit based system. Reservation should result in less inequality and increased confidence of women. Women if encouraged to participate through reservation will emerge even in nonreserved constituencies. Once women emerge, we can revert to a merit based system. Also, the argument that women's reservation is a play of the upper castes to bring their women into Parliament is not true. Schedule Castes and Scheduled Tribe and OBC men have come into Parliament either through constitutionally mandated reservations or by being given tickets by their parties, they have significant representation in Parliament within their party organisation. It is upto the 'same people' to ensure that party tickets are given for women from minorities and disadvantaged communities.

The possibility that 33 per cent reservation will ghettoise women, has its own reasoning. In the face of the fact that women today are already marginalised, this provision alone could arrest this trend. It will provide them an opportunity to escape from ghettoslation imposed upon them by patriarchal norms and practices.

Reservation reflects the will of the people. It is the part of the common minimum programme of all parties, which make up the United Front (UF) government. The then prime Minister had himself introduced the 81st Amendment Bill in Parliament The leader of the opposition has fully endorsed the bill in his public address to the nation. The national Policy on women of the Ministry of Human Resource Development (HRD) has stressed the need for more women to be part of the political decision-making process.

The national alliance of women's groups have strongly articulated the need for reservation for women in Parliament and the assemblies. Even after looking at over 100 submissions including the attorney general, the law ministry and the national commission for women, the select committee made up of representatives of all parties from both houses has strongly recommended that the bill as amended, be passed without delay and that necessary legislation to give effect to the provisions of the bill may be brought before Parliament at the earliest. So how can it be reiterated that reservation for women is the demand of only a few urban elite women and does not reflect the will of the people? It was indeed surprising, when a positive response in favour of bill, came from a male MP, Anand Mohan, on the fateful day of July 14, 1998. He seemed to be the only honest male politician in the house to have questioned amidst revolt, "speaker sir, what about the women's reservation bill?"

The bill would bring roughly 181 women in Parliament. The integration of women in the political process at all levels of political life is essential for the democratisation of politics. Although it is known that some sections of people in the country including the women should take more active interest in public life, this cannot be ensured by a system of reverse preference to ensure a quota for women in legislature. This is the surest way of ensuring that women do not achieve equal status in life. The idea is to bring about a qualitative change with women's participation in these fora rather than bring the level of functioning down further with women simply joining as puppets in this enterprise.

The Education Factor

In future electoral contests, parties that show themselves to be sensitive - voluntarily rather than under compulsion - to the need for greater female representation could well reap a proportional harvest. This would salvage the issue of gender justice from the detritus of caste prejudice that today surrounds it. Another strategy would be for a diligent study of the patterns of social representation that have emerged from the women's quota in local bodies. The large number of women who have recently assumed office as mayors of Important cities is an index of the substantive impact of this measure. Objective observers are convinced that in their social origin, the women who have gained seats in local bodies are as representatives of the underlying caste sub-stratum as are the men. If the appropriate lessons are avidly disseminated before the extrapolation of the principle of reservations to legislative institution many of the political Insecurities that have recently emerged well be placated. The more the women and educated and enlightened, the more, they would benefit from the reservation facilities.

PART — SIX

Islamic Viewpoint

FOURTEEN

State of Minorities

The education of the minority communities in India have been very much neglected except perhaps in the case of the Christian community. The worst sufferers are the women of the Muslim community. Because of poverty and purdah the Muslims have avoided sending their daughters to the schools. The Muslim clergy is by and large opposed to the liberal education of the girls. According to them the education of the women should be confined to the reading of the religious texts and to those activities which are performed by them for the maintenance of their households.

The Christians on the other hand, have a tradition of educating their daughters. The missionaries have opened a number of good institutions where the Christian girls get quality education. The girls of the Sikh minority except of the Sikhs who fall in the category of Dalits are able to get fairly good education. Hence the Muslim minority is the one which has not been able to educate its daughters to the extent to which they should have been educated. We shall examine in this chapter the socio-psychological factors that have affected the education of the Muslim girls.

The Muslims feel that it is ordained in holy book Quoran that the women are kept under purdah. It is often quoted:

> And say to the believing women
> That they should lower
> Their gaze and guard

Their modesty; that they
Should not display their
Beauty and ornaments except
What (must ordinarily) appear thereof

(Quoran 24:31)

According to the above verse among Muslim women veiling or Purdah is projected as the preferred code of conduct. They are supposed to remain veiled whenever they go out or face the males. They are thus restricted to go to those institutions in which they have to discard their veil. The choice of schooling, therefore, remains very limited. Because of pardah Muslim women are also restricted from undertaking jobs in the factories or offices. Their rightful place is considered home and their responsibilities are the domestic work and rearing of the children. It is, therefore, not surprising that very few Muslim women are employed in Government or factories or business services.

Trauma of Partition

It may be mentioned that the Muslim community in India has undergone the trauma of partition. No doubt that to some extent the community in India was partly responsible for the partition of the country in 1947 but once it took place this community suffered a lot. Its elitist, well to do members, shifted to Pakistan and those who were left were separated from many of their near and dear ones who migrated to Pakistan. The trauma of partition that separated the families is very effectively projected in the movie Garam Hawa. The affluent businessman of shoe market at Agra found his relations migrating to Pakistan and ultimately decided to leave the country. It was a difficult and much pain producing decision but there was no escape route. In many other stories and novels including Bhisham Sahani's Tamas, a Television serial, the trauma of partition with which Indians suffered has been dramatised. The effect of it on the Indian Muslims was that they retreated into a world of their own and tried to preserve their culture and religious ideology as interpreted by not very well educated Mullas. The community thereby instead of taking a progressive outlook fell prey to obscuration ideas and values. The worst sufferers of this situation were the Muslim women who were forced to embrace ignorance.

After Independence many laws were made to give equal rights to the Hindu women. The Hindu Code Bill conferred almost equal rights to women in the sphere of property and marriage etc. Unfortunately there has been complete absence of reform in Muslim family laws. The Indian constitution envisaged a single civil code for all the citizens of the country. But because a large section of the Muslims were extremely critical of a common civic code it could not be enacted. Muslims do not want that any changes be made in their personal law. But there are many provisions and interpretations of the Shariat, which go against the interests of the Muslim women. So while the Hindu society is on reformist trending the Muslim clergy favours the status quo. The outcome is that the women are sufferers. It may, however, be noted that there is no feminist movement worth the name sponsored by the Muslim women for the removal of any law that places them in an inferior position than men. The reason for this may be found in the Muslim women psyche. They have been so groomed that to raise any objection to the interpretation of the Shariat by the Ulemas is unthinkable. The restrictions on their education keep them perpetually in the sphere of ignorance.

The enactment of the Muslim Women's (Protection of Rights on Divorce) Bill in 1986 by the Indian Parliament was done because controversy arose over a case that came up for review in the Supreme Court. It is better known as Shah Bano's case. In this case the earlier judgment of the Supreme Court was, that a husband was responsible of maintaining his wife. The orthodox argued against this judgment that is goes against the spirit of Shariat. A wife is entitled for her Mehar only. About this Bill Maitrayee Mukhopadhyay writes: "The Muslim Women's Bill constitutes a major attempt at codifying Muslim personal law, setting up boundaries delineating what Muslim women are entitled to in the event of a divorce. In the process Muslim women's entitlements have been redefined and men's responsibilities to their divorced "fixed" in a way that disempowers Muslim women". It may be asserted that the Muslim women's fight for a fair treatment by their male counterparts faces very tough opposition in the name of keeping the separate identity of Muslims and in the name of not involving any other agency than what Ulemas consider as the right interpretation of religious texts.

Huma Ahmed-Ghosh writes: "The lifestyle, attitudes and cultural identity of Muslim women in India are an outcome of their socio-economic condition, and a tenuous relationship the Muslims share with the Hindus". She in her article entitled "Preserving identity: a case study of Palitpur" examines the various indicators of the socioeconomic status of Muslim women in Palitpur, a village in Meerut district, north India. She found the Muslim community in Palitpur as economically backward. But the economically depressed, Muslim men in Palitpur "Flaunted a moral and cultural superiority over the Hindus." In them there was a feeling that they belonged to the ruling (royal) class, (referring to the four-century rule of India by the Mughals). They felt that due to the creation of Pakistan they have been neglected or harassed by the government and Hindus because they stayed back.

The above finding shows that the Muslims after partition ascribe to their backwardness the neglect by the government and blame the Hindus also. They have a sort of defeatist mentality. They want to keep their Islamic identity not by progressive education but by remaining rooted to the traditional education given in madrassas. In Palitpur there were only two schools, one the government school and the other the madrassa. Muslim children attended the madrassa that only imparted Islamic education. It is through such education that they wanted to keep their Muslim identity. In spite of this there was a sense of helplessness among them. They considered that their future was bleak.

The Muslim women in Palitpur were victims of "their gender as well as their minority status". They were uneducated and conservative. In them the idea of good education was not at all inculcated. They considered the reason for their low socio-economic status lie in their victimisation by the Hindus and the neglect by the government. According to Ghosh: "Education which was the only way out, was still not encouraged. The sense of victimisation was very strong. For the women, conforming to Islamic tenets as rigidly as their socio-economic conditions would allow, was not only perceived, as an improved lifestyle but also the only escape from their 'disadvantaged' situation".

The case study of Palitpur may not be the representative of all the Muslims in India since there exists a diversity of culture and lifestyle among Muslims in different regions and states of India. But certainly it throws some light on the social status, aspirations and motivations of Muslim women of rural India. In Palitpur Muslim community aspires for upward mobility but not through learning or further understanding of the Quran, Hadith or Shariat. They try to achieve it by means of emulating the lifestyle of the Ashrafs, that is those who belong to higher social echelon.

The Indian Muslim women's lower status and position is due to many factors. Some of these we have outlined above. The women are guided by the zeal resulting from their adherence to Islamic tenets as preached by male Muslim leaders. Many of their interpretations of the religious texts go against their interests but because of their ignorance and upbringing they are incapable of raising their voice against them. They also suffer from the feeling of helplessness for improving their lot. They are also fed with the propaganda that their plight is the result of a conspiracy by the Hindu fundamentalists which make them more rigid in the observance of the religious practices and the obedience of religious injections. The Mullahs and Muslim politicians have a stake in keeping them backward and so they feed them with those notions that perpetuate their backwardness. The plight of Muslim women can improve only if they are encouraged to have liberal education and to think independently and assert their individuality.

Co-education

It is not difficult to understand the attitude of Islam with regard to co-education, if one realises that its conception of sex equality is founded on a differentiation of functions as between men and women. Islam insists on married life both for men and women. It regards the home and domestic life as the natural and most important sphere of a woman's activity. It dislikes the free intermingling of men and women except under the strain of a serious emergency. It is, therefore, obvious that co-education is opposed to the whole tenor of Islamic teachings, because the system rests on presuppositions and postulates which are quite different. Co-education is based on the assumption that there are no psychological and temperamental differences of any great consequence between man and woman, that after completing their education they have to pursue like careers and enter identical spheres of activity and that no sexual aberrations are likely to occur from the herding together of boys and girls in the same institution, or if they do occur, their consequences for, the stability of the family, the happiness of married life and the general character-formation of men and women are not serious enough to warrant social condemnation. All these assumptions are very questionable and since the modern education of girls has been mostly based on them, the results have been none too happy, as the following paragraphs will show.

In the earlier phase of the movement for women's emancipation in England, the British feminists did not allow their aspirations to run amuck. They had a practicable and sane ideal of women's freedom which did not run counter to the fundamental traits of feminine nature. As early as 1864, Miss Emil Davies wrote in the *Year Book of Education:* 'We are not encumbered by theories about equality and inequality of mental powers in the sexes. All we claim is that the intelligence of women, be it great or small shall have full and free development. . . the object being the awakening and strengthening and adorning of the human spirit.' Totally different have been the ideas of later feminists whose educational and other ideals have fallen in the same line with men. Under the assumption that the female brain was capable of intellectual pursuits equal to the male, the modern educational system for girls is a copy of the educational system for boys. The results of this policy have been commented upon in the report of the committee appointed in England in 1923 to consider the differentiation of curricula between the sexes in secondary schools. The authors of the report remark: 'Basing their policy on the belief that girls could equal boys at least in intellectual matters if favourable conditions were afforded, the leaders of the (women's) movement implicitly assumed that what had been done for and by boys was in general suitable for both sexes.' A complete lack of feminine ideals and a thorough imitation of masculine ideals have been the most outstanding features of the educational system for girls.

To a considerable extent this defect in the education of girls is the outcome of co-education. When boys and girls are made to learn and receive their education under the same teachers and in the same schools, it is naturally difficult to give sufficient consideration to their psychological, emotional and temperamental differences and yet these differences are deep, abiding and all-pervading. Let us examine them one by one.

In his book entitled *The Psychology of Education*, Professor Wilton points out that while man lives by reason, woman's outlook is moulded and determined by feeling. 'She approximates the emotional temperament even when she does not show it in all its fulness. Intuition is a special quality of woman; and therefore she does not care for abstract thought. It is not that she does not generalise, but that she generalises without preparatory analysis.' He cites the example of so eminent a woman as Hume de Sevique who acknowledged that 'abstract reasoning was repugnant to her.' Man, therefore, he points out, analyses and applies principles deductively, but a woman takes the special case and its value for feeling. The differences in the mental outlook of the sexes become, according to the observations of this author, clear from early life. A little girl of four is essentially a little girl; and a little boy, a little boy. The girl, says he, is precocious in speech, is less often troubled with stammering. Her play has not the force and expansion of movement which characterises the boy's: it is comparatively quieter and assumes a definite meaning.

Wilton sees intellectual distinctions also. Intellectual distinctions colour the learning of the two sexes as soon as the studies provide an opportunity for their respective intellectual qualities. Thus, girls do well in all that demands neither originality of thought nor abstraction. They, therefore, keep pace with the boys, or even surpass them, in the earliest school studies most of which are concerned with concrete wholes. They learn by heart with ease, take delight in neatness and in the embellishment of their written exercises, they work out with accuracy all detailed processes with the general form of which they are familiar or which they can imitate from example. They appreciate beauty of feeling and of form; and that is why study of literature has a special appeal to them, and they can show here more progress at an earlier age than what boys could do.

These mental and intellectual differences, says Wilton, are sadly ignored by the advocates and promoters of equal education to the sexes. He is, therefore, opposed to co-education. Boys and girls, he says, may be taught together in the same subjects only in the earliest age, say, up to ten years of age, because in these years 'the matter put before them gives little scope for their characteristically different modes of apprehension'. But the intellectual differences come into prominence with advance in age. Soon boys and girls begin to retard each other's progress, the girls being held back for slower boys in some subjects and, in their turn, impeding the advance of the boys in other subjects, So, different schools for the sexes with different curricula would seem to give the best intellectual results. And this, he says, is very marked out by my own somewhat extended observations.

One point, however, Wilton makes clear. It states that it must never be supposed that woman is an imperfectly developed man. That woman differs from man in intellect does not mean that she is in any way intellectually inferior to him. To deduce intellectual inferiority from woman's ineptitude for abstract thought is to apply a false standard to reach a wrong conclusion. 'Neither is inferior to the other. Each is essential to life; and in this difference of attitude, as in all that follows from it, man and woman are complementary. There is no question of superiority or inferiority: and any course of action based on the assumption that woman should try to become intellectually like man rests on a very insecure psychological foundation.'

Another ground on which Wilton proposes a different type of education for women is their functional difference from men. The functions of men and women, he says, are essentially distinct. Evolution does not mean the identification of sex qualities, but their more perfect mutual adaptation. 'Equality in value of complementary functions, not the obscuring of differences already established, is what the whole course of man's evolution leads us to expect.' In his book, *What Do We Mean by Education*, he sadly deprecates the tendency of the course of women's education which seeks to prepare them for various forms of professional and commercial life which, he points out, involves strenuous intellectual application during the years of adolescence and thus becomes trying on their nerves. In his opinion the present education on the same lines as that of males disturbs the nervous equilibrium of girls and thus injures their health. This breakdown of health may become serious in the rough and tumble of competitive examinations, and still more so when the competition is with boys.

In his book, *The Mixed School*, Howard comments on the psychology of women. Howard does not admit much intellectual difference between the sexes, but he lays special emphasis on temperamental difference. He says that boys are less emotional and more practical. The girls are more subjective in their outlook while the boys are more objective. Similarly, the girls are distinguished by greater passivity so that they are inclined to rely more on authority than on reason and argument. The girls have also a certain power of rapid intuition. They jump to conclusions all too easily and reason back from them to test their accuracy. Howard, therefore, advocates a different system of education for girls and boys. He bases his conclusion on the fact that girls are liable to fatigue more readily after puberty when the amount of haemoglobin in the blood becomes lessened. This fact, he says, is of far more importance than is generally believed. For this, he cites Dr. Adams who has summarised his observations as follows. Girls in general are (1) not so strong physically as boys; (2) highly strung and liable to nervous strain which possibly is associated with the fact that physiologically they are liable to heavier drains upon the circulating calcium of the blood, and (3) with their thinner blood with lowered haemoglobin content after puberty, they are nearer to the threshold of anaemia.

This consideration of her physiological aptitude, in the opinion of Howard, must weigh when laying down a particular system of education for girls. 'The sex-changes during adolescence are followed in the girl by recurring periods of strain when general efficiency may temporarily be impaired.' He, therefore, fears a risk of overstraining the girls through unsympathetic treatment at this period. Moreover, there is a definite risk which, in his opinion, may fail to do her abilities full justice at a moment when she specially needs it.

Howard, therefore, suggests that, as far as games and physical exercises are concerned, the sexes should be entirely separated as soon as their physical differences become significant. As regards intellectual education, first boys and girls may be separated for those subjects which are usually only studied by one sex; secondly, wider choice of optional subjects may be given in girls' schools; and, thirdly, overstrain on the part of the girl may be minimised by an easier optional subject.

Mrs. Dora Russell says in her book, *Hypatia*, 'Is there something wrong with the education of women and, if so, what? I think we must judge that there is. The reason lies in, the sense of inferiority bred in women by so much operation, and the natural result that their chief aim, as they struggled upwards, was to prove that they could jolly well do without men. This effort is mistaken. Each sex has that to give to the common stock which alone it can give, and robs itself and community by inferior imitation.... Feminist ideals of education, then, had the defect that they did in a certain measure deny sex or ignore it.'

That there is such a thing as a female mind is proved beyond doubt by psychologists. And this female mind requires a suitable education for its own culture and development, irrespective of what the corresponding standard is for men. As Dr. Rabindranath Tagore pertinently remarks in an article published in *The Nineteenth Century and After* (August 1927): 'If woman's nature were really the same as that of man, it would be a superfluity, a mere tautology.... If women acquire the view that sex' difference is only physical, and that mentally and spiritually they are of the same nature as men, and if they act on this assumption- (thus giving life a one-sidedly masculine form), then our civilisation would sink into utter confusion and chaos.'

Vital Defect

The most vital defect of co-education, from the point of view of female nature and woman's special functions in society, is that it prevents the training of woman for motherhood. How can a common educational institution run alike for boys and girls make adequate provision for training women in those arts and branches of knowledge which are necessary for her future life as a mother? Education for motherhood is the crying need of the world today. Because the vast majority of girls become mothers in after-life, every girl should be required to specialise for a definite time "in those subjects which will make her a good mother. When the whole curriculum of girls is hopelessly congested with subjects on the line of boys which cost them their mental equilibrium and physical health, their essential function in life is allowed to pass off in ignorance. Girls expected to manage somehow, without any adequate training, their function of motherhood on which in a great degree depends their own happiness and the preservation and welfare of the race. As a woman herself writes: 'The human mother gives poisonous mixture to her infant in place of Nature's food. She feeds its lungs with poisoned air in overheated, stuffy rooms, whilst its nervous and physical vitality is undermined by the noises and distractions of over-civilized life. Teach, train and direct instinct in women if you will, but supplement it with knowledge that is essential for child bearing in our social organization.'

Not only is there a thorough lack of training in maternity, but, on the contrary, that female education today incapacitates women for motherhood and marriage. It is because the strain of higher education is so enervating and exhausting that they cannot bear the strain of childbirth. Dr. Cyrn. Esdon has remarked on this point: 'Many- educated women are so exhausted before marriage that after bearing one or two children they become wrecks.' Dr. Taylor writes very much in the same strain in his book, *The Nature of Women*. He says: 'This much we do know that probably at no other time in history has childbirth been so difficult, so unhealthily difficult, as now, and that this has manifested itself chiefly in the last fifty years, a period of increasing educational strain for girls.'

Similarly, Dr. Knealy writes in *Feminine and Sex Education:* 'When adolescent girls are strained by athletics, by over-culture or industrial exhaustion, the vital resources are so diverted from the evolution of function as to cause incapacitation in them, partial or complete, for wifehood and for bearing of fine offspring.' Finally, the author of *Whither Woman*, Y.M. Rege, says:

> No feminist of however extreme views-can deny motherhood to be the flower of all woman's individuality, physical and psychical. If higher education on male lines has done anything wrong to women, it is this: it has by arresting the full development of her physique, by enervating her nerves, made her incapable of attaining the full growth of womanhood of which motherhood is the final symbol. There is no surprise that the graduates of English and American universities, with their physical energies sapped for any healthy reproduction, should come out in the world with a-maternal feelings and should try to cover this up with false pretentions that their unmarried state is due to their desire to devote their lives to some social service. It is really a pity that many a fine girlhood which, if spared of this overstraining education, would blossom into fine womanhood and would give real service to society by giving it healthy

> and vigorous children, is victimized under an entirely false and misguided idealism.

All these defects in the modern system of female education can be remedied if co-education is entirely given up, separate institutions for boys and girls are set up and, consistent with the special needs of each sex, two parallel systems of education and curricula of studies are evolved, so that the large mass of girls who are to be the future mothers of the race may receive preparatory training for their special calling. A limited number of women there will always be whose special gifts may entitle them to a different kind of education, but the interests of the many should not be sacrificed for the chosen few. And even these women of special gifts and endowments should not refuse the call of motherhood because they can reproduce and enlarge their gifts by becoming mothers. In a country which is backward like our own, there may be difficulties in obtaining the requisite number of female teachers for higher arts and branches of knowledge, but this difficulty does not tilt the scale in favour of co-education. Islam allows men and women of advanced age who have lost sexual attraction to mix with members of the other sex, under the stress of social or religious necessity. To prepare and train women teachers in the higher branches of knowledge, male teachers and professors of advanced age can be employed in sufficient numbers. When an adequate number of women have been trained, the need for even this amount of co-education will disappear.

FIFTEEN

Education under Islam

As per Islamic perspective, in dealing with women's education, it is recognised that wider issues pertaining to a modern Islamic curriculum have not been addressed. The latter is, indeed, a crucial issue, but our concern here has been one of the key questions of principle that should surely guide current attempts to formulate an authentically Islamic education system, namely the approach to women's education in such a system.

Long as the education system is governed by the spirit of Islam throughout, there will be a harmony between, these two modes of social activity, permitting women to express themselves in accordance with their natural dispositions, and to be given the respect and honour which is so central to the real social message of Islam.

Knowledge and education are, highly emphasised in Islam. Both are integral parts of the Islamic religion. Islam encourages its followers to enlighten themselves with the knowledge of their religion as well as other branches of knowledge. It holds the person who seeks knowledge in high esteem and has exalted his position). In reality, the entire aim of the Divine revelation and the sending of prophets to humankind has been stressed in the Quran as the communication of knowledge. The Book says: 'The Prophet recites unto people God's revelation; causes them to grow and imparts to them knowledge, and wisdom'. The Divine desires every believer to be well educated in religion, to possess wisdom and broad intellectual knowledge.

The purpose of raising a prophet in a nation is to teach and to impart knowledge.. The Quran is full of verses which praise learned people, encourage original thinking and personal investigation and denounce unimaginative imitation. It also emphasises the importance of the study of nature and its laws. According to the Quran, learning is an unending process and the entire universe is made subservient, to man, the agent of God, who has to abide by the truth and not by narrow notions of hereditary customs and beliefs. The verses in the Quran which enjoin people to learn and observe nature outnumber all those related to prayer, fasting, and pilgrimage put together.

In the Hadith literature, knowledge is highly appreciated and encouraged also. The Prophet Muhammad always emphasised the importance of knowledge to his followers and encouraged them to seek it. Learned people are regarded as the inheritors of the prophetic wisdom. In this connection, the following Hadiths can be quoted: 'The prophets leave knowledge as their inheritance. The learned ones inherit this great fortune. 'Search for knowledge though it be in China'.

Studies were conducted in the Mosques, circles of discussion (*halaqat*) were set up; and teachers were simultaneously students learning from their superiors and, in their turn, teaching their own students. Education was considered a matter of religious duty-a manifestation of the Muslim's submission to the will of Allah and an act of piety which could lead to a deeper knowledge of the Creator—the One. Hence we find that all members of society participated in that process. Since education was free of charge, opportunities were available to everybody, rich or poor alike. The Prophet said 'Treat equally poor and rich students who sit before you for the acquisition of knowledge'. Gifted students were helped and highly encouraged to continue their education, so that they would be able to fulfil their aspirations.

Moreover, the seeking of knowledge was not circumscribed by age limitations; the Prophet said 'Seek knowledge from the cradle to the grave'. Therefore, we find that the companions of the Prophet sought knowledge even when they were at an advanced age. Also, there was considerable academic freedom; in the classes, the students were entitled to ask questions and to discuss themes with the teacher-indeed, their reputation depended heavily on their success in such sessions of debate and discussion.

Initially, the learning process of the Muslims started with the Prophet who himself used to teach his companions the principles of Islam. When he migrated to Medina, he immediately started the process of eradicating illiteracy. His mosque also served as a centre for Muslim learning. He was so interested in this matter that, soon after the victory of Badr, he instructed each of the Meccan captives, who were literate, to teach ten Muslims how to read and write as a condition for their release. He also sent teachers and missionaries to different parts of Arabia so that they could teach the newly converted Muslims the principles of Islam. He also set up circles of learned men to study and teach the Quran. Later, mosques were set up in every locality and since then have remained as the essential location for educational activities among the Muslims. The Prophet's example as a teacher constituted a sacred precedent for his followers. Hence they considered it their duty to set up mosques and schools in their domain. In the course of time, the simple pattern of the Prophet's school developed into a comprehensive and coherent educational system, fully integrated into the social and economic way of life. This educational system was based on moral and spiritual qualities. It recognised no separation between sacred and secular. Indeed it 'breathed in a universe of sacred presence'.

Whatever was known contained a profoundly religious feature, not only because the object of every type of knowledge is created by God, but also because the intelligence by which man knows is in itself a Divine gift. The education system therefore dealt with the whole being of the person whom it sought to educate. Its aim was not only the training of the mind but also the entire personality of the student. The teacher in this system was the transmitter of knowledge as well as the trainer of souls. Even the term 'teacher' in itself gained the meaning of trainer. It was embodied with ethical connotations which in the modern world have almost disappeared from the process of teaching and the transmission of knowledge, especially at the higher levels of education.

The Islamic educational system neither separated the training of the mind from that of the soul, nor regarded the transmission of knowledge or its possession to be legitimate without the possession of proper moral and spiritual principles. Indeed, the acquisition of knowledge without these principles was regarded as very dangerous both to individuals and society.

However, despite the fact that the Islamic educational system encompassed the whole life of traditional Muslims, certain distinct phases can be discerned. The first stage started at home where both parents acted as teachers in matters such as religion, language, culture and social customs. This period was followed by the Quranic schools (al-Kuttab) corresponding to elementary school. The aims of these schools were to enable the child to read and write the Quran, and to master the language as well as learn other subjects such as proverbs, poetry and, later, arithmetic. These schools formed the preparatory stage for higher studies where the students could then attend the Madrasah.

The Madrasah often incorporated the Jamiah which can be said to correspond at one and the same time, to secondary school as well as to college and university education. The activities of these Madrasahs were divided into two parts. The religious or the transmitted sciences, and the intellectual sciences. The religious sciences included the study of the Quran, the Hadith, linguistics and theology and they dominated the educational activity of most Madrasahs. The intellectual sciences included the study of logic, mathematics, and the natural sciences, as well as philosophy. These divisions of the sciences were reflected in the curriculum of the Madrasahs and were taught alongside each other. These Madrasahs enjoyed a high position in society and, in the course of time, they developed into fully fledged educational institutions performing an important role throughout the Muslim world, such as the Qayrawan in Morocco and al-Azhar in Egypt. Later on, we find the development of a university system with several campuses such as al Nizamiyyah and al-Mustansiriyah in Baghdad and al-Nuriyyah in Damascus.

In addition to the Madrasahs where theoretical learning was conducted, there were a number of observatories and hospitals. Some of them acted independently as institutions of scientific learning and experimentation, others were appended to the colleges. Al-Mamun's famous Shamsiyyah observatory was a most remarkable example. It was followed in many other cities. Moreover, these higher institutions continually provided society with its intellectual elite, and socio-political thinkers.

No Priority

There is no priority for men over women in relation to the right to education. Both are equally encouraged to acquire education, as already shown, 'from the cradle to the grave'. Indeed all the Quranic verses which relate to education and which advocate the acquisition of knowledge were directed to both men and women alike. In accordance with the all-embracing concept of Tawhid-Oneness-when Islam elevated women physically by abolishing female infanticide, it could not overlook the need for their mental and spiritual elevation. By contrast, Islam would view the neglect of these dimensions as virtually tantamount to murdering their personality. The Quran says: 'They are losers who besottedly have slain their children by keeping them in ignorance'. Neither the Quran nor the sayings of the Prophet prohibit or prevent women from seeking knowledge and having an education.

Prophet was the forerunner in this regard, in declaring that seeking knowledge is obligatory upon every Muslim man and woman. By making such a statement, the Prophet opened all the avenues of knowledge for men and women alike. So, like her male counterpart, each woman is under a moral and religious obligation to seek knowledge, develop her intellect, broaden her outlook, cultivate her talents and then utilise her potential to the benefit of her soul and of her society. The interest of the Prophet in female education was manifest in the fact that he himself used to teach the women along with the men; he also instructed his followers to educate not only their women but their slave girls as well. The following Hadith puts it thus: a man who educates his slave girl, frees her and then marries her, this man will have a double reward. The wives of the Prophet, especially Aisha, not only taught women, they taught men also and many of the Prophet's companions and followers learned the Quran, Hadith and Islamic jurisprudence from Aisha.

There was no limitation placed on women's education. Women were allowed to learn all the branches of science. She was free to choose any field of knowledge which interested her. Nonetheless, it is important to stress that, because Islam recognised that women are in principle wives and mothers, they should also place special emphasis on seeking knowledge in those branches which could help them in those particular spheres. In accordance with the dictates of the Quran and the Hadith encouraging women to develop all aspects of their personality, it was believed that an educated Muslim woman should not only radiate her moral qualities in the environment of her home, but she should: also have an active role in the broad fields of social, economic and political development.

The Quran, in particular, commands men and women to perform their prayers, pay their poor-tax and enjoin good and forbid evil in all forms: social, economic and political. This means that both have an equal duty to accomplish these tasks. In order to do so, they must have equal access to educational opportunities. For how can a woman uphold good social and economic policies or disapprove them if she is intellectually not equipped for the task? Following the injunctions of the Quran and the Sunnah concerning female education, early Muslim women seized this opportunity and laboured to equip themselves in all branches of the knowledge of their time. They attended classes with men, they participated in all cultural activities side by side with them and managed to win their encouragement and respect. Early Islamic history is replete with examples of Muslim women who showed a remarkable ability to compete, with men and excelled them on many occasions.

Religious studies was the favourite subject for women in early Islam, and a considerable number of Muslim women managed to become notable figures among traditionists and jurists. On top of the list was Aisha, the wife of the Prophet. She was a renowned scholar of her time. Her foresight and advice in the affairs of the Islamic community were regarded as highly important by the early Islamic rulers. She was credited with thousands of traditions received directly from the Prophet and is to the present day considered a great authority on Islamic Jurisprudence. Another famous name in this subject was Nafisah, a descendant of Ali who was a prominent jurist and theologian. It is mentioned that Al-Shafi, the founder of one of the schools of Fiqh used to attend her lessons and public lectures. Shuhda as well was a renowned name in the subject of tradition, especially Hadith, which is a branch of Muslim science which was thought to be exclusively for men.

Muslim women proved their ability to master in Literature and achieved a high reputation among their contemporaries. In the forefront was al-Khansa, the greatest poetess of her day. Her poetry has survived into the present period. She was admired by the Prophet himself when he said that her poetry was unsurpassed. In addition one could mention Qatilah who composed a famous elegy on the death of her brother which, again, was praised by the Prophet.

The humanitarian duties were performed by women in all the battles fought in Islam. It was a custom that Muslim women accompanied the troops, so that they could bandage the wounded, fetch the water, transport the casualties back to Medina and instil courage in the men whose spirits were sagging. It is said that when the Muslim troops were preparing to conquer Khaiber, Umayyah bint Qays-al-Ghaffariyyah, with a group of women, asked to be allowed to accompany the army. The Prophet granted: them his permission and they performed their duties well.

In addition, Muslim women attained a high status as medical scholars such as Zainab of the Bani Awd tribe who was a prominent physician and an expert oculist. Umm al-Hasan hint al-Qadi Abi

Jafar al-Tanjali was a renowned woman of broad knowledge in different subjects, and was especially famous as a doctor.

Muslim women proved to be good warriors and they fought side by side with men. They achieved a considerable degree of success, and on occasion played very important military roles. In this respect mention should be made of Nusaiba, the wife of Zaid Ibn Asim, who took part in the famous battle of 'Ohud'. In that battle she fought vigorously and in the critical time when the Prophet was left alone she fought alongside him and wounded 11 persons with her sword. In the same battle, Nusaiba hint Kab al-Mazinia headed the Prophet's army against the enemy forces and at a crucial moment managed to minimise the losses of the Muslim army.

In addition, Muslim women also proved their ability to play a constructive role in other activities of the community. For example, they were involved in the political issues of the time and their opinions in political affairs were highly respected. They often took part in the process of choosing the Caliph. They also enjoyed full freedom to express their ideas and were encouraged to participate in the social life of the community. Public life was like a stage where both men and women were actively involved. In the early period of Islam women used to discuss and debate with the Prophet and his companions and even protect their rights if they were breached. It is said that during the time of the second Caliph Omar, a woman expressed her disagreement with him publicly in matters relating to the women's dowry and managed to correct him.

The Quran encourages women to speak their minds and not to be silent; nonetheless we see today some fundamentalists propagating the unfounded slogan that the voice of woman is A'wrah (private parts to be covered up) and therefore arguing that it is in her best interest to keep quiet. For how can a woman learn and grow intellectually if she is not allowed to speak and communicate with others? How can she widen her understanding of things around her and speak forcefully and impressively if she is prevented from debating with others publicly?

On the contrary, Islam granted woman the right to hold a job and to involve herself actively in trade and commerce. She is entitled to work outside her home and earn a living. During the early Islamic period women often helped men in their outdoor work and were allowed to move about freely among men. Asma, the daughter of the first Caliph Abu-Bakr, used to help her husband in his field work. The Prophet himself praised women who worked hard and well; he also encouraged women, including his wives and daughters, to engage themselves in gainful work. He used to say 'The most blessed earning is that which a person gains from his own labour'.

Women in early Islam even held formal posts of authority in the community such as al-Shafa bint Abdullah who was appointed by the second Caliph Omar as superintendent of markets in Medina many times. Hence, women can work as teachers, doctors, lawyers; they can work as employers or senior managers and they can work as Judges. It must be stressed that up until the present time and in most Muslim countries with the exception of Tunisia and Malaysia, the position of Judge is still regarded as a male domain. Women in these countries have traditionally been prevented from assuming this position.

The ban has no legal foundation in either the scripture or the Sunnah. On the contrary, Aisha, the wife of the Prophet, was the forerunner in undertaking the position. She acted as a Judge during the era of the first three Caliphs. Also, Abu Hanifa, the founder of one of the schools of law states that a woman might become a Judge; and consider all matters except the ones that are under the penal code. Jarir al-Tabari, the famous commentator on the Quran, gives women the right to be appointed as Judge without any conditions. However, despite the fact that the external work of the woman was allowed and respected, a house- wife, unable to work due to domestic responsibilities, did not feel that her contribution was less honourable and less fruitful.

The high status granted to women by the Quranic reforms which prevailed during the early Islamic period did not last long.

Firstly, certain pre-Islamic customs reappeared, especially during the Abbasid period; secondly, various social attitudes infiltrated Islamic culture from conquered peoples, and were assimilated as norms and then identified with Islam.

The status of Muslim women started to deteriorate. This was accelerated by catastrophic historical events such as the Mongol and Turkish invasions and the ensuing decline of the Islamic civilisation. The ambience generated by these conditions served to undermine the position of Muslim women who became less and less part of social life in general. They were neglected and treated as sex objects, assumed heavy veiling and were confined to their small circle of womenfolk with no contact outside their homes; they were prevented from participating in the public life of the community and excluded from public worship in the mosque. But the worst deprivation of all was the denial of their right to receive education. It was believed that basic awareness of the religious rites and memorising part of the Quran was sufficient for women.

While girls were welcome to all religious instruction especially in the lower grades, they were prevented from having further knowledge and education. In fact, the opposition to female education reached its peak when condemnation was voiced against teaching women the art of writing: 'He the teacher must not instruct any woman or female slave in the arts of writing, for thereby would accrue to them only an increase of depravity'. Thus, their role in society centred mainly on preparing them to be good and obedient wives and mothers. Later, when modern education became available, women were denied access to it and only schools for boys were initially developed. Female education was constrained by inherited social customs.

Education for women came to be viewed as being of secondary importance to keeping the home and the family. 'A woman's mission is to be a good wife and a compassionate mother... an ignorant rural woman is better for the nation than one thousand female lawyers or attorney generals'. Female education was viewed as a threat to the traditional customs and the way of life of these societies. Indeed, educated women were feared and mistrusted as they could communicate potentially destructive or innovative ideas. Educated women were considered to be obtrusive and assertive. They did not appeal to men who expected them to serve them obediently. In addition, leaving home to go to school was in contrast with the idea of women segregation. The Islamic ideal of women's education and intellectual development was thus distorted, confused and actively opposed. The result was a disaster.

The illiteracy of Muslim women reached a peak and became a widespread phenomenon in the world of Islam. Consequently, women throughout the Muslim world became ignorant not only of outside affairs, but also of their legal rights in terms of marriage, divorce and inheritance. Very often due to their ignorance of these rights, they were cheated, deceived and misled. This rendered Muslim women unable to claim and defend the rights guaranteed them by Islam. This situation continued up to recent times, until efforts were made to improve female education in different parts of the Muslim world. However, despite these efforts and the rapid progress which has been achieved in the past four to five decades, the opportunities for women's education in the Muslim world, especially in the Middle East, still lag far behind those for men. Nothing substantial has been achieved, despite the fact that all Muslim countries have encouraged the spread of female education, stated that their aim is to try and raise the educational level of women, and proclaimed their intention to attain universal literacy. The accomplishment of these goals seems very far off.

Influence of Modernity

The gap between female and male literacy rates in several places is increasing and the overall level of illiteracy is extremely high. The Islamic world, especially the Arab world, is amongst the areas in the world which has, the highest rate of illiteracy amongst women, the lowest level of schooling for girls and the smallest number of women in paid employment. In 1991, the illiteracy rate among females in Afghanistan was 86 per cent, in Pakistan 78 per cent, in Egypt 66 per cent and in Iran 56 per cent. Although women's literacy varies enormously from country to country and also from area to area in any particular country, women in the Arab world are still a small minority among the student population. In every country the rate of male literacy is much higher than female literacy. Even in those countries which have initiated some reforms, there are still considerable disparities between male and female literacy, as well as major discrepancies between the type of female education offered and the socio-economic needs of the various Arab countries. This has been caused by many factors such as: family attitudes toward female education which still prevail, especially in the rural areas, where the majority of the Muslim population lives; and the high female drop out rate due to the inequality between urban and rural education.

But the most important factor so far has been the historical interpretation of the jurists. This has taken the shape of a clear deviation from genuine Islamic principles by its strong opposition to female education. This factor is still very strong in Muslim society, particularly Arab society, and it influences government policy on education options and opportunities for women. Saudi Arabia presents a clear example where Islam has been used to first deny and then discourage women's education.

In Saudi Arabia, a highly selective and narrow interpretation of Islam have had a restrictive impact upon the lives of women. Traditionally, religion has been used as an excuse to justify the seclusion of women from the educational process. The rigid influence of the conservative theologians has played a critical role in: suffocating female education for several decades through maintaining that girls should be prevented from all state primary and secondary schools.

The extremists argued that education of women would create immorality through corrupting their thinking and diverting their attention away from their essential role as good wives and mothers. They also voiced their fear that the outcome of the conflict of values brought about by such an educational transformation would result in discontent and instability both in the home as well as in society. It was under such pressure that public education for women in the Kingdom did not start until 1960.

Female education was introduced in Saudi Arabia in 1960, when the former King Faisal took the decision to set up schools for girls. Initially, the attempt met with strong opposition from the extremists who demonstrated their disagreement by gathering at the gates of the schools, expressing their displeasure with the new schools and with those who registered their daughters in them. National Guards had to be called to restore order. The opposition continued, unabated, until the government made two essential concessions: first, the government pledged that female education would be in line with Saudi customs, especially that of rigid segregation.

Secondly, it set up a special body called the 'General Presidency for Girls' Education' to be responsible for girls' education. As a gesture of its commitment to preserve Saudi customs, the government placed this body under the control of the Saudi religious authorities who, since then, continue to supervise the education of girls in the Kingdom.

With this compromise, opposition to female education was finally mitigated and schools for girls were eventually established. The idea of schools for girls seems now to be accepted and the number of females enrolled in the educational process is increasing every year. However, despite the fact that female education in Saudi Arabia is becoming popular, and the statistics show that significant gains have been accomplished, equal opportunity between men and women is still far from being reached. This is even more the case in respect of female education in the rural areas, which is an elusive goal yet to be attained.

In fact, the policy of female education in Saudi Arabia has been founded on limited bases, aimed more at discouraging than promoting the learning process; this process neither satisfies the needs of Saudi women nor corresponds to the socio-economic requirements of the country. In the elementary schools, for example, girls mostly learn those courses which are assumed to be suitable for them in their traditional role in Saudi society. These courses emphasise mainly the Arabic language, home economics, child caring and religious instruction.

Although the elementary schools have been set up almost everywhere in the Kingdom, the proportion of female drop out after this primary level is still very high, and is a cause of great concern. As the level of education increases, the opportunities for girls to advance or progress become fewer. This is due to the fact that not all levels of knowledge and education available are at the location where the girls happen to be living, and also because in Saudi society women are not allowed to live alone in a residential campus. Hence it is difficult for them to move close to the educational institutions. Secondary schools, for instance, are not available everywhere in the country, neither are colleges.

Vocational education too has been extremely limited except for nursing schools and tailoring centres. As regard university education, the situation is no better. The universities in Saudi Arabia are mainly for males, although some of them have branches in their departments for females. In these branches there is strict segregation of the sexes in classes and all teachers are female. Sometimes, due to the lack of suitable female teachers, the learning process is accomplished through the use of closed-circuit television. This enables male professors to lecture and answer female questions, without coming into contact with them.

Awakening in Middle East

In speaking of the remarkable general progress of education in Iraq several years ago one of the officials in the Ministry of Education summed up the great contrast between the present development and that under the Turkish regime. "Very little was done for girls. The Central Girls' School in Baghdad which was established for the daughters of Turkish officials was like a foreign school, and did not benefit the girls of Baghdad. There were practically no foreign governesses, even in the better Baghdad families, such as you would have found in Istanbul or Cairo. Only a few sent their daughters to the Catholic convent for a smattering of French and embroidery, but education for girls in the real sense did not begin until after the Mandate. At first it developed slowly, but now is going with a rush." What is meant by a rush is evident from the fact that elementary schools are crowded in towns like Baghdad, Mosul and Basra, and each year brings an added demand for more girls' schools. The number of girls, which is at present about one-third of the number of boys, is increasing more rapidly than the number of boys in school.

The actual number of girls entering school in 1932 was more than the number of boys entering. The enrolment of girls in primary education has increased 105 per cent. But even though the relative rate of increase of girls is greater than that of boys, there will be for a long time the disparity in the education of girls and boys that is characteristic of the East. The desire that eventually this should not be the case is evident from the new requests each year for more girls' schools.

This urge for girls' education is passing out of the few cities exposed to modern ideas into the smaller towns, where today a girls' school attracts an increasing number. Even from Najaf and Kerbela, the two shrine cities of Shi'ah Islam, requests for girls' schools were sent several years ago to Baghdad, but the reactionary forces in these Shi'ah strongholds stirred up such an opposition that the requests were withdrawn. More open to new ideas are the semi-nomadic tribes of the desert.

Growth in education may be measured not only in geographical extension and in the larger number of schools and of girls enrolled, but also in the ascending level of girls' education. It has moved steadily up from the little Quran school under the Mulla to the primary school, then to intermediate and secondary schools.

The Central Girls' College in Baghdad has extended its course from eight to ten players, and now gives the most complete education for girl's in Iraq. For the small town the new attitude toward girls' education is evident in the numbers in the primary school; in Baghdad the Central College is the index of the Muslim response to education for girls since over eighty per cent of the students are Muslim, and many do not live in Baghdad. The registration in this school each year exceeds the facilities so that a large number must be turned away. In Iraq conservatism has been disarmed by promoting the education for girls within the sanctions of Islamic tradition.

The Baghdad school is a good illustration of the general situation. Purdah conditions in this institution are carefully observed, the school following rather than directly promoting social change. But the atmosphere of the school is steadily becoming less purdah. At the beginning there was no man servant; now a young man janitor moves about the school freely. At first, no men visitors were allowed, not even the English Director of Education; now they are admitted but only with special permits from the Ministry of Education. When they were first admitted, all the girls veiled; now perhaps only one or two out of forty ever cover their faces before visitors.

Although none of the older girls take part in the school exercises, there is a tendency for parents, proud of their daughters, to waive their conservatism and let them appear in public even after they are really past the age of veiling. For example, a well-known family still allows a talented daughter of fourteen to perform in public. She is rather small for her age, and passes without criticism.

The consciousness of the veil is still very evident, however, outside the school. Visit the Baghdad School near closing time and you will find a group of old women, perhaps a few men, hovering about waiting to take the girls home. The older as well as the younger girls must have a special guardian, since according to Muslim custom, a veiled woman is helpless outside her own home. These caretakers are often disregarded by the girls; or perhaps "parked" somewhere while the girls manage to shop or go to the dressmaker on the way home.

An extra gift or bakshish smooths the way for this suspicious freedom and then the girl appears at home properly chaperoned. The elderly chaperone is required also to accompany the girls on 'The school excursion, a regular annual event for each class, and a great sign of advancing freedom. These excursions are an interesting illustration of the old and new. The girls go in motor cars, veiled, as far as the outskirts of the city, then up go the veils. Their regular attendants' a nurse or a chauffeur, or some old family retainer, enjoy watching the games and incidentally have a good exposure to modern ideas. "These caretakers," as the Principal of the school remarked,' "are much more aware of the present-day schoolgirl's problems than are the girl's parents."

The slightest innovation in the Baghdad school, as in other schools in Iraq, must be carefully considered in reference to conservative opinion. The need for such care is illustrated by the protest which was made against having a lecture given at the Girls' College by a professor from the Men's Normal School.

One of the students commented on having heard a very interesting lecture. The father, a reactionary Muslim, reported it to the Parliament and the Minister of Education. Since then, the further use of men speakers has not been possible. Indicative of progress, however, is the occasional attendance of a group from the Girls' Normal School at lectures, cinemas or special national celebrations at the Men's Normal School. The girls are, it is true, carefully chaperoned, and sit as a group in the balcony without any individual contact.

The limited social milieu of girls' education in Baghdad is determined not only by public opinion, but also by the attitude of the authorities. King Feisal was very definitely interested in girls' education but believed that it should, be promoted within the social sanctions of Islam. King Ghazi has continued his father's policy. The advance of education, for girls, as for boys, will doubtless continue to receive, the patronage of the Palace, but without any idea of changing social customs.

The change in the programme of girls' education along a number of lines indicates growth in effectiveness. Teachers are beginning to be aware that girls need other courses than the stereotyped programme required by an identical system for boys and girls. The difficulty of introducing new content in education becomes obvious from the fact that a girl in a civics class, working on a "Know your City" project, could not visit the post office, because girls are not supposed to go out and have no reason to see public buildings. In spite of difficulties new ideas are making headway. Physical education is, progressing, even though slowly because of the veil.

Physical education is now interpreted in the larger meaning as an emphasis on normal recreation-clubs, school excursions, and general creative activities. This represents an entirely new idea in education as a whole, but especially in the education of girls. The use of the school as the centre for entertainments, recreation, cinema and radio performance is being promoted. The old Oriental idea of the crowds being entertained by the storyteller furnishes perhaps the germ for the new community usefulness of the school. Some teachers realize the need for vocational education for girls, but the time does not yet seem ripe for this emphasis.

Differentiation in girls' education, however, is emphasized through courses in home sciences, including homemaking, child care, sanitation and personal hygiene. With these new emphases the necessity for a closer relationship between the home and the school is obvious to thoughtful teachers, who realize that the real job of the modern school is social.

The Principal of the Baghdad Central College summed up the problem of the difference between the teaching of the school and the home thus: "Every Muslim girl who goes to the Baghdad School is exposed to two streams of influence which affect every act of her life—sleeping, dressing, and undressing at night, eating, walking, and thinking. The school teaches physical and mental activity; the home, passivity and fatalism. The school must seek to bridge the gap between its influence and that of the home."

This contrast between the ideals of home and school have led to a recognition of the need for adult education. There are some developments of adult education for the lower classes to raise the level of literacy, and also the higher level along the lines of social education. At the other extreme from adult education is the promotion of the modern kindergarten, an entirely new emphasis in Iraq. These kindergartens are in striking contrast to the Mulla schools for little children, where they sat all huddled up together before an old sheikh or an uneducated elderly Muslim woman, chanting the Quran in high shrill voices, swaying back and forth in rhythmic accompaniment. The kindergarten in the Girls' School in Baghdad, which serves as a training centre for kindergarten teachers, would compare favourably in equipment with nine-tenths of modern American kindergartens. Another problem about which educators for girls in Iraq express concern is the question of social relationships. Under the regime of the veil the school does not encourage social contact, but the content of the teaching, as has been shown, lead toward the idea of unveiling.

Social change and education inevitably go together, since, as an Iraqi educator said, "You can't 'stagger' social advance" until the educational process is finished, and you cannot advance in education without some idea of social reform. The major difficulty in promoting a programme of modern education or even education along conventional lines in Iraq has been the securing of teachers. The steady development of a staff of trained women teachers in a decade has been accomplished to a large extent by the importation of Syrian teachers. The salaries paid by the Iraqi Government to these Syrian teachers have been very high, in comparison with salaries in Syria, but the need was urgent.

A real pioneering spirit and keenness for adventure together with their technical preparation for teaching, have been required of these Syrian teachers, who have been building a school programme for girls in a new country. This group of young Syrians has established the teaching profession in Iraq on a high educational level, has given prestige to teaching as a career and made it worthy of even the most conservative upper class. Their influence however has not been limited to the schools but has permeated the social environment.

Undoubtedly to the younger generation of Iraqi young men and women, the Syrian group of men and women teachers has presented, by their normal social relationships, a whole new way of life and inspired the desire in the younger generation of Iraq to be released from their traditional social restraints. The heyday of the Syrian teacher's opportunity, both for men and women—for there have been many of each has now passed.

The Syrian women teachers are now only in secondary and normal schools and are there much less than before. Eventually, perhaps in four or five years, they will be entirely replaced, as it is considered desirable, both because of national economy and national amour-proper, for Iraq to have her own teachers. The preparation of Iraqi girls for secondary schools is being accomplished by sending them abroad to Syria or elsewhere on Government scholarships. The extension of Government subsidies to girls in itself signalizes progress in girls' education.

Until 1928 these foreign scholarships were limited to men. Since 1928, when the first group of eight girls went to Syria, their number each year has steadily grown. Now thirty or more girls are studying abroad, mostly in Beirut at the American School for Girls and the British Syrian Training College, also in the American junior College for Women and the American University of Beirut.

Naturally, the problem of sending girls is more difficult than boys because of social conditions. Furthermore, there is less certainty of direct benefit to the Department of Education, since educating girls is something of a lottery because of the high probability of their marriage.

However, as an investment, not measured in direct returns to the schools, but to the community as a whole, this system of foreign scholarships has had great value. Especially worthy of note is the increase of Muslim girls on foreign scholarships. At first, only Christians were available, as Muslim parents could not think of sending their daughters abroad. The number of Muslim girls has increased; now about half the number or more are Muslims.

The attitude of Muslim parents has distinctly changed. Now training abroad is becoming every year a more natural thing, although it must still make quite a stir in a Muslim family to send a daughter five hundred miles across the desert, for ten months' study each year for several years, in a Christian Mission School. Muslim girls now go abroad for study not merely on Government scholarships, but also on private funds to gain a higher education, as a few Muslims as well as Christians have felt the urge for something beyond the Baghdad School. These Muslim girls from Iraq who are studying abroad are already exerting a social influence in their home environment. They come back from Beirut each spring with new ideas showing Anglo-Saxon influence in points of view and clothes of the French style. Often while abroad they have perhaps indulged in a vacation from the veil. All of these broader outside influences cannot fail to have their effects in Baghdad or in Mosul. Up to the present time the needs for higher education both for men and women in Iraq have been met by study abroad, in very large measure in the American University of Beirut, which has become the university for the Arabic speaking world. There has been some agitation in Baghdad for the establishment of a university but this is not considered probable for sometime, since this would involve an unwarranted expense for the small number of students who are as yet ready or desirous of higher education.

A medical college in Baghdad is, however, regarded as necessary to solve the most pressing national problem of health. The training of men and women in medical service is fundamental to the economic progress of Iraq and in the near future should be carried on in Iraq.

The admission of Muslim girls to the coeducational medical school in Baghdad would be an interesting parallel to the fact that the first university coeducation in Egypt was for women medical students. One of the special influences that has favoured the promotion of girls' education, especially in Baghdad, is the presence of a number of educated Turkish women, wives of prominent Iraqi officials. Their example has stimulated a spirit of competition in Baghdad mothers to have their daughters well educated and thus make a good marriage. The marriage motivation which is evident throughout the East in promoting girls' education, has thus an added force in Baghdad, because of the Turkish influence in the situation. The group of advanced Turkish women has created a desire among some of the Baghdad women for social progress. The contrast between the freedom of Turkey and the social conservatism of Iraq has made a special impression because the Turkish women are Muslims. The combined effect of the Turkish and Syrian groups has undoubtedly been influential in creating in Baghdad a certain dissatisfaction with existing social conditions and in stimulating the urge for change. In the development of modern education in Iraq, Anglo-Saxon-British and American-influence has played an important role. British ideas furnished the basis of the educational system which was organized during the first years of the mandate.

American educational influence has been evident in the later developments in Iraq, largely due to the fact that most of the Syrian teachers were graduates from the American institutions in Beirut and a number of them also had studied in America. Moreover, the majority of the Iraqi students on foreign scholarships have also studied in Beirut in the American schools and hold key positions in the educational system of Iraq.

As a natural result of the predominance of Anglo-Saxon influence in Iraq, English is the second language. Compared with other countries of the Near East and Middle East, the work of foreign educational institutions in Iraq has been very limited. Girls' education, however has been directly affected by the three American Mission Schools for girls in Baghdad, Mosul and Basra. These three institutions have contributed to a number of Muslim girls a sound educational preparation and have stimulated public appreciation of the value of girls' education. The primary impetus for general progress in Iraq and this, of course, affects the educational advance of women has come through the vigorous spirit of nationalism awakened since the World War. The example of Turkish nationalism, strong, aggressive, successful has been undoubtedly a stimulant for Iraq.

Leaders in Iraq repeatedly express the idea that the retarded development of women is a real handicap to the development of children and hence to the progress of the State. Iraq has adopted democratic institutions such as a constitution and Parliament, which are an anomaly in an illiterate country. Hence, the problem is to raise the whole educational level. The spirit of almost breathless nationalism of Iraq has stirred the public consciousness into a sense of need for education, and especially education for Muslim girls.

Scene in Iran

Education in Iran has always in the past been identified with religion, largely connected with the mosques and maintained by the clergy, created an unfavourable atmosphere for promoting the education of girls. The general public has always considered it useless to educate girls.

The idea expressed in Iranian philosophy that education should be highly selective for those who can profit by it, has always been the current opinion and has debarred girls from educational privilege as expressed in the saying, "Where the innate capacity is good, education may make an impression, but no furbisher knows how to give a polish to bad iron." Although the new spirit is overcoming the old prejudicial attitude toward girls' education, such a handicap is not soon overcome.

The number of Government boys' schools, primary and secondary, is about four times the number of schools for girls, and the total enrolment of boys in all schools in Iran is slightly more than three times that of girls. More than half the education of girls in Iran is carried on by private schools, which have contributed also very greatly to boys' education.

Teheran of course represents the high-water mark of interest in both girls' and boys' education. Rural education receives little attention and girls' rural schools are practically nil. The opening of ten primary schools of three grades for boys and girls is not only a numerical advance but also also represents social progress in adopting coeducation. The teachers of these mixed primary schools are all women and over half the pupils are girls.

Education for the great majority of girls is limited to the elementary schools, which means a maximum of six years but often only a four-years' course. There are only a few middle schools and one normal school for girls, offering an eleven years' course and about thirty private middle schools, also of eleven years.

The American Mission institution for girls in Teheran, Nurbakush, with a course of twelve and sometimes thirteen years represents the top level of education for girls in Iran. Girls' education in Iran of any kind is the product of only about two decades and education on a modern basis is the result of only a decade. Viewed over a period of years there are distinct signs of advance. The fact that education for girls has begun is in itself the most hopeful evidence of progress. Apart from the growth in the extent of girls' education in Iran, it is worthy of notice also that education for girls has risen from the floor of the Quran school to the level of seats and desks of the modern primary school.

From the dull, damp room connected with some mosque with its crowd of little boys and girls huddled together on a mat in an atmosphere of disorder and all-talk-at- one-time casual heterogeneity under an old sheikh, whose method was to keep up an unbroken chanting of the Quran—from such a school it is a far cry to the present-day primary school with its well-ordered school room, its maps and blackboard, its orderly atmosphere, and young teachers, such as one finds in most of the schools in Teheran today. The fact, however, that some girls' schools are still held in private dwellings, ill-adapted for school use. And that many of the teachers are inexperienced, makes one, realize that schools for girls, even in Teheran, are of recent origin.

The eagerness of girls for education and the inadequacy of their facilities are also evident when one visited a Teheran primary school, and found three girls wedged tightly in each seat in a room with fifty children, which could not comfortably hold more than thirty or thirty-five. With girls clamouring for places in school, it is easy to understand the statement that the Parliament does not disagree over the necessity to expand education for girls.

When the first girls' school was opened there, a private venture of a wealthy Muslim woman, the key-bearded city fathers raised a strong opposition. "Why should there be a school for girls?" They said: "Who believes that they can learn?" The answer to their protest was a model small town school, an attractive new building, very spacious playground and an alert young teacher from Teheran, well trained according to the present standards.

Any doubt as to whether girls can learn is dispelled by the bright-eyed little Iranian girls, one hundred or more, learning the elements of modern education, and also the useful vocation of carpet weaving, if they choose. The eager response of the girls must give deep satisfaction to the founder of the school, who herself is illiterate and therefore, perhaps, more keenly appreciates the value of education. She must feel that her annual expense for the school, the entire income from one of her villages, is a sound investment. But the city fathers doubtless still shake their heads at such rank and futile extravagance. In such a reactionary environment, modern education had been planted with great care.

The physical schools have been developed along the more formal type of gymnastic exercise. The creative forms of recreation through various extracurricular activities are scarcely known. New emphases, however, are being introduced by an American adviser to the Ministry of Education. A class of thirty-two young women in 1935 finished a course of three months in scouting as a preparation to develop this work in the girls' schools. Another group has been trained in sports to offset the programme of conventional calisthenics.

An effort is also being made to introduce more social plays, and games, and especially music, all of which are innovations. The programme of athletics in girls' schools has been given a great deal of newspaper publicity through frequent pictures of Girl Guide troops and girls in, active games and exercises. Thus, the public is being effectively educated to this new idea of girlhood. School hygiene is also receiving attention.

A special medical officer visits the schools, inspects the sanitary conditions, examines the children and sends those needing special attention to the clinic or hospital where free treatment is given. But since these visits are not very frequent, perhaps only once a month, the regular teacher is expected to emphasize the fundamentals of health. A distinctive feature of the teaching profession in Iran has been the work of the women inspectors. The system of having women inspectors, which was established when the private schools were brought under Government supervision, was necessitated by the fact that it was impossible because of the veil for men to visit girls' schools. Thus, a social handicap has led to a constructive educational benefit.

The women inspectors, many of whom are graduates of the American School for Girls in Teheran, represent a high type in the teaching profession. One of the best known of the women inspectors is Khanum Doulatabadee, the pioneer in girls' education already mentioned, who was one of the first women from Iran to study abroad.

As Iranian girls at that time did not leave their own country alone, the ever watchful police held up at the border this eager student on her way to Paris, until verification could be received from Teheran. Today Iranian women students as well as men pursue higher education abroad. But women students have not yet received Government scholarships for foreign study. For over eighty years Iranian boys have been sent abroad for foreign study. Practically all of the present leaders of Iran have studied in Europe, the large majority in France.

An increasing number have been sent from the different ministries—Education, Health, Justice and others. Although, some of the other Ministries are still sending students abroad the Ministry of Education has now discontinued these foreign scholarships, at least temporarily, and is concentrating on the development of stronger institutions of higher learning in Iran. When a law was passed authorizing too foreign scholarships annually for five years for young men but making no provision for women students, the obvious inequality evoked a vigorous protest from some of the advocates of women's education. Ten to twenty scholarships for teacher training were urged for women. The question became the subject of heated discussion carried on in the Press. The opponents argued on the basis of unpreparedness of girls and the danger of Western contamination, contending furthermore that Iran offered adequate training for girls.

The advocates of foreign scholarships for girls, among whom were several women, cited as proof of the capacity of girls the number of successful candidates in Government examination, and maintained that women would be less contaminated morally than men have been by foreign contact. They emphasized the necessity of training in Europe because of the backward conditions in Iran, which make adequate training impossible.

The discussion brought into sharp relief the conflict in Iran today between conservatism and progress. In spite of a strong tide in favour of foreign scholarships for girls, the opposition prevailed. No girls have been officially included on the Government lists, but a few, six or eight, have been partially helped by Government funds. However, quite a number of Iranian girls, perhaps sixty or more, are now studying abroad, mostly in Europe on private funds.

Recently, higher education in Iran for girls has been the subject of much public discussion. The conservatives in Iran as elsewhere East or West have advanced the argument that girls not only do not need advanced education but should not have it, since they are required for home life. But quite aside from the opposition against higher education for women, there seems to be as yet on the whole very little demand for it in Iran. Nurbakush, Sage College, meets the needs as yet of the small minority who desire to go beyond the secondary school. The Government University will be eventually opened to women students in departments, beginning first with dentistry and pharmacy, for which courses several women students have already applied.

The prevailing lack of urge for higher education up to the present time is doubtless related to the fact that the interest in professional careers in Iran has not yet in any sense cut across the idea of marriage. Aside from teaching which, as has been said, is considered as an economic necessity rather than a career, there is practically no profession open to Muslim girls in Iran. Marriage is the main career. To ensure a good marriage, education up to a point is regarded as desirable. This explains in Iran as elsewhere the increasing number of girls in school beyond the primary and secondary stage. But higher education is not considered an additional marriage asset; perhaps this explains the lack of desire for it.

The fact that the education of girls is being extended, however, through the secondary stage is very important. The longer period of education and later marriage age point to the eventual solution of one of the major problems of Iran and of the East as a whole—the disparity between the literate husband and illiterate wife. Some few attempts are being made in private schools in Teheran to meet the problem of the present generation of illiterate wives, many of whom are pathetically eager to bridge the gap between themselves and their husbands. Some of them are beyond the schoolgirl stage and can only laboriously overcome the handicap of illiteracy.

Many are still the age of schoolgirls and eager to attend the regular schools, which, however, are already overcrowded and cannot admit married women or girls. A few private schools for married women have been started such as, for example, the one carried on by a Women's Association in Iran. These schools are small but significant, showing what should be done on a much larger scale to meet this important social problem.

The growing consciousness of this problem—the disparity in education between men and women—is one of the main secrets of the present awakening of interest in education for girls and women in Iran, whether it finds expression in the primary or secondary schools or in meagre adult education efforts. A few years ago there was not as at present this poignant awareness of the fact that Iranian women without education are under a terrific handicap.

The social and intellectual cleavage between men and women in Iran was not questioned. But today there is a growing consciousness of a need for change. The younger generation of educated men want educated wives in Iran as elsewhere. The Iranian mother desires to see her daughter well married, and enjoying an equality in marriage such as she, herself, has been denied. Perhaps just as in Baghdad the increase of foreign wives in the higher circles has made some Teheran mothers realize the desirability of educating their daughters.

Doubtless, Muslim women in Iran, especially in Teheran, have been affected also by a comparison of their social and educational position with that of women in other communities. The Armenians, in giving up the chaddur a number of years ago and availing themselves freely of educational opportunity have furnished a progressive example.

The Zoroastrian community with its freedom from social handicaps for women, and its active promotion of girls' schools may have also had an influence, although the forward movement of Zoroastrian women has produced no outstanding women leaders. More significant for Muslim women perhaps has been the example of the women of the Bahai community, who though still veiled, are quite free behind the veil, representing thus a halfway stage of progress.

The fact that in many communities the Bahai Girls' was the first and only school for a long time has undoubtedly stimulated Muslim educational effort, but the Bahaist influence is less important today than in the earlier period. The Muslim woman's desire for education and general advance has also been greatly affected by the social reforms in Turkey.

A direct influence on the educational progress of Muslim women had also come from the Anglo-Saxon schools, the British and American Mission girls' schools in different parts of Iran and especially Nurbakush in Teheran. These institutions had effectively presented to the community the highest value of education for girls. Without discussing freedom or apparently promoting freedom for women, they produced an atmosphere in which freedom is the natural result. At the commencement of Nurbakush in May 1929 for the first time the three Muslim unveiled graduates delivered their graduating 'addresses to an audience of eight hundred people, and were received with enthusiasm and applause.

The Mission Schools for Girls in Tabriz and Hamadan had deeply affected a whole area. The Shiraz Girls' School, formerly a Mission institution but now under private auspices has been a distinctive influence for education along modern English lines. It represents an adaptation of Anglo-Saxon ideals. Alborz College in Teheran, the American College for Men, has without question been a great force for the social and educational progress of women, in that it has given to its large student body of young men from all over Iran new social ideals.

The increasing penetration of Anglo-Saxon ideas, as represented in the British and American schools in Iran, is an interesting evidence of the new trend in Iran away from the European model of life and thought. For over eighty years French influence has been dominant. French is the second language; the educational system is modelled on French lines; Paris has always been the Mecca for Iranian students. But in the present period of awakening, a migration from French to Anglo-Saxon influence is evident, which is having a pervasive effect on the social and educational advance of women.

Although foreign influences, French and English, are exerting a subtle force toward change in various phases of Iranian life, the impelling motive of the present renaissance, of which the advance of women is a part, in Iran as in Iraq, is the newly aroused spirit of nationalism. This has for Iran the special meaning of a growth in the consciousness of national unity and a new appreciation of Iranian culture. The building of roads has facilitated travel and brought hitherto isolated cities into closer contact. The divided provincial loyalties of the past are being supplanted by a national loyalty and pride, which demands that Iran should not have an inferior position in the East. A few leaders in Iran recognize that the advance of women is a necessity for national progress and are therefore vigorously promoting girls' education. Even by the less thinking majority, education for girls is being accepted as a natural part of the new era. However, the situation changed to a great extent, following the Islamic revolution.

Situation in India

The obvious reason for the lack of education among Muslim women is purdah and general Muslim conservatism, an interrelated cause and effect. Purdah lays a detaining hand on the Muslim girl's education. It interferes not only after the veil is assumed, which is usually not until the age eleven or twelve years, but also before that age; the prevailing purdah psychology often prevents even little girls, not yet veiled, from attending the primary school, which does not have a woman teacher. Because of the dearth of women teachers in the primary schools many Muslim girls never cross the threshold of a school.

The direct effect of purdah on the number of girls in school is shown by the fact that in purdah-bound provinces like the Punjab and the United Provinces, the attendance of girls in school is lower than in other provinces. Apart from the fact that purdah undoubtedly curtails the school privileges of Muslim girls, it presents very practical difficulties in education. At the opening or closing hour, or in a smaller town like Bhopal, the covered bullock-carts lined up at the school door, and have watched the shrouded figures scuttle from the entrance of the school compound into the curtained safety of the conveyance.

In addition to the purdah conveyance, the necessity for a female attendant to accompany the girl to see to it that purdah is not broken on the way to school, and the elaborate precautions necessary for preserving strict purdah in the school, for example requiring even the elimination of all male servants from girls' schools — these restrictions have vastly complicated school life for a Muslim girl in India.

Other social customs characteristic of India, but not peculiar to Muslims, have prevented Muslim girls, as well as Indian girls of other communities, from having full educational privileges. Although child marriage is especially associated with Hinduism, early marriage among the masses of Muslims is also quite common.

In 1921 out of eight and a half million brides under fifteen years of age one and a half million were Muslims. This means that number of girls were cut off from any education beyond the early primary grades. With attention concentrated on early marriage for their daughter, the Muslim parents' chief concern naturally is to find a suitable son-in-law. Hence, attendance of girls in the primary school seems unnecessary and in the middle school is obviously impossible. As girls are withdrawn from school just at the time when they begin to mature in mind as well as body, this not only cuts off the majority from ordinary education but reduces to a minimum the number of Muslim girls who might become teachers.

The education of Muslim girls has been impeded not only by the specific handicaps of purdah and early marriage, but frequently by the conservatism of the Indian Muslim community. This conservatism has been strengthened by the Nationalist Movement. Muslim India in its fear of absorption by the Hindus, has shown a reaction similar to the attitude the Muslim community in Palestine in reference to Zionism. Some Muslim leaders have always insisted on having special privileges in schools for Muslims, unwilling otherwise to avail themselves of the regular facilities of education in India.

The general situation, of education for Muslim girls shows a very slow but steady advance both in the number of schools for girls and of girls in schools. After 1920 the curve of elementary and secondary schools begins to ascend. This period marks also practically the beginning of higher education for Muslim girls, although the number of Muslim girls is still negligible. Isabella Thoburn College in Lucknow, and Kinnaird College for Women in Lahore, which may be taken as valid criteria, show a steady increase of Muslims as also of girls from other communities. The few Muslim women who are well educated often hold positions of unusual prominence.

A widely known Muslim woman in the Punjab, the first woman to take her doctorate, has an important post as an inspectress for girls' schools. She has maintained strict purdah and thus proved that in spite of the purdah, advance in education is possible. But it may also be questioned whether by such a policy she has not sacrificed an opportunity to exert greater influence for social advance, as the first highly educated Muslim woman in her part of India.

Of the widespread desire of Muslim parents for the education of their daughters there is no question today; even more evident is the eager response of Muslim girls themselves to these new opportunities.

The renaissance in education is affecting not only the extent but also the character of the Government programme for girls' schools. Under the old system the few girls who entered college found themselves well prepared for equal competition with men in professional careers; but preparation for marriage, the primary career for the great majority in India, as elsewhere in the East, has received little attention. The regular Government schools and the majority of private girls' schools have been bound by the straitjacket of the examination system.

Homemaking subjects, physical education, and hygiene have been only optional and difficult to promote, since the parents, as well as students, regard the school certificate based on the regular requirements as the final seal of education. There is, however, some loosening of the straitjacket bonds, through the beginning of vocational training and homemaking courses, and more physical education.

A certain amount of vocational education has been developed in connection with the regular schools. Some of the Mission schools have pioneered in this field attempting to coordinate girls' education more closely with the needs of practical life.

The most distinctive development in the Government system is the Government Zenana Industrial Schools in Lahore of which there are now fifteen. In addition to regular elementary education these schools offer courses in home arts and crafts along very modern lines. Although these schools are open to girls and women of different religions, and social levels, and different ages they especially serve Muslims and offer particularly the uneducated *purdahnashin* a belated opportunity to overcome her lack of earlier educational development by the right type of useful vocational training. The response of Muslim schoolgirls to education, keen as it is, perhaps is not as eager as is the desire of some young Muslim women, who were married at an early age and thus deprived of education.

The growing demand for more educational facilities for Muslim girls today reflects in no small measure the effect of some of the non-Muslim communities — the Parsees because of their social freedom of women; the Brahma Samaj community because of its aggressive social reforms; and the Christians because of their widespread facilities for education and the large number of Christian women pioneers in professional life have in different degrees helped to stimulate the social and educational advance of Muslim girls. A few outstanding Hindu reformers, men and women, have also undoubtedly exerted a strong influence in the advance of Indian women as a whole affecting Muslims as well as Hindus. Undoubtedly one of the main forces that has steadily promoted the educational and social development of Indian women of all, communities, has been the Christian institutions for girls. These schools were very often the first school for girls in a community, and today they still constitute a large part of girls' education in India.

The study of progress in the education of girls and women in India, is virtually a study of the educational efforts of Missions.

Certain institutions have had a special effect on the education of Muslim girls, notably the two Christian Colleges in North India already mentioned Kinnaird College and Isabella Thoburn College, and the Women's Christian College in Madras. The increase in Muslim students in Kinnaird College is a special indication of a breaking down of conservatism since the Government College observes purdah strictly. A growing number of Muslim fathers desire the more liberal type of education.

In 1925 two Muslim girls, swathed in shroudlike white burqas were awarded their diplomas from Isabella Thoburn College which issues its diplomas at the convocation of the University of Lucknow. In 1929 three Muslim girls on the same platform received their diplomas, unveiled with all the other men and women students. Their names were read off in the alphabetical list and no one in the audience paid any attention to whether they were Hindu, Muslim, or Christian.

Since that time all Muslim students have received their diplomas publicly in the Lucknow University. In the liberalizing atmosphere of these colleges for women, such an advance is regarded as merely the natural result of a modern education. Some of the men's colleges are also exerting a progressive influence on women's education.

The major factor in the promotion of educational and social progress today is the influence exerted by Indian women themselves, both individually and through collective effort. A decade ago, only a few Indian women were conscious of their responsibility as a force for advance. Today there are a growing number of educated leaders who are devoting themselves to the crusade of education for the hundreds of thousands of uneducated women who, still behind the purdah, are voiceless to make known their needs.

In the small minority of highly cultivated leaders, who are advocates of education, one can single out from different parts of India the few outstanding Muslim leaders who are devoting themselves untiringly to the promotion of woman's education and social reform.

A number of women's organizations in India have as their primary objective education and social reform, and through collective effort are influencing public opinion and official policy. Viewed in the light of statistics, the appalling illiteracy of Indian women, the comparatively small number of girls in schools, the withdrawal from school of many girls after but one year, the growing disparity in education between men and women, the dearth of women teachers—and with all of these facts intensified in reference to Muslim women the situation does indeed seem depressing. But the upward curve in the education of girls, Muslims as well as others, has begun. Official and private agencies are increasing the educational facilities for girls. The general public, including even the conservatives, has awakened to the need to educate girls as well as boys. The eager response of girls to these new opportunities is everywhere evident. Progressive influences, foreign and Indian, are working unitedly on this common problem of education for girls.

Ideals in Egypt

Due to the slow development of education, Egyptian women did not begin to emerge from illiteracy until after a spirit of nationalism asserted itself in 1919. Popular education, properly speaking, either for boys or girls, had its beginning in Egypt after that date. The previous unimportant position of education in Egyptian policy is shown by the fact that Lord Milliners's book *England in Egypt* devotes only a few pages to education and the *Encyclopaedia Britannica* gives it barely a page in small type. Up to this time popular education meant for the most part native schools, largely under untrained and even illiterate teachers, whose main qualification was their ability to chant the Quran. Under these conditions the figures for illiteracy and the disparity in education between girls and boys, are not surprising. Many of the women teachers could neither read nor write.

Anything above elementary schools for girls was obviously not considered. The Government in 1920 had only five primary girls' schools with 843 pupils. Since that time there has been a definite forward movement in education. The new Constitution of Egypt, proclaimed in 1923, provided for free and compulsory primary education, with 1935 set as the objective date for realizing this educational aim. Obviously this achievement has not been possible in such a limited period, but the country is moving toward that goal. There were in 1929 in contrast to 1919 almost twice as many elementary schools, and more than twice as many girls in elementary schools; almost three times as many higher elementary schools with almost three times as many higher elementary students; nine times as many schools for teachers' training for elementary schools with a little less than six times the increase in students; three times as many kindergarten schools and seven times the number of children; four times as many primary schools and four times the number of primary pupils.

This period marked also the beginning of secondary education for girls and the addition of a special college for girls; the transition from the old style makeshift school, often held in a mere hovel and taught by an illiterate teacher, to a well-organized modern school under a trained teacher; and the introduction of modern kindergartens on the Friable model. But the most significant progress of this first decade of the twentieth century lies in the fact that it marks the beginning of modern education for girls and its advance from the elementary grade to the college and university level.

The real landmark as regards girls' education is the year 1925 when girls' secondary education was officially established. Before 1925 a great gulf divided the status of boys' and girls' education. The fact that lower standards were required for teaching in girls' primary schools than in boys' schools, illustrated the inferiority of girls' education. Teachers for the boys' schools had to complete their secondary education before being admitted for teachers' training; whereas women teachers for girls' schools obtained the primary certificate after only four years' study in primary schools, and in addition the four years' course of a training college. Graduates of unusual ability were sent to England, but few won this opportunity, because of their short period of training and limited scope of knowledge. Girls not desirous of teaching suffered from the lack of general cultural values in the course.

Egyptian leaders, however, have recognized the inadequacy of the preparation for teachers of girls' schools and the resultant inequality of the educational status of boys and girls, and have accordingly promoted the addition of secondary schools for girls. To serve the two types of girls—those of the leisure class, desiring general education, and those preparing to teach secondary education was differentiated into two types of courses.

Some of the educators who are directing the policy of girls' education in Egypt, recognize the desirability of more differentiation in girls' education, especially in the secondary schools. The objectives of education for girls are not adequately met by the prescribed curriculum which was built to serve the needs of boys. Education of boys has been directed largely toward a Government Job and therefore based on the "white collar and clean hands" idea of education.

Such a system, which no longer fits the needs of boys, is obviously unsuited for girls. The difficulty of achieving differentiation in girls' education, however, is obvious because of the hidebound examination system. If equality in education for girls and boys means identical standards then differentiation in the girls' programme is impossible.

The important question is whether the special needs of girls can be met without sacrificing the principle of true equality. Opinion is divided on this subject. Some teachers advocate more attention to vocational education such as the industrial arts. An industrial Arts Course is offered in the Elementary Teachers' Training Schools, but as a whole, general vocational training is not yet considered necessary since the usual vocational lines, which constitute in the West the means of economic livelihood for the masses, do not exist for the Muslim girls. The girls' schools of

Egypt are, of course, primarily geared to the needs of Muslims, because of the very large proportion of Muslims in the population.

Commenting on the question as to the need for vocational training for girls, the Director of Girls' Education some years ago said: "The public is not ready for economic liberty for women. It will be another twenty-five years before women will be in many professions in Egypt. We are pushing vocational training for boys, of course, as an economic necessity."

A gymnastics exhibition of two thousand primary schoolgirls under the supervision of the Egyptian Directress of Physical Education, illustrated the development of physical education for girls in Egypt. The complete freedom of the Egyptian girls at that time seemed refreshing in contrast with the veil-restricted life of schoolgirls in most of the other Muslim countries. This exhibition, the Second Annual Exhibition of the Physical Education Department in Cairo was held in the Gezireh sports grounds before a very large and representative gathering.

The children, with complete abandon and schoolgirl enthusiasm, carried out the varied programme, which showed incidentally the influence of the Supervisor's training in England—relay races and games, English country dances, drills and marches. The Muslim Director was assisted by a group of teachers, all Muslims, a fact which one recognized by their neatly bound scarf head-dress, which to the casual observer did not suggest a special Muslim style but gave only the impression of a distinctive fashion worn in preference to the hat. There was no suggestion of the veil or the psychology of the veil in their manner. And yet, one knew that it could not have happened a few years earlier in Cairo and at that time was possible in no other Muslim country except Turkey. Today Iran, as we have said, also endorses this full measure of freedom. Although the Islamic social customs have greatly changed, modernism in Egypt has not meant secularism in the schools. The teaching of Islam in the girls' schools is still being carried on but in a modern way by young teachers trained in the tenets of their religion.

The modern method of teaching religion in the Egyptian schools is appreciated in other countries. Palestine has occasionally turned to Egypt for a trained woman teacher of religion. The religious teaching in the training schools is given by sheikhs, not the elderly type as formerly, but often young sheikhs, some of whom have been trained in Europe. These younger sheikhs are the products of the new reforms of Al Azhar, the great intellectual centre of the Muslim world. The study of science and comparative religions in Europe can scarcely fail to have its effect.

Today the inclusion of the teaching of Islam in the school programme is a formal recognition of religion, one feels, rather than a vital endorsement of Islam, such as would characterize Muslim teaching in India. Girls in Normal School have always been supposed to keep their heads covered in classes taught by men, but this is no longer observed. Moreover, now they do not have the attitude of passive acquiescent deference before the sheikh as in the past. Sometimes the sheikhs have to call in a woman teacher to help in discipline. The freedom of the Muslim schools of Cairo today is in striking contrast to the general conditions fifteen or twenty years ago, as related by one of the English inspectresses, who had taught for a number of years in a private school in Lower Egypt. "Formerly the girls were always brought to school in covered conveyances; men clerks could not be employed. The girls were all closely veiled, visited very little even in the homes of girls with whom they had been special friends in school, and after their marriage rarely saw each other. There was no need for more than primary schools as early marriage was the rule. Contact with foreigners was very slight; in fact, the Egyptians were afraid of foreigners." This, she explained, was not true of Cairo, but of Zagazig, a typical 'Large town in Lower Egypt. "When I opened the Girls' School in Zagazig twenty years ago," she continued, "the little girls were very much frightened.. One little girl especially would not allow me to do anything for her for three days. Then when she finally allowed me to undo the little Quran amulet to wash her neck, I knew that her fear had been broken."

What a striking contrast to that day of seclusion and fear of contact one finds in modern Egypt today with its crowded primary and secondary schools and its public gymnastics exhibitions. The social conservatism of the authorities does not in any way seem to retard the educational development of girls. The schools remain technically in the frame of Islam, but each year the frame is widened. The modern spirit dominates in spite of the adherence to certain traditions. Undoubtedly, one of the greatest difficulties in promoting rural education in Egypt is the placement of teachers. As in India and elsewhere the difference in living standards and in social mores makes it practically impossible for young women teachers to live in backward village areas. Furthermore, trained women teachers are reluctant to leave the interests and amusements of the large city. There are few special inducements offered for rural service; quite the contrary, in fact, as positions in Cairo are often given as the reward for merit and students of lower scholarship are sent to villages. This problem is a subject for serious consideration. The most noteworthy advance in girls' education in Egypt during the last decade and a half has been the successful establishment of a trained teaching staff. The growth from two training colleges for women elementary teachers in 1920 to fifteen in 1934 with an increase in students from 447 to 1,132 shows that women teachers have been poured out in increasing volume.

In spite of the rapidity of the process, a high standard of training has been maintained by the English supervisors and English principals of the training colleges. The teaching profession has been made especially desirable. Egyptian women students in the training schools have received free board, and free tuition and sometimes even a stipend; whereas men in training have had only free tuition.

Women teachers have received better salaries in Egypt than teachers in any other part of the Near East, and often better than men in Government service. As a result, the supply has caught up with the demand, and in the elementary colleges even exceeded it. The definite Government endorsement of teaching has undoubtedly encouraged Muslim girls to enter the profession. Women have been given more official recognition in education than in any other field.

A Muslim woman teacher some years ago was on the Government Education Board.

One of the inspectresses of women's education recently commented on the number of women teachers in evidence at the Ministry of Education and called attention especially to their complete freedom of expression. "There is no feeling of inhibition before the Director of Education; in fact, most of the women teachers would be quite free to express an opinion even to the Minister of Education."

The self-assurance and spirit of independence of Muslim women teachers in Egypt is especially worthy of comment because of the fact that Egyptian women have so recently entered professional life. Such an attitude is in sharp contrast to the hesitant attitude which is often characteristic of Muslim women of the old-fashioned type. The woman teacher typifies this new freedom of Egyptian women. In the establishment of the teaching profession for women, the system of foreign scholarships has been an important factor. From 1922 to 1930 the number of scholarships for women increased from ten to forty. The increase of applicants has made possible more careful selection, first from each school, then from the best from all the schools. Muslims, because of their larger number of applicants, have a practical though not theoretical preference.

Various lines of training are followed—Froebel kindergarten courses, Domestic Science, Art, Physical Training, and regular courses for the B.A. degree. These students are naturally sent to England because of the language and the general English basis on which education in Egypt is being developed. English headmistresses are now being replaced by Egyptian headmistresses, of whom a number have been chosen since the appointment of the first Egyptian headmistress, Mine Mansour Fahmy, a widely known educator. One of the distinctive forces promoting educational advance for women in Egypt is the Feminist Union of Cairo which, from its inception, has promoted as one of its primary aims, equality of educational opportunity for girls, requesting first the opening of girls' secondary schools, later the admission of women into the university, and the granting of foreign scholarships to girls. Through lectures, a woman's magazine, and in various other ways the Feminist Union has sought to promote the intellectual and moral advance of women as a necessary preparation for political and social equality.

The Feminist Union is also carrying on an interesting educational project—an industrial school where two hundred girls of the poorer class are given a general education, also domestic science, needlework and carpet making, as a means of earning a livelihood. There have been some interesting developments in adult education in Egypt. Several years ago a very ambitious programme of lectures for women was promoted by a movement called the Reconstruction Education Movement. We have already referred to the lecture on the advance of women given by Madame Hoda Sharawi Pasha at the American University of Cairo. Lectures of this type are a regular part of the programme of the University Extension Department, which has as its objective the education of the public along lines that are of national interest. There can be little question of the educational and social influence of having a Muslim woman deliver an address on the status of women before a mixed audience of perhaps a thousand people with two hundred women and a large number of white-turbaned sheikhs.

Foreign influence has had a more pervasive effect on educational and social advance in modern Egypt than in any other country of the Near East, exerting its influence with less shock. But French influence has been dominant ever since Mehmet Ali imported the body of French savants and Ismail followed a policy of conscious exposure of Egypt to French culture. The second language is French, the atmosphere and prevailing culture is French. As far as women are concerned, the upper class especially has been greatly influenced by French styles and French culture through private education, social contact and travel. It is interesting that British culture has not been the dominant influence in Egypt in view of the long period of occupation.

At the present time, however, there is a distinct increase in English influence, which is exerted primarily through the public school. English specialists in education, English methods of education. Egyptian students studying in England, the general use of English in the schools—all these are significant evidences and causes of the increase in English cultural influence. The Anglo-Saxon influence has been, in general, very favourable to a growth in social freedom and the educational advance of women.

Anglo-Saxon influence has affected Egypt not only through English, but also through American channels, especially through the American Mission schools. Many of these institutions antedate the Government schools and have been an outstanding educational force over a long period. The first girls' school in Egypt was opened by an American Mission seventeen years before the first Government school for girls was established by Ismail. The Assiut Mission School through educating a large number of Coptic women as well as a smaller number of Muslims had imparted education to girls in Assiut recognized as a necessity.

The American College for Girls in Cairo, a junior college, the most advanced institution for girls in Egypt, has demonstrated the value of higher education and prepared leaders for various professional careers and for lives of general usefulness. The College has for a long period had a large proportion of Muslim students. The American institutions for men, Assiut College and the ,American University at Cairo, which admits women to its courses, have played an important part in promoting the advance of women by educating young Egyptian men to a proper understanding of the position of women in society. One can scarcely speak of Syrian influence as foreign in relation to Egypt because of the cultural unity between the two countries established through the language, but as an outside influence coming into Egypt, Syria has played an important part. A number of early Syrian leaders, who have contributed greatly to the thought life of Egypt, have now become entirely identified with Egypt. Syrian influence is recognized as a definite element of progress.

The effect of modern Turkey on progress in Egypt, especially on promoting the development of women, has been less direct and obvious than in Iraq or Persia. Although the Turkish reforms have not been taken as a goal in Egypt as in other countries, there is, however, little question of the indirect effect of Turkey, as an example of a progressive Muslim country. The day has passed in Egypt when foreign influence is needed to promote either directly, or by example, the appreciation of girls' education.

National pride actuates modernists and reactionaries alike to promote education for girls as well as for boys as part of the programme of progress. Nationalism in Egypt is not merely a political passion. It has had the deeper meaning of a birth of national consciousness. This new spirit has generated the dynamic power for national advance. But unlike Turkey, Egypt has not considered advancement of woman as a sine qua non of national progress.

Movement in Palestine

Under the Turkish regime very little attention was given to the education of Muslim girls. Some improvement began after 1908 with the opening of a few girls' schools by the Government. But as the language of the schools was Turkish, they had a limited effect in an Arabic-speaking country.

For the great majority of Muslim girls education was confined as elsewhere to the very heterogeneous Quran schools. A few girls of the upper classes received from the convent schools a somewhat sketchy education, consisting of a smattering of French, and a bit of handwork and embroidery. A smaller number was given instruction of sorts at home, but the foreign governess did not play as important a role in Palestine, as in Egypt and Turkey, in bringing the education and culture of the West into the harem. Hence, comparatively few of the higher class Muslim girls in Palestine had any educational advantages. The situation for Christian girls was quite different because of the large number of Mission institutions in Palestine.

These Mission institutions practically left untouched the Muslim communities; hence, there was a great contrast in the educational advancement of Muslim and Christian women of the pre-war generation. This explains the fact that the literacy of women of the Christian community is approximately eighty per cent in contrast to five per cent for Muslim women. There is a similar difference in the literacy of Christian and Muslim men, of ninety per cent for Christians and ten per cent for Muslims. The post-war period marks the beginning of the new regime in education for all, but especially for Muslim girls. Since that time a Government programme has been vigorously promoted and the Muslim community also has undertaken education for girls as well as for boys.

The growth through the Government programme is clearly shown by the steady increase in the number of girls in attendance in schools since 1919. More than twice as many girls were in the Arabic public schools, the Government system, in 1932-33 as in 1920. This increase in the girls in Government schools marks primarily an increase in Muslim girls who are being educated, since the great majority of Christians attend private institutions.

The lack of education for Muslim girls, however, is shown by the contrast between the number of Christian and Muslim girls in school. In 1932 a little less than half of the total number of girls in schools of Palestine, both public and private were Muslims, a fact which has special meaning since seventy per cent of the population of Palestine is Muslim.

A further evidence of the lack of education for Muslim girls is the difference in the number of schools for Muslim girls and boys, and also in the enrolment of each sex. In 1932-33 there were almost ten times as many schools for boys as for girls in the Arab public system, and in rural Palestine, one girls' school for thirty boys' schools.

As to the enrolment the total number of Muslim boys in school in both public and private institutions, was four times that of Muslim girls in schools of all kinds. The difference between the education of Muslim girls and of Muslim boys offers a significant contrast to the situation in the Christian community where there is practical equality in education for boys and girls.' Education for girls in Palestine is still in the primary stage.

The Government policy has been to promote primary-schools throughout Palestine for the masses before raising the level of education for the few, who may be ready for the higher grades. In carrying out this policy of promoting primary education, the Government is developing village schools as rapidly as the villages will assume the cost of buildings.

The rural programme will benefit Muslims especially, as the rural population is very largely Arab. The great majority of rural schools, however, are as yet for boys. Muslim girls would receive more education if social conditions made possible co-education.

The policy of developing education in harmony with general needs is shown by the emphasis on practical subjects. There is as yet no vocational training except courses in domestic arts and homemaking. In several places practical instruction in infant welfare is provided through visits of the students to the infant welfare clinic under the supervision of the doctor and trained nurse.

Emphasis in the Government schools is also given to physical, education, singing and games, and drill. Interscholastic netball matches are held every year.

The Girl Guide Movement has been very popular in Palestine. There are over one thousand Guides—guiders, brownies and rangers. All of the companies except the Y.W.C.A. companies, are connected with schools. The Girl Guide displays and prize-giving programmes are limited to women and must be carried on under careful harem restrictions.

Training camps for leaders and small groups of girls which are held every year, make a marked appeal. A Western visitor to one of these camps finds it especially interesting to watch the arrival of Muslim Guides at camp; they arrive black-veiled and black-clothed and reappear from their tents completely different in their grey uniforms and picturesque white head-dresses. This transformation is a symbol of the effect of the Girl Guide Movement, which unites girls of different religions and gives them all a wider, freer outlook.

In developing the general system of education for girls, Palestine faced the common problem of the East—the dearth of trained teachers. In 1932-33 there were only 172 women teachers in a total of 827 teachers in the Government schools.

The special importance of the Teachers' Training College is, therefore, obvious and the growth of this college is an index of the steadily ascending curve of girls' education. This institution, which has always had an English Principal, has shown a continuous increase in the number of students and especially in the proportion of Muslim girls. Some years ago it was necessary to take the Muslim girls free of charge. Only girls of the middle class, and those merely because of economic necessity, were willing to enter.

Today the inducement of free tuition is no longer necessary; the applicants for admission include daughters of some of the best families in Jerusalem. Hitherto teaching has been considered as a respectable profession, but in the general public mind no girl would enter teaching except as an economic necessity, and certainly no girl of social position would teach. The Training College is successfully changing this idea. In the beginning trained Egyptian and Syrian teachers were enlisted for service in Palestine. Now they are being replaced by graduates from the Training College.

The need for primary teachers was so urgent that the requirements at the beginning could not be too high nor the selection of candidates too rigid, but now higher standards for admission are required and greater care can be taken in selecting candidates for training. A more advanced course has also been developed, in addition to the regular teachers' training, in order to meet the need for a secondary school for paying pupils.

In promoting this programme of steady growth the Teachers' Training College has been very careful to stay within the conventions of the veil, which are still widely observed in Palestine. There are of course Christian students who do not observe Muslim customs but the general atmosphere of the school is in harmony with Muslim ideas. By its distinctly harem conditions the Training College has achieved its primary objective of winning the confidence of even conservative Muslim parents, and attracting Muslim girls for training.

Apart from the Director of Education, who visits the school freely, no men are allowed. But when the Director later visits the schools where the training students teach, often the teachers veil. This is an interesting contrast between Egypt and Palestine, as Egyptian teachers have never veiled before the Directors on their visits to the schools. When other men visitors come to the Training College, the girls are told in advance and given the opportunity of veiling. The girls are not allowed to receive any male visitors except the immediate family or relatives. The commencement exercises, sports, contests, and other school gatherings have only women audiences. For the classes in the Quran the girls all have their faces covered even though the sheikh is often an elderly man. In the Training College these elderly religious leaders have not been replaced by young sheikhs as in Cairo. But some of the girls' schools now have women teachers. It is safe to surmise that no ethical teachings along modern lines are injected into these Muslim classes in religion.

Although the Training College carefully avoids promoting modern social or religious ideas, it is steadily laying the foundation for a future social freedom which seems inevitable. The impact of modern ideas is irresistible so that the individual girl is unconsciously being led toward social change. In order that the excellent training given at the College may not be lost, a careful plan of supervision during the first year of teaching is followed and the final certificate is withheld until after that apprenticeship is satisfactorily completed.

The allocation of graduates from the Training College to their teaching posts presents in Palestine as elsewhere a serious problem. Prevailing social attitudes make it difficult and often impossible for a girl to teach outside of her own village. Christian as well as Muslim teachers insist on teaching at home, or perhaps the parents insist. For example, the parents of a girl living in Safe were unwilling to have her teach in Tiberias, less than an hour's distance away.

Muslim communities that are especially reactionary such as Hebron and Nablus, demand a Muslim teacher but social conditions make it difficult for a Muslim woman from outside to live in these places. Christian teachers often find difficulties in teaching in an entirely Muslim town where social conventions make life very restricted. For what might pass as harmless in Jerusalem is often considered to be questionable morals in a centre of greater conservatism. To meet the need for teachers in the village schools, the Training College in Jerusalem has established a Rural Training Centre in Ramallah which is about twelve miles from Jerusalem. The curriculum includes mainly practical subjects-Domestic Science, Needlework, Gardening and Care of Poultry.

All of the students for the first year, thirteen in number, are Muslims. The standard of living in the school is that of a village, with the same type of convenience but with an emphasis on health and cleanliness. The Department of Education has established a small number of foreign scholarships for girls. Several have had training in Egypt, in the American University of Beirut, and in England. Palestine has not, however, promoted the foreign scholarship plan as vigorously as have Iraq and Egypt.

The major task has been the training of women teachers for the primary schools, which is being achieved in the Training College in Jerusalem. Secondary education has not been undertaken and therefore the preparation of secondary teachers by training abroad has not yet been promoted.

In spite of evidences of conservatism, which one finds with interesting variation in different places, and in reference to different questions related to girls' education, there is today a general acceptance of the idea of education for girls as well as boys.

Even in reactionary centres like Hebron a distinct change is evident as the demand stage had already begun in 1930, when the pressure for a new school was being felt. The keen interest in girls' education in Jerusalem represents the other end of the scale from Hebron. The Directress of the Mamuniya School, a Syrian Christian, commented on the increase of Muslim girls in the upper grades, as shown in this leading Muslim girls' school in Jerusalem. Interest is also growing in education for girls beyond the elementary stage. As has been said, the Government has not as yet provided secondary schools for girls. But the Teachers' Training College has a two years' course and the Jerusalem College for Girls and also the Friends' School at Ramallah offer secondary education. These two institutions represent Christian effort of a very high type; the Friends' School is a Mission institution, the Jerusalem College for Girls, a private Christian enterprise with missionary cooperation, and some Government support. The latter, founded in 1918, is the highest institution for girls in Palestine, offering a fourteen years' course, which extends from the kindergarten through the secondary grade to teachers' training and the first year of university. The American Friends' School for Girls in Ramallah, the first school for girls in Palestine, which was founded in 1869, has been a most convincing argument for girls' education.

As a boarding school with girls from all over Palestine, its influence has been widespread and very beneficial. Obviously these two private schools cannot long satisfy the demand for secondary education of girls in Palestine. In the last decade of Government primary schools the number of Christians who have attended Government primary schools has increased and therefore the demand for free secondary education has grown steadily.

Through the Government schools, moreover, an entirely new Muslim client for girls' primary and therefore also for secondary schools has been created. Today Palestine has passed beyond the period in which private schools can adequately meet the needs for girls' education. The growing demand for both primary and secondary schools is the real criterion of progress in girls' education in Palestine.

Apart from the educational facilities for girls, provided by Government schools and private Christian agencies, girls' education in the elementary stage is also being advanced by the Supreme Muslim Council, through funds from the mosque endowments. More money is expended for boys' schools, but the necessity for girls' education is recognized, and also the need for education on modern lines, which is shown by the effort to secure well-trained Muslim and Christian teachers from Syria.

In addition to the regular Government programme these schools of the Supreme Muslim Council stress especially Arabic and Islamic teaching. The objective in these schools, both for boys and girls, is to strengthen the Muslim infiuence and safeguard Islamic culture, which Muslim leaders have felt to be endangered by the, Zionist influx since the Mandate. "Strictly Muslim education is necessary," as the secretary of the Supreme Muslim Council explained, "because the Government cannot give the Arabic language adequate emphasis; nor Muslim tradition its full value. "Although the veil is carefully maintained in these Muslim schools under the Supreme Council, the need for a modern programme and for modern methods of education is fully realized.

Whatever may be the reason, well-trained teachers are employed in these Muslim schools; games, guide activities, dramatics are all encouraged as a part of the programme. The Supreme Muslim Council has also taken a very advanced step in establishing a number of foreign scholarships for Muslim girls; four in Helouan Training College in Cairo, and one in the Sidon Mission School for Household Economics in Syria, the only school of its kind in the Near East.

In addition to these foreign scholarships, a scholarship has been granted for nurses' training in the Jerusalem hospital. The influences which are producing an active interest in girls' education on the part of Muslim leaders are an interesting complex of conflicting tendencies.

Undoubtedly the presence of an aggressive Zionist minority, which is increasing in numbers and power, has affected the Muslim attitude and strangely enough along two opposing lines. The necessity for competition on an equal basis and consciousness of a lack of education and general Muslim lag, have spurred the Muslim community to progress.

The contrast between the educational development of Muslim women with that of the women from other communities, also furnishes the urge to promote education for Muslim girls as a necessary part of their general advance. On the other hand, the presence of an entirely different civilization nothing could be more different than the conservative Muslim and the modern Zionist—has aroused a fear of absorption, and has therefore produced a defence psychology that tenaciously protects Arab and Islamic culture; hence the extreme social conservatism of the Arab community in Palestine, which adversely affects the position of women.

A leading citizen of Jerusalem who voices the policy of the Supreme Muslim Council expressed very clearly this double motivation of progress and conservatism: "Zionism brought an awakening of national consciousness and a sense of necessity for social uplift which must affect women. To oppose Zionism we have realized the necessity for the same weapons that the Zionists have. The Jews maintain a high educational level both for men and women. Hence, to bring up the Arab level we must educate Muslim women."

The inner life of Palestine, until after the World War, was singularly unaffected by foreign influence. The Christian groups from abroad which were concentrated in Jerusalem did not fuse into the life of the country as a whole. The very fact that Jerusalem is the sacred city of three great faiths has always divided the community into compartments.

The adherents of each religion leading segregated lives, Muslims and naturally most of all Muslim women, were quite isolated from the other currents of life, practically cut off from contact with the outside world. But the post-war period has brought Palestine as a whole, and especially Arab life, sharply into contact with modern forces.

The impact of foreign influence has not aroused as keen a desire for change as in Iraq. But the insistent exposure to modern life is undoubtedly having its effect. The promotion of school's for girls as for boys by the Government has presented the opportunity and thus stimulated the desire of the Muslim community to .advance. Education for girls will doubtless develop more slowly than boys' education, but the forward movement seems assured.

The fact that in Trans-Jordan education is the third item in the Government expenditure is an evidence that it is of primary interest in this newly formed political entity but very old country. Schools in Trans-Jordan under the Turkish regime were few and far between- seventeen schools for boys, four for girls, the traditional Quran schools. Practically all that remains of the Turkish school system now is the war-wreck of a rather good school building in Kerak, the former Turkish seat of government. The rest of the country seems to have been untouched by education save for a few Mission schools, which were and are very meagre in comparison with Mission schools elsewhere. But the postwar period has brought to Trans-Jordan, along with cinemas and automobiles, the development of education both for boys and girls.

For girls especially, the present period represents a clear gain over the pre-war period, and steady progress in overcoming the disparity between girls' and boys' education. Fortunately Adib Wahby has remained Director of Education for a number of years and has been able to witness the results of his efforts. In 1930 there were eight times as many boys' primary schools as primary schools for girls; today the proportion is three to one. There is as yet, however, no girls' secondary school but four for boys.

In the beginning it was necessary to import women teachers from Syria and Palestine and pay them higher salaries than were paid to men teachers. The lure of the desert —Amman is just on the edge of the desert—did not appeal to the girl from Beirut or Jerusalem, accustomed to more "civilization." Today over half the women teachers are from Trans-Jordan, and their salaries are no longer higher than those of men. Progress in education has equalized the salary standards so that the women teachers have lost their advantage. To attract Trans-Jordan girls of the better class into teaching has apparently not been very difficult, as there is less prejudice to break down in this breezy town of Amman on the desert's edge than in many more sophisticated cities. Moreover the well-paid young teachers from outside, representing the latest styles of Beirut or Jerusalem, doubtless have made the teaching profession singularly attractive for girls of the first families. The difficulty in training Trans-Jordan girls has been, until the present time, solved by scholarships in Jerusalem or Syria. Six girls are now studying in Jerusalem. But eventually there will doubtless be a training school for women teachers in Trans-Jordan. The danger of a purely academic education, unrelated to the simple environment of Trans-Jordan girls, is recognized. But a special Arts and Crafts school for girls, corresponding to the very modern Trade School for Boys, although frequently discussed, has not yet been achieved.

In the promotion of the new educational programme Trans-Jordan presents an interesting contrast to Palestine. In Trans-Jordan the programme depends entirely on local initiative. The English Adviser for Trans-Jordan has no direct relationship to internal affairs; such as, health and education. The primary interest of the Mandate in Trans-Jordan is in the problem of security, without which, of course, there could be no constructive development along any line.

The attention of the Mandate is centred in the air over Trans-Jordan, rather than on the land itself, as the maintenance of the air route across the desert through Trans-Jordan and Iraq is vital to the route to India. The English Adviser, although personally interested, assumes no direct responsibility for social or educational developments.

In Palestine, education is directly promoted and administered by the Mandate under a more direct foreign administration than in any other country of the Near East. Efficiency of method and speed in promotion are the result. The desire of the people, however, under the direct foreign promotion in Palestine is no keener than in Trans-Jordan.

Position in Syria

In Syria there is a lack of any united system of education and therefore a divergence of cultures and educational trends. This means that there is not merely a difference between the backward and progressive sections as in other countries, but also a distinct variation in the type of education and culture in different parts of the country and even in the different communities in the same section. The lack of a single educational system has retarded the education of Muslim women much more than the Christian, especially in the Lebanon, since Muslim girls for the most part have not taken advantage of the many Christian schools. Before the war, a few Muslim girls of the upper class in the Catholic convent schools and the Protestant schools, were the great exception.

Since the war the number of Muslim girls in foreign schools and in Muslim schools has increased but they represent a selected class, which are less conservative and not averse to foreign influence. The great middle class of Christians as well as Muslims has felt a lack of free public education, since the middle class in any country is cut off from educational advantages as long as there is no public system. During the war, an interesting attempt was made to lay the foundation for a school system on definite national lines. The leading educator from Istanbul, Halide Edib, was sent to Syria with a staff of fifty or more teachers to establish primary, secondary and normal education for girls. Schools were opened in Beirut and Damascus on very modern lines, with Arabic as the basis for instruction and French and Turkish as additional languages. This excellent effort, however, was brought to an abrupt close by the fortunes of war, but has left permanent results, as the present Government system is based on these schools.

Under the French Mandate, schools have been promoted through the local governments, on French and Arabic lines. An attempt is being made to standardize courses and certificates according to the French system. There has been no interference with the programme of foreign schools, although it is to the advantage of their students that the foreign schools meet the requirements of the French school certificates for different grades.

The foreign schools have remained practically autonomous and constitute as a whole the major educational influence in Syria. The Government schools do not compete with the foreign schools; the main value of the Government system consists in its extension of education to the masses.

The Muslim Philanthropic Educational Society has been recently developing facilities for secondary education of girls. Thus, education on modern lines is reaching down further into Syrian life. Muslim girls especially are profiting from the development of Government schools. It is estimated that at least ninety-five per cent of the girls in Government schools are Muslims; since the girls and also boys of the Christian population, especially in the Lebanon, are educated in the various Christian schools, local and foreign. Hence the Government schools have had their primary benefit in reaching the Muslim community.

That this extension of education for Muslim girls is greatly needed, is obvious. Although the Muslim population of Syria is over one-half the total, the proportion of Muslim girls in schools was only a little more than one-fourth of the total enrolment in 1928. The hopeful feature in the situation, however, is the trend of increase. The number of Muslim girls in both the Government and private schools is practically a clear gain in view of the meagre pre-war Government facilities and small pre-war attendance of girls in private or public schools. A distinctly constructive new factor in the situation is the active promotion of girls' education, both primary and secondary by the Muslim Philanthropic Education Society.

In addition to promoting primary education for girls, the Government has provided a certain amount of secondary and higher education for girls; in the Lebanon the New School with secondary grades and two years of normal training; in Damascus, a normal school and the Syrian University open to women; in Aleppo, a secondary school and normal school. Secondary education for girls in Syria is largely provided by foreign institutions, the majority of which are in Beirut. The beginning of secondary education in the Government school in Beirut is a hopeful trend, as it is primarily intended to provide secondary education for girls of the middle or poorer class, who cannot afford the private school.

The Government schools for girls in Syria give the impression of a decided mixture of French and Arabic. The atmosphere is distinctly French with Arabic as a second language and culture. In the kindergarten the picture of a French kitchen, a French home, a French barnyard, build up the child's vocabulary in a French atmosphere. The group of little five-year olds sing with great enthusiasm C'est la musique du Moulin. But they also sing with equal fervour the anthem of the Lebanese Republic, a good example of Syrian adaptability.

Muslim girls after leaving school, which is usually not later than the fifth grade, are cut off from any educational influences. The eager and grateful appreciation of some of these ex-primary schoolgirls throws light on the empty veiled leisure of the average Muslim girl's life. Those who are in touch with the problem of girls' education in various, parts of Syria, it is interesting to note, find certain similar signs of progress, however different the actual situation may be. There is little question that the best educational facilities for girls in all stages—primary, secondary and college—are afforded by foreign institutions.

Before the war these schools were largely attended by girls of the Christian community; since the war there has been a marked increase in the attendance of Muslims. Schools such as these offer an interesting index of the present attitude toward secondary education for girls. The need for higher education for girls, Christian and Muslim, is being met by the American Junior College for Girls, and by coeducation in the American University of Beirut. Originally a part of the American Girls' School, the Junior College is now an independent institution, preparing girls to enter the Junior Year of the University of Beirut. Its influence is steadily increasing.

As the highest institution for girls in the Arabic-speaking countries, exclusive of Egypt, the Junior College attracts students from Iraq and Palestine on Government scholarship and also on private support. Of the twenty-five Muslim graduates from the Junior College, a number are holding important teaching positions. Aside from the regular academic college course, the Junior College stresses homemaking, health, recreation and community service, such as a special club project for a group of forty to fifty homeless Muslim boys. Summer programmes of village welfare carried on in the Lebanon villages, by groups of Muslim and Christian students under faculty supervision, illustrate a creative approach to major problems of rural education. Such attempts to bring students in direct contact with backward village life, may have a helpful bearing on the problem which is caused by the growing cleavage between the educated urban minority and the underprivileged rural population, one of the critical problems of the East as a whole.

Co-education at the American University of Beirut has met with a favourable response as is shown by the increase in numbers each year, although the demand for higher education for women is still very limited. Of the twenty eight women students in 1934, two were Muslims. The first Muslim woman graduated in 1929, Madame Ihsan Shakir el Kousy, an Egyptian, whose example doubtless encouraged other Muslim women students to enter a coeducational university. The fact that she was studying with her husband, prevented any adverse reaction to the idea of an unveiled Muslim woman attending classes with men.

Co-education for Muslim girls is still distinctly in the pioneering stage in Syria. There is perhaps little awareness of its significance; in some quarters there may be active opposition. But the student body has accepted co-education as an established fact, recognizing women students on an equal basis, as members of the same classes with men, and in the normal relationships of study and discussion group contacts. Women share also in student activities and also hold student offices; for example, a woman student, the only one in a class of fifty, recently was elected class president. Viewing the present situation of education in Syria with special reference to Muslim girls, one is conscious of a general awakening of interest, not only in advanced but in backward areas, and a slow but sure advance from the primary school to the university. Foreign influences have played a larger part in this advance in certain areas of Syria than in any other Eastern country. The absence of foreign contact in some parts explains perhaps in large measure the greater divergence in Syria in the development of different sections than is characteristic of other countries of the East.

The growing awareness of the disparity in education between men and women; the marriage motif, which causes parents to realize the impossibility of their daughters' making a good marriage unless educated; the presence of the more advanced educated Christian community, especially in the Lebanon, which stimulates in Muslim girls and women the desire for progress; the urge to adopt modern ideas, due to the irresistible pressure of Western life; and finally the spirit of keen nationalistic self-determination and aroused self-respect these are the conscious and unconscious motivation, for progress in Syria.

A composite of progressive influences and personal desires is thus actively operating in favour of the educational advance of Muslim women of Syria. The forces for education are not, however, *pari passu* leading to an immediate social transition as symbolized by unveiling. Nationalism under a Mandate Power is driven back into itself and seeks defence for its own traditions. The assertion of self-determination which is politically discouraged finds its outlet in the insistence on its own social conventions. The Muslim community in Syria and Palestine, in the presence of foreign influences, tends to become socially conservative; and social conservatism in Islam is not conducive to a change in the social status of Muslim women.

Revolution in Turkey

Education for girls in Turkey was the sudden product of the new regime. The almost passionate drive to educate the masses is the distinct result of the new republic, but a period of preparation came before. A few Turkish women of the upper class began to receive the private cultural education of the home soon after Turkish men came under the influence of French ideas, even as far back as Mahmud the Great (1809-39). Later, during the period of the Tanzimat reforms (1839-79) foreign governesses were introduced into the harem for the privileged few. Even the severity of Abdul Hamid could not stop the flow of Western influence, although it dammed up the outlet and made the open acceptance of Western ideas and attendance at Western schools difficult, especially for girls.

For the great majority of Turkish women, however, aside from the Quran schools and a girls' normal school for training elementary teachers, attended primarily by orphans and poorer girls, there was no real educational provision for girls, until after, the Constitution in 1909. The first serious efforts at more than mere elementary education for girls came in 1913 with the establishment of a coeducational or secondary school for girls by Bayan Nakiye Elgun, for over thirty years the outstanding educational leader of Turkey, now a Deputy in the Grand National Assembly. The extension of primary education followed, and also the reorganization of the Evkaff (Mosque Foundation) schools was undertaken and effectively carried out by Halide Edib and Bayan Nakiye. These schools were consolidated in 1916 under the Ministry of Public Instruction. The adverse fortunes of the World War—the period of despair and defeat that followed, the Allied Occupation, the Turkish struggle and triumph in the Greek War constitute the all-absorbing, later sequence of events, in which the interest in education was lost in major issues. Then came the birth of the New Nation, and the realization of the necessity for strengthening its foundations.

Under the new regime, education has been assumed as a vital national responsibility and, as a consistent part of the promotion of general education, girls' education has moved steadily forward.

The decade between 1913 and 1923 shows a gradual development and improvement of girls' education but with no distinctive change in direction. The next decade between 1923 and 1933 reflects not only the strenuous drive for increasing girls' education, but also the introduction of coeducation.

Most of the elementary education for Turkish girls is now provided through mixed schools. As a primary mean of solving the tremendous problem of the disparity in education of girls and boys, Turkey adopted co-education in 1925, beginning with the elementary schools, later introducing it to a certain extent in other stages. The success of co-education, as a national programme is shown by the rapid increase of girls in primary schools, an achievement which would have been obviously impossible under the system of separate schools because of the double expense as well as the lack of teachers.

In the adoption of co-education, Turkey differs from all other Eastern countries, which have not yet cut the Gordian knot of their difficulty in promoting general education and especially education of girls. A trip through Asia Minor from Marash to Marsovan several years ago revealed how widely co-education is being extended. Strangely enough or perhaps naturally enough, co-education has been introduced especially in the Interior rather than in Istanbul. The primary reason is doubtless economic. The only possibility of extending education has been through the economy of mixed schools. Hence, not only primary but also some middle schools and lycees in the Interior are co-educational; whereas in Istanbul there are separate girls' middle schools and lycees, and co-education has not replaced the already well-established system. But if new schools are built in Istanbul as elsewhere they will doubtless be co-educational.

In addition to its economic value, co-education is serving a definite purpose as a leverage in lifting social conditions, especially in the Interior. Since one still sees veiled women in Asia Minor, the idea of co-education may seem strangely incongruous, but the very fact that the veil has not entirely disappeared in the Interior is a logical social reason for co-education. The present generation of women in Asia Minor may not all discard the veil, although there are indications that unveiling may be more aggressively promoted.

In order, however, that the best social as well as educational values may be safeguarded in the co-education system, certain wise precautions are being taken. Only mixed activities that belong properly to the school programme are encouraged. Mixed dramatics and mixed recreation are under careful guidance and subject to certain restrictions; for example, in school plays no girls can take boys' parts, or vice versa. Moreover, care is taken that teachers shall not present extremes in modern social customs. Rouge and lipstick and lurid fingernails are frowned upon, and a frown often equals an order. Teachers, moreover, are not allowed to enter the Turkish beauty contest. The need for careful social guidance of co-education in order to meet its inherent difficulties and avoid possible social dangers, is fully recognized by thoughtful Turkish teachers in mixed schools.

One of the major problems in Turkey, in the extension of schools in rural areas, is the provision of trained teachers. To allocate an individual teacher to rural schools is always difficult, because of the social adjustment to an isolated village life. This problem is being met in some places in Turkey by the appointment of a married couple to a village. The married couple conducts the school on modern lines, creates a modern home, which invites imitation, and adds greatly to the general community life.

As a further effective use of teachers in rural areas, to facilitate the spread of rural education, the idea is being developed of establishing a school with a number of teachers and a boarding home for students in a central village, perhaps also a clinic and small hospital, the whole unit thus serving the needs of the surrounding area.

The boarding school is required as a modification of the usual consolidated school because of the lack of bus lines and the great distances between the villages. A very interesting demonstration of this concentrated plan of rural reconstruction in education and health has already been achieved in Etemetsu, a model village half an hour's distance from Ankara. To see the very up-to-date, small, but adequately equipped hospital with a keen young doctor in charge, and an attractive midwife, and to visit the modern school and boarding home near by, staffed by several young married couples, was like catching a glimpse into the future of rural Turkey, if such a plan could be carried out more widely. The alternation of the regular school programme with practical work for boys, several hours each day in the garden and fields, and for the girls, the same amount of time spent in weaving and sewing, showed that this modern school was avoiding the danger of educating village children away from village life.

The boarding home for more than a hundred children, some of them under the special support of the Child Welfare Society, showed that the influence of the school was extended into villages beyond walking distance. Adjoining the school, but with a separate entrance and a small garden, was an attractive building for the teachers, in which each married couple had a little private apartment. Such a plan undoubtedly ensured the continuity of the teaching staff and their full contribution to the community life. Between this small group of teachers and the people of the village evidently there is an intimate contact, as a visit to several homes clearly showed. The way one of the young mothers proudly displayed her baby to the midwife for her approval was an evidence that the home and hospital are closely related. The promotion of education in the new Turkey has meant the modernization of the whole educational programme.

Of central importance in this process of building Turkish education on a modern basis is the policy of secularization of schools. The starting-point for all of the reforms in education was the elimination of the power of the ecclesiastic authorities. For example, co-education, which has increased especially the education of girls, could scarcely have been accomplished under the old regime, when schools were dominated by religion.

Following out this policy, the schools have been completely secularized.

The Turkish girls of today, therefore, have no formal religious instruction in the school. The chanting of the Quran, the teaching of the Islamic formula, the proper ritual and prayers, as far as the schools are concerned , are all things of the past, since definite religious instruction is regarded as the function of the home, not the school. Religion as such is not repudiated, but is regarded as an entirely individual matter. Not only in reference to religious teaching but in general because they did not assert complete independence, there is a distinct trend in education away from the old traditional ideas.

One of the most important developments is the introduction of physical education on modern lines, given by well-trained teachers. Mild calisthenics directed by the regular class teacher in high-heeled shoes, giving her commands passively in a colourless voice, constituted the physical education of the earlier period.

Today one finds a vigorous young Turkish Physical Director, well trained, conducting her class in a regular uniform and flat-heeled shoes, issuing commands in vibrant tones and actively leading the gymnastic exercises. The present teachers of Physical Education are graduates of the course given in Ankara at the Men's Normal School, or at the Istanbul Normal School.

The course in Ankara is one of the most recent developments in co-education. The lectures in theory for men and women students are held together; the courses in practical gymnastics are separate. The men and women students use the same gymnasium, but at different times. At one end are the dressing-rooms and showers for men; at the other, those for the women. The freedom of this joint physical education training course for men and women is the natural result of the new social attitude in Turkey.

Another significant emphasis in the education of Turkish girls is the promotion of vocational education. A number of excellent vocational schools have been established to teach practical arts, as their name Sanat schools signifies.

The Ismet Pasa Institute in Ankara serves as a model for the rest of Turkey for schools of this type, with its fine modernistic building, its excellent classrooms and laboratories, its splendid equipment, adequate dormitory facilities, and well-trained staff. In addition to regular middle school subjects, a primary certificate is required for entrance-two main courses are offered, household economics and a clerical course.

The Household Economics Course is very complete, including home arts, sewing, tailoring, embroidery, cooking, laundry and millinery, which has a rather special interest in Turkey, because of the discarding of the veil. As the veil was less expensive than the hat, there is a distinct economic value in having Turkish girls learn millinery. Two enterprising graduates of the school have set up hat shops in Ankara and are doing a flourishing business. The Clerical Course also meets a timely need in view of the recent entrance of Turkish girls into business life. In addition to one of these two special courses, Home Economics or Clerical Training, all of the students have a simple course in Home-making and Child Care, taught by a well-known young Turkish woman doctor, a specialist in child welfare. This Institute offers an interesting illustration of the consistent year-by-year growth of education in Turkey. In a five-year period it has become established in its very spacious new building. The French Directress has been replaced by a Turkish Director, with a Turkish woman assistant, both of whom have studied in Europe. Turkish teachers, several trained abroad, have replaced all of the foreign teachers except one, the French specialist in millinery. In addition to the clerical course at the Ismet Pasa Institute, training along commercial lines is offered for girls in the very up-to-date Ankara Commercial School, a co-educational institution under a Russian Principal. This school has a number of modern emphases in education; such as student cooperatives, student savings department, a student shop and the student management of the library.

In the development of Turkish education along modern lines, the problem of the training of women teachers is receiving serious consideration. Training for primary teachers is provided in a number of normal schools throughout Turkey; training for secondary teachers is given in the Higher Normal School in Istanbul, connected with Istanbul University. The requirements for teaching have been advanced: to teach in a lycee, a diploma from the university is necessary; for the primary or secondary grade, a normal school certificate. The relationship of the teacher to the community is a vital question for Turkey today.

The young normal-school graduates from Istanbul, fully emancipated young Turkish women wearing hats, fond of dancing and a normal social life, face a difficult problem of social adjustment when they find themselves planted in backward communities, where perhaps some of the women are still veiled and old social customs are still observed. Moreover these young teachers in the Interior have the responsibility of interpreting by their own example the meaning of social freedom. For all this they must be adequately prepared. Hence, the task of the normal schools is not merely to give academic training in methods of teaching, but to socialize education and interpret the career of teaching on a very high moral level. Some of the directors of the normal schools and teachers have grasped the significance of the problem, and are working creatively to develop in every way possible the social values in education.

The young graduates on their part, eagerly take advantage of all opportunities, especially extracurricular activities, such as folk-dances and games for recreation, in order to prepare themselves for the varied demands of teaching service in the Interior. In addition to the regular training courses in normal schools, which are given on a Government scholarship for a contract of five years, obligatory service in the interior, the plan of short-term summer training courses, especially designed for the untrained village teachers, of whom there are still many, has been developed within the last few years.

For foreign scholarships to prepare for teaching along special lines, women students compete on equal terms with men. The competition for foreign scholarships is open primarily to lycee students both boys and girls, but in some special cases, students in the orta mektep, junior high school, also compete. The principle of equality of boys and girls for foreign scholarships does not necessarily mean that the same number of Turkish men and women students receive foreign scholarships. The needs of Turkey for special types of service naturally have a direct bearing on the situation.

Higher education in Turkey is open to women on a basis of full equality with men. Women were admitted to the university in 1915 during the World War, but attended at first as quite a separate section; the men's classes were held in the morning, the women's classes in the afternoon. This involved a duplication of time and effort on the part of the faculty, and hence a double expense.

In the summer season of 1921 accordingly mixed classes were begun, with men and women students on different sides of the room and with no contact outside of classes. The women students entered the classes veiled, raised their veils during the class, and lowered them when leaving.

The fact that this first group of pioneer women students was in a conspicuous and difficult position, was shown by their extreme care in the details of veiling. These early days of co-education in Turkey are typical of the present situation in some countries in the Muslim East, where co-education is regarded as a doubtful social experiment.

Since 1922, when the Medical Faculty was opened for women, there has been a continuous increase in the number of Turkish women in the University of Istanbul, studying law, science, letters, medicine, dentistry, pharmacy, and even engineering. In 1934 the total number of women students was over one-fourth the number of men students.

An interesting evidence of the increasing response of Turkish girls to the opportunity of a higher education is the number of out-of-town students now attending Istanbul University. It is a distinctly new development for a hundred or more Turkish women students to come from the Interior to Istanbul for higher education. Many of these non-resident women students live with relatives or friends, but soon a regular dormitory provision for them will doubtless be needed.

Apart from the opportunities for higher education offered at the university, facilities for cultural studies are provided in special schools in which women students are registered together with men. A Government school for the training of teachers of music in Ankara usually has an equal number of men and women. This school of music is of interest because it shows the present effort being made to westernize the music of Turkey. The students from this school will fill positions in teaching music all over Turkey.

The study of art, also on Western models, is offered in the Beaux-Arts School in Istanbul, situated in one of the palaces on the Bosphorus, which shows the way the old regime serves the new. There is a fair proportion of women students in the various departments. Girls from the lycees compete for entrance. Commercial art, poster making, interior design are all given special attention. In addition to promoting regular education in all its phases, Turkey has vigorously attacked the problem of general adult education.

The illiteracy of Turkey some years ago was estimated at eighty-five per cent; the general illiteracy of women was higher than men, as is usually the case. The adoption of the new Turkish script in 1928 presented the opportunity and drastic necessity for a nationwide drive for literacy. The change from the old to the new letters meant for the time being that the whole nation was reduced to the level of illiteracy. It was immediately necessary for all-the learned and the unlearned-to go to school.

Consequently, a campaign for literacy, unparalleled perhaps in world history, was launched. In October 1928 the nation's schooling began, including Kamal Ataturk, Cabinet ministers, officials, teachers, peasants, men, women, and children of all classes. Attendance at these National Schools in the first year was compulsory for everyone between the ages of sixteen and forty. As soon as the student learned to read and write and could pass an examination, a certificate was issued which served as exemption from further study.

Enforcement of the law was vigorously prosecuted by the Turkish police. The course was taught by regular teachers, who received a small supplementary salary for this extra teaching. School buildings and other public buildings were utilized. The courses were held outside of regular school hours, classes for women for the most part were held in the daytime; and for men, at night.

The courses during the second year were of two types: the simple course for literacy, and a more advanced course including geography, higher arithmetic, additional reading, letter writing and civics. Women constituted over half of the million students in the National Adult Schools, which were established in September 1928, when the new language was officially adopted, and continued during two years.

According to reports, women made equal progress with men. Women of all classes took advantage of the opportunity to learn to read, even mothers attended classes with babies in their arms. The upper class of women, highly educated in the old Turkish language, entered into this pursuit of literacy in new Turkish with zest as in a game, studied at home or in one of the national schools, passed their public examinations along with the masses, and proudly received their diplomas with their pictures attached as on a passport.

The women of the people especially have profited by this drive for learning the new letters. Illiterate before, with little thought of ever learning to read and write, they have suddenly, through the national schools, been awakened to an idea of their ability, hitherto unknown. The number of women reading newspapers on the trams and boats is a visible proof of their new literacy.

Foreign influence has permeated the life and thought of the country. It is difficult to estimate what was the full measure of this foreign influence silently pervading the Turkish harem, and bringing glimpses of a different world, for such subtle influences are not summed up in statistics. In the later period foreign schools began to play their part in the education of Turkish women.

Throughout the Interior of Turkey the American Mission Board has had a chain of girls' schools for a considerable time, until recently when their number has been reduced and their influence concentrated in a few selected centres. Although these schools have been attended primarily by girls of the non-Muslim population, they have undoubtedly benefited the cause of education in Turkey as a whole, giving a successful demonstration of modern girls' schools at a time when the need for education for girls was not generally recognized.

The French and Italian convents have contributed primarily to the education of girls of their religious community with also a limited contact with the Turkish population. The influence of the convent schools has been mainly along the lines of home-training and culture. None of the foreign institutions perhaps has exerted a greater influence on the education of girls over a longer period than Istanbul Women's College, which was founded as a high school in 1875 and became a college in 1910.

Through its general influence and through the individual example of some of its distinguished graduates, this college represents one of the major educational forces which has prepared for the forward movement of the Turkish women. The last decade shows an increased number of Turkish women students in the College, a fact which indicates the growing interest in higher education for Turkish women. The Turkish graduates and former students at the College are contributing in many ways to the life of Turkey; as homemakers, women in business and professional life, in public affairs, and more recently in the Councils of the State, as the recently elected group of Turkey women deputies includes several graduates of the College.

In the promotion of higher education for women, Istanbul Women's College has exerted an influence not only in Turkey but widely throughout the East. In relationship to the work of Istanbul Women's College, Robert College for men has had a direct effect on the education of women in Turkey, through creating an understanding of modern social values and an appreciation for the necessity of a higher educational and social status of women.

Foreign educational influence in Turkey are working in close relationship with the Turkish Ministry of Public Instruction, seeking to make their distinctive contribution in accordance with the educational policy and ideals of Modern Turkey.

The national system of Turkish education, highly centralized and closely integrated in all of its branches, determines the general trends as well as specific emphases of the present programme. Turkey differs from other countries in the East in its general attitude toward foreign influences.

In contrast to the *laissez-faire* attitude in Syria, or the unconscious absorption and assimilation of foreign influence in Egypt, or the acquiescent acceptance of foreign educational benefits in Palestine, the New Republic follows a policy of careful selectivity and appraisal of foreign influences. There is little question that Turkey recognizes certain values in the educational systems in Europe and America.

The presence of foreign educators in the Turkish school system is ample proof of this fact; for example, an American woman specialist in primary education, made a practical demonstration of modern methods in a Turkish primary school; an American specialist in teaching English to foreigners gave a series of courses to Turkish teachers of English; several American teachers of English are at present in Ankara schools, and a few in Istanbul.

A large group of noted German professors are aiding in the re-establishment of the University of Istanbul on advanced modern lines. French and Russian specialists are contributing in their special technical and cultural fields to the educational development of Turkey on modern Western lines.

But modern Turkey today does her own shopping for education and culture and for scientific progress—it may be in Berlin, or Paris, Moscow, London, or New York. It has been of special significance to the education of girls that this process of selecting foreign values has indicated a definite interest in Anglo-Saxon and perhaps especially in American methods.

In speaking of European culture and education, a former Minister of Public Instruction said in a personal conversation that the culture of Europe was more suited to the old regime than the new. Turkish girls have come out, of the harem and need now an education of practical emphasis and social value, so that they may be better fitted for civic and national responsibility.

It is important, however, that one should remember that the choice of foreign values is only a means to an end. The primary basis of Turkish education and culture is not foreign but Turkish. The sense of direction in Turkish education as in Turkish life is singularly clear.

Background

Before the advent of Islam, Arabs were groping in the darkness of ignorance. There was no importance of life for them. Their main aim was to acquire more and more material progress for worldly pleasure. The realities of life were beyond the range of their thinking.

Islam, explained to them the real philosophy of life and provided the complete code which included moral restrictions and the principles of right and wrong. It gave them the clear concept of Heaven and Hell. It taught them to obey Allah and His Messenger, Muhammad (S.A.W.).

When these Arabs gradually accepted the teachings of Islam, a new society came into existence. It was refined and free from all vices. During the evolution of Islamic Society, a commandment of Allah was revealed:

> "O Prophet, if believing women come unto thee, taking oath of allegiance unto thee that they will ascribe nothing as partner unto Allah, and will neither steal nor commit adultery nor kill their children, nor produce any lie that they have devised between their hands and feet, nor disobey thee in what is right, then accept their allegiance and ask Allah to forgive them. Lo ! Allah is Forgiving, Merciful." (60 : 12)

In this verse of the Holy Quran, woman has been directed to follow certain principles of Islam. However, it becomes essential for woman to educate herself in order to understand and follow the principles in letter and spirit. She has been categorically instructed to obey the Holy Prophet (S.A.W.). This commandment made women to think and seek the knowledge of Islamic teachings. The Muslim- women practised the principles of Islam and acquired honourable status in the society. Hazrat Ayeshah (R.A.A.) says:

> "The Ansari women were wonderful ! Nothing could check them from understanding of Islam." (Muslim)

The women during the times of the Holy Prophet (S.A.W.), acquired profound knowledge of teachings. Hazrat Ayesha (R.A.A.) says:

> "We used to memorise, not only but injunctions of every verse of the Holy Quran revealed to the Holy Prophet (S.A.W.). (Al Iqdul Farid)

The real place of woman's education is her home. Therefore, Islamic Shariah directs the parents to educate their daughters so that they may be able to distinguish between right and wrong. It is the duty of the parents to educate their daughters in order to provide them an honourable status in the society. Without education, it is not possible for a woman to understand the teachings of Islam and mould her life accordingly. The Holy Prophet (S.A.W.) has encouraged the education of women and thus earn the pleasure of Allah, in these words:

> "Whosoever brought up three daughters, taught them manners and etiquette, got them married and treated them well, Heaven is for him." (Abu Dawood)

The foundations, of the family in Islam are blood ties and marital obligations. No other type of relationship, like "Adoption" "Mutual Alliance", "Common Law", "Trial Marriage" or "Mutual Consent" to sexual intimacy, will constitute family in the Islamic sense. Islam appreciates the religious virtues, the social necessity and the moral advantages of marriage. There are many verses in the Holy Quran and sayings of the Holy Prophet (S.A.W.) which go as far as to say that when a Muslim marries, he has thereby perfected half of his religion; so let him be conscious of these religious obligations and be careful with the other half.

There are many statements of the Holy Quran and traditions of the Holy Prophet (S.A.W.) that prescribe kindness and equity, compassion and love, sympathy and consideration, patience and goodwill. The Holy Prophet (S.A.W.) goes as far as to declare that the best Muslim is the one who is best to his family, and the greatest, most blessed joy in life is a good and virtuous wife.

These ethical principles allocate to the wife certain rights and corresponding duties. It is the husband's duty to behave with his wife in an equitable and kind manner. He is bound for the full and adequate maintenance of his wife, a duty which he must discharge cheerfully, without reproach, injury, or bickering.

The Holy Quran says:

> "O ye who believe ! Ward off from yourselves and your families a fire whereof the fuel is men and stones, over which are set angels strong, severe, who resist not Allah

in that which He commandeth them, but do that which they are commanded." (66 : 6)

Malik-bin-Huvairis says that he, alongwith some other youngmen, stayed with the Holy Prophet (S.A.W.) for twenty days to acquire the knowledge of Islam. When he (S.A.W.) realized that we were anxious to go home, he (S.A.W.) said, "Go to your wives and children and live with them and teach them the principles of Islam and order them to practise." (Bukhari)

Hazrat 'Umar Farooq (R.A.A.) wrote to the people of Koofa "teach them Surah Noor."

The Holy Prophet (S.A.W.) said, "There are three types of men who will be rewarded twice as such. One of them is that man who has a maid and teaches her good manners and imparts her better education and after freeing marries her." (Bukhari)

Once, the Holy Prophet (S.A.W.) got a woman married to a very poor man. The Holy Prophet (S.A.W.) asked him to teach the Surah of the Holy Quran that he knew to his wife in lieu of dower. (Bukhari)

Sometime, the Holy Prophet (S.A.W.) instructed the men to teach particular portions of the Holy Quran to their wives. For instance, he (S.A.W.) said, "Undoubtedly, Allah has completed Surah Baqarah (The Cow) with two verses which have been given to me from the treasure which is under Heaven. So you learn and teach them to your wives also." (Darimi)

A daughter of the Holy Prophet (S.A.W.) says that while teaching her, the Holy Prophet (S.A.W.) used to say, "When you rise in the morning say that Allah is Holy and that He alone can provide the power to praise Him. Whatever Allah wishes it happens and whatever He wishes not, it happens not. Remember, Allah commands everything and He is the Knower of everything." (Abu Dawood)

Legal Rights

The well-known Maliki scholar and jurist Allama Ibn Alhaj has written:

> "If woman demands her right in respect of Deen (Islam) from her husband and approaches the 'ruler of the time for the issuance of an injunction in her favour for the acquisition of religious education which is her legal right, that is, either the husband himself should educate her or allow her to go out and study, then it is obligatory upon that ruler to order her husband to fulfil her wishes, as he (The ruler) does in case of worldly rights. Because the religious rights are more important than the material."
>
> (Al Mudkhal Ibn Alhaj)

Imam Fakhruddin Hasan Bin Mansoor Hanafi (d. 295 A.H.) in his famous fatwa, says, "A woman has no right to participate in any literary sitting without the prior permission of her husband, when any problem arises, she should consult her husband. If the husband is not a learned man, he should solve the problem with the help of other learned men, then she must not leave her house without his permission. However, if the husband fails to make research and solve her problem, then she can visit any educational institution without his permission and get the problem solved. Because it is incumbent upon both, man and woman, to acquire knowledge. Specially, when the wife is helpless, her right to acquire knowledge will have priority over the husband's right."

(Fatawa Qazi Khan)

Result of Educational Facilities for Woman

Islamic Shariah provides all facilities to woman to acquire knowledge. It intends to develop her mental powers in order to become a useful member of the society. Islam emancipated woman from ignorance and made her position dignified and honourable. 'Urwah bin Zubair, (R.A.A.) says about Hazrat Ayeshah (R.A.A.) :

> "Hazrat Ayeshah (R.A.A.) knew more about the injunctions of Holy Quran, poetry and literature, the History of Arabs and their hierarchy than any other person."

Moosa bin Talha says:

> "I have not come across any other person more eloquent than Hazrat Ayeshah (R.A.A.)." (Tirmizi)

Ibn Abee Malkah (R.A.A.) asked Hazrat Ayeshah (R.A.A.), "We are not much surprised by your knowledge of prose and poetry because you are the daughter of Hazrat Abu Bakr Siddique (R.A.A.) whose literary status is well-known. But from where did you learn the medical science?" She replied, "Whenever the Holy Prophet (S.A.W.) fell sick, the medical team prescribed medicines for him. I learn the use of these medicines from them."

Hazrat Ayeshah was so apt in accounts that the senior companions of the Holy Prophet (S.A.W.) used to consult her on matters of inheritance.

Umrah bint Abdur Rahman was one of the students of Hazrat Ayeshah. (R.A.A.). Ahmad Ibn Hambal says about her, "The Jurist, Umrah bint Abdur Rahman was brought up by Hazrat Ayeshah (R.A.A.). She related a great number of hadis through her which are authentic. Her memory is sharp." "Ibn Hibban testifies about her, "She has learnt most of the hadis from Hazrat Ayeshah."

Allama Ibn Abdul Birr (R.A.) says about Hazrat Zainab (R.A.A.), "She was a great jurist of her time."

Abu Rafay Sa'igh says, "When I talk of any woman jurist of Madina, I at once remember Zainab bint Abi Salma."

Ummul Hassan, a maid of Hazrat Umme Salamah (R.A.A.) was a great scholar who preached and delivered sermons to women.

About Ummul Momineen Hazrat Safiyah, Imam Navavi says, "She was one of the wise and intellectual women."

It is said that Fatima bint Qais (R.A.A.) argued with Hazrat 'Umar (R.A.A.) and Hazrat Ayeshah (R.A.A.) over a juristic problem for a long time but they could not change her view. The other scholars also gave preference to her thought. Imam Navavi has said about her, "She was one of those who migrated in the earlier period and was a versatile genius."

Hafsa Bint Seerin (R.A.A.) of Basrah completed the study of the Holy Qur'an when she was just twelve years old. The famous Judge of Basrah, Ayas-bin-Muawiya says about her;

> "I did not come across any other person whom I could give superiority over Hafsa Bint Seerin."
>
> (Tahzib-al-Tahzib)

Sayeed bin Musayyab had married his daughter to his pupil. The next day her husband was preparing to attend the literary sitting of her father. She said to him, "Be at home, what Sayeed bin Musayyab can teach you there, I can teach you here."

Similarly, the daughter of Imam Malik (R.A.) was a learned lady. If a student made a mistake while reading Moatta, she used to knock at the door of her room from inside. Imam Malik had full confidence in her knowledge, therefore, he used to ask the erring student to repeat it correctly.

About Umme Varaqa Bint Naufil (R.A.A.), it has been said, "She had studied the Holy Quran, therefore, the Holy Prophet (S.A.W.) had allowed her to lead the prayers of the female members of her family."

A famous Maliki Imam, Ash'hab (R.A.) once bought some vegetables from a maid. In those days it was a custom to give bread to the seller in lieu of money. Ash'hab (R.A.) had no loaf at that time. Therefore, he asked the maid to come and collect the loaf from him in the evening when he' would get it from the baker. She replied that it was not fair because according to the Shariah, the exchange of commodities must take place on the spot.

(Al-Mudkhal, Ibn Alhaj)

The history shows that most of the Muslim women not only knew reading but they were well versed in writing as well. They were competent to write letters and note down various problems.

Contribution to Education

Educated Muslim women made great contribution to the cause of education and learning. They became the source of guidance and enlightenment for the society. Imam Ibn Qayyim says:

> "The Companions of the Holy Prophet (S.A.W.) who were competent to issue religious decrees (fatwas) were about one hundred and thirty. This number includes men and women both." The persons who issued most of the Fatwa included Hazrat Ayesha (R.A.A.) and Hazrat Umme Salama (R.A.A.).

The other women who issued few Fatwa are:

Umme Atiya, Hazrat Hafsa, Hazrat Umm Habiba, Hazrat Safiya, Laila bint Qaiyim, Asma bint Abi Bakr, Umme Sharik, Khaula bint Towait, Umm Darda, Atika bint Zaid, Sahla bint Hazrat Juwairia, Hazrat Maimoona, Hazrat Fatima bint Qais, Hazrat Umme Salama, Zainab bint Umm Salama, Umm Aiman, Umme Yusuf and Ghamadiya (R.A.A.).

These wise and learned women made a great contribution to the cause of Islamic teachings and helped in the uplift of the society.

Hazrat Ayesha (R.A.A.) was a renowned scholar of Ahadis She has narrated two thousand, two hundred and ten Ahadis ' Her knowledge was so apt that sometimes she corrected Hazrat 'Umar (R.A.A.) and Abu Hurairah (R.A.A.) Hafiz Ibn Hajar says :

> "Hazrat Ayesha (R.A.A.) had learnt a great many things from the Holy Prophet (S.A.W.) and lived for fifty years after him (S.A.W.). People were greatly benefitted by her. Many principles were related through her and it is said that one-fourth of the laws of Shariah were related by her."

Suhairah bint Huzair has said about Hazrat Safiyah (R.A.A.), "I, alongwith some other women, went to Madina after Hajj and visited Hazrat Safiyah (R.A.A.). There were already some women from Koofa. We requested her to explain to us the laws regarding the relation of husband and wife and other relevant topics."

> The knowledge of the Holy wives of the Holy Prophet (S.A.W.) greatly helped in the solution of the problems which puzzled the Companions of the Holy Prophet (S.A.W.). Imam Ibn Qaiyim (R.A.) says : "When there was any difference of opinion amongst the Companions of the Holy Prophet (S.A.W.) and any of the Ummahatul Momineen quoted any hadis, then they accepted it and forgot their differences." (Zadul M'aad Vol. 4, Page-221)

> About Umme Atiya (R.A.A.), Allama Ibn Abdul Bir (R.A.) has said : "She attended the after-death bathing ritual of the daughter of Holy Prophet (S.A.W.) and she explained the principles of bath (Ghusl) very efficiently. Her hadis regarding bathing of dead body has become the fundamental principle (for Muslims). The Companions of the Holy Prophet (S.A.W.) and their disciples in Basrah learnt the rules of the bathing of the dead body from her; and there are many other Ahadis also, which have been related through her by Ans-bin-Malik, Muhammad bin Seereen and Hafsa bint Seereen." (Al Istiab)

Bibliography

Agrawal, Usha, *Indian Women Education and Development*, Ambala, The Indian Publications, 1995.

Altekar, A.S., *The Position of Women in Hindu Civilization*, Varanasi, Motilal Banarsidas, 1962.

Anastasi, Anne. *Psychological Testing*. London, Collier Macmillan Publishers, 1982.

Anne, Roe. *Psychology of Occupations*. New York, John Wiley and Sons, 1956.

Anshen, R.N., (ed.), *The Family, Its Functions and Destiny*, New York, Harper & Row, 1959.

Arbuckle, Dugld S. *Counselling, Philosophy, Theory and Practice*, Boston, Allyn and Bacon Inc., 1965.

Aruna, Asaf Ali, *'Women's Suffrage in India," Our Cause*, edited by Shyarn Kumari Nehru, Allahabad, Kitabistan, 1937.

Asthana, P., *Women's Movement in India*, Delhi, Vikas Publishing House, 1974.

Badel, Auguste, *Women, Past, Present and Future*, New York, Bone and Liveright, 1918.

Baig, Tara Ali, *India's Woman Position*, Delhi, S. Chand and Company Pvt. Ltd., 1976.

Bala, Usha, *Indian Women Freedom Fighters*. New Delhi, Manobar Publication, 1986.

Barot, Jyoti, *The Indian Family in the Change and Challenge of the Seventies*, New Delhi, Sterling Publishers, 1972.

Barrie, H. et al. *The Theory and Practice of Vocational Guidance*. London, Pergamon Press. 1968.

Bebel, August, *Women in the Past, Present and Future*, ed. By

Mukerjee, Subrata and Rama Swami, Sushila, New Delhi, Deep and Deep Publication, 1996.

Beck, Carlton, *Philosophical Foundations of Guidance.* Englewood Cliffs, New Jersey, Prentice Hall, 1964.

Bennett, Margaret E. *Guidance and Counselling in Groups.* Second ed. New York, McGraw Hill, 1963.

Berdie, R.F. *"Counselling—An Educational Technique"* 1949.

Bernard, H. W. and Fullmer, D. W. *Principles of Guidance, A Basic Text* (Indian ed.). New Delhi, Allied Publishers Private Ltd.

Bhasin, K. (ed.), *The Position of Women in India*, Bombay, Leslie Sawny, 1971.

Bhushan, Jamila Brij, *Muslim Women*, New Delhi, Vikas Publishing House, 1980.

Billington, Mary Frances, *Women in India*, Delhi, Amarka Book Agency, 1973.

Blalock, H.M. and Blalock, A.B., *Methodology in Social Research*, New York, McGraw-Hill, 1969.

Blocher, Donald H., *Developmental Counselling*. New York, The Ronald Press, 1966.

Bose, Moni Mohan, *Female Education in India*, Kanpur, B.B. Gupta Publication, 1921.

Brewer, J.M. *Education as Guidance.* New York, Macmillan Co. 1962.

Caplow, *T., Sociology of Work*, New York, Mc-Graw Hill, 1954.

Carden, Maren Lockwood, *The New Feminist Movement*, N.Y. Russall Sage Foundation, 1974.

Carstairs, G. Morris, *The Twice Born*, Bloomington, Indiana University Press, 1958.

Cattell, B.B. *Abilities, their Structure, Growth and Action.* Boston, Houghton Mifflin Co., 1971.

Chakrapant, C. Kumar-S. Vijaya (editors). *Changing Status and Role of Women in Indian Society*, New Delhi, M.D. Pub., 1994.

Chattapadhya, Kamladevi, et. al. *The Awakening of Indian Women*, Madras, Everyman's Press, 1939.

Chaturvedi, Geeta., *Women Administration in India, A study of the socio-economic background*, Jaipur, RBSA Publication, 1985.

Chauhan, S.S. Principles and Techniques of Guidance, New Delhi, Vikas Publishing House, 1982.

Coe, William C. *Challenges of Personal Adjustment.* San Francisco, Rinehart Press, 1972.

Cofer, C.N. and Appley, M.N., *Motivation Theory and Research,* John Wiley and Sons Inc., 1964.

Cormack, Margaret, *The Hindu Women,* Bombay, Asia Pub.. House. 1961.

Cottle, W.C. and Downie, N.M. *Preparation for Counselling.* Englewood Cliffs. N.J., Prentice Hall, 1970.

Cottle, W.C. *Interest and Personality Inventories.* New York, Houghton Miffling Co., 1968.

Crites, J.C. *Vocational Psychology.* New York, McGraw Hill, 1969.

Cronbach, L.I. *Essentials of Psychological Testing.* New York, Horper, 1970.

Crow, Lester D., and Crow, A. *An Introduction to Guidance Principles and Practices.* New Delhi, Eurasia Publishing House, 1962.

Das, Ram Mohan, *Women in Manu's Philosophy,* Jalandhar, ASB Pub. 1993.

De'Souza Alfred, *Women in Contempurury India and South Asia,* Delhi, Manohar Pub., 1980.

Deckard, B.S, The Women's Movement, Harper and Row, New York, 1979.

Desai, Neera and Patel Vibbuti, *Indian Women,* Bombay, Popular Prakashan. 1975-85.

Devasia, L. and Devasia, V.V, *Empowering Women for Sustainable Development,* New Delhi, Ashish Pub. House, 1994.

Dowing, Lester N. *Guidance and Counselling Services.* New York, McGraw Hill, 1964.

Drucker, P.F., *An Introductory View of Management,* Harper College Press, New York, 1977.

Dubey. S.C, *Men's and Women's Role in India, a Sociological Review,* in Women in the New Asia, ed. by Barbara Ward, Paris, UNESCO, 1968.

Dugan, W.E., *Guidance in the 1970s. The School Counsellor.* 1963.

Engineer Asghar Ali, *Islam and Liberation Theology,* New Delhi-Sterling Pub., 1990.

Erickson, Clifford E. *A Basic Text for Guidance Workers.* Englewood Cliffs, Prentice Hall, 1955.

Evan, M. William, *Organizational Theory Structure, Systems and Environments,* Wiley Interscience Publications, John Wiley and Sons Inc, London, 1976.

Everett, J.M., *Women and Social Change in India,* Heritage Pub., 1979.

Frank, H. Krouse. *Counselling Technique with Youth.* Ohio, Charles and Mervil, 1960.

Freeman, Frank S. *Theory and Practice of Psychological Testing.* New Delhi, Oxford and IBH Publishing Company, 1965.

French, Elizabeth, G., *Effects of Interaction of Achievement Motivation and Intelligence on Problem Solving Success,* American Psychologist, 1951.

Friedan, Betty, *The Feminine Mystique,* N.Y., W.W. Norton, 1963.

Froehlich, C.P. and Hoyt, *K. Guidance Testing.* Science Research Associates Inc. 1959.

Fuster, J.M. *Psychological Counselling in India.* Bombay, Mac Millan, 1964.

Gandhi, M.K. *The Role of Women* Bombay, Bhartiya Vidhya Bhavan, 1964.

Garret, A. *Interviewing, Its Principles and Methods.* New York, Family Service Association of America, 1942.

Gaur, J.S. and Saraswat, R.K. *Occupational Literature, An Annotated Biblography.* New Delhi, NCERT, 1978.

Ghadially, Rehana, *Women in Indian Society,* New Delhi, Sage Pub., 1988.

Ghiselli, Edwin E. *Personnel and Industrial Psychology.* New York, McGraw Hill Book Co., 1955.

Goldstein, Rhoda L., *Indian Women in Transition, A Banglore Case Study.* New Jersey, The Scarecrow Press Inc., 1972.

Good, W.J., *World Revolution and Family Patterns,* London, Collier MacMillan, 1963.

Gorwaney, N., *Self Image and Social Change, A Study of Female Students,* Delhi, Sterling Publishers, 1977.

Guilford, J.P. *Fundamental Statistics in Psychology and Education,* New York, McGraw Hill, 1965.

Gullahorn, J.E. *Psychology and Women in Transition.* New York, John Wiley. 1979.

Gupta, A.K. *Women and Society,* New Delhi, Criterion Pub., 1986.

Gupta, A.R. *Women in Hindu Society,* Delhi, Jyotsna Prakashan. 1985.

Gupta, J.L. *Challenges to the Fair Sex,* Delhi, Gyan Pub., 1988.

Hahn, M.E. and Maclean, M.S. *Counselling Psychology.* New York, McGraw Hill, 1955.

Hamrin, S.A. *Initiating and Administering Guidance Services.* Bloomington, McKnight and McKnight Publishing Company, 1959.

Hansen, James C. *Counselling ,Process and Procedures.* New York, Mac Millan, 1978.

Hasan, Zoya (ed.), *Forging Identities, Gender, Communities and the State,* New Delhi , Kali for Women, 1994.

Hatch, Ramend, N. and Steffle, Buford. *Administration of Guidance Services.* Englewood Cliffs. New Jersey, Prentice Hall, 1958.

Hate, C.A. *Hindu Women and Her Future,* Bombay, New Bombay Co., 1948.

Hate, C.A., *Changing Status of Women in Post-Independence India,* Bombay, Allied Publications, 1969.

Herr, E.L. and Cramer, S.H. *Vocational Guidance and Career Development in the Schools, Towards a Systems Approach.* Boston, Houghton Mifflin, 1972.

Hollis, Joseph William and Hollis, Lucide. *Organising for Effective Guidance.* Chicago, Science Research Associates, 1965.

Hoose, William N. Van (ed.). *Counselling and Guidance in the 20th Century.* Boston, Houghton Mifflin Co., 1979.

Hoppock, Rebert. *Occupational Information—Where to Get It and How to Use It in Counselling and Teaching.* New York, McGraw Hill Book Co. Inc., 1957.

Horney, I.B., *Women in Buddhist Literature,* Kandy, Buddhist Publication Society, 1961.

Horney, Karen. *Feminine Psychology,* N.Y., W.W. Norton & Co., 1967.

Humphrey, J. Anthony and Traxler, Arthur E. Guidance Services. Chicago, Science Research Associates, Inc., 1954.

Indra Prof. *The Status of Women in Ancient India,* Lahore, The Minerva Book Shop. 1940.

Inkeles, A. and Smith, D., *Becoming Modern,* London, Heinmann Educational Books Ltd., 1974.

Jain, D, *Indian Women*, Delhi Publication Division, Government of India, 1975.

Jain, P.C., Jain. Shashi and Bhatnagar, Sudha (eds.), *Scheduled Caste Women*, Jaipur, Rawat Pub., 1997.

Jain, Pratibha and Mahan, Rajan, *Women Images*, Jaipur, Rawat Pub., 1996.

James, A.R. Vocation, *Education and Guidance, A System for the Seventies.* Columbus, Ohio, Charles E. Marril Publishing Co., 1970.

Jayal, Shakambari, *The Status of Women in Epics*, Delhi, Motilal Banarsidas, 1966.

Jayashree, *India and Indian Women*, Aligarh, Granthayan, 1980.

Jogdand, P.G. (ed.), *Dalit Women, Issues and Perspectives*, New Delhi, Gyan Publishing House, 1995.

Jones, A.J. *Principles of Guidance and Pupil Personnel Work.* New York, McGraw Hill, 1963.

Kalarani, *Role Coriflict in Working Women.* New Delhi, Chitra Pub., 1976.

Kapur, Promilla. *Marriage and the Working Woman in India*, Delhi, Vikas Pub., 1975.

Kapur, Promilla, *The Changing Status of the Working Woman in India*, Delhi, Vikas Pub., 1974.

Keeton Kathy and Basrin Yvonne, *Woman of Tomorrow*, N.Y., Harvard Univ. Press, 1985.

Khanna, G. *Indian Women Today*, New Delhi, Publishing House, 1978.

Kidwai, Shaikh M.H., *Women under Different Social and Religious Law*, New Delhi, Seema Pub., 1976.

Kirpal, Viney (ed.), *The Girl Child in 20th Century Indian Literature*, New Delhi, Sterling Pub., 1992.

Kishwar Madhu, *Off the-Beaten Track Rethinking Gender Justice for Indian Women*, New York, Oxford, 1999.

Knapp, Robert H. *Practical Guidance Methods for Counsellors, Teachers and Administrators.* New York, McGraw Hill Book Co., Inc. 1953.

Knight R. *Intelligence and Intelligence Tests.* London, Methuen and Co. Ltd. 1943.

Kroth, J.A. *Counselling, Psychology and Guidance.* Springfield, Illinois, Charles C. Thomas, 1973

Krumboliz, J.D. and Thoreasen, C.E. *Counselling Methods.* New york, Holt Rinehart and Winston, 1976.

Kuppuswamy, B., *Social Change in India,* Delhi, Vikas Publishing House, 1972.

Lateef. Shahida, *Muslim Women in India, Political and Private Realities,* 1890-1980s, New Delhi, Kali for Women, 1990.

Law, Bimla Churn. *Women in Buddhist Literature,* Ceylone, N.E. Bastian, 1927.

Lederer, Wolfgang, *The Fear of Women,* N.Y., Arun and Strattan, 1968.

Long L. and Mehta, P.M. (editors). *First Mental Measurement Handbook for India.* New Delhi, NCERT, 1967.

Mahler, C.A. *Group Counselling in the Schools.* Boston, Houghton Mifflin, 1969.

Marshall, Katherine, *Employed Parents and Division of Housework, Perspectives,* Autumn, 1993.

Matarazzo, J.D. *Wechsler's Measurement and Appraisal of Adult Intelligence,* Baltimore, Williams and Wilkins, 1972.

Mathewson, Robert H. *Guidance Policy and Practice.* New York, Harper and Row, 1962.

Mehta, Hansa, *Indian Woman,* New Delhi, Butala & Co., 1981.

Mehta, Rama, *Socio-legal Status of Women in India,* Delhi, Metropolitan Book Co., 1982.

Mehta, Raman Lal, *The Western Educated Hindu Woman,* N.Y., Asia Pub. House, 1970.

Mehta, Raman Lal, *Thesis on the Legal Rights of Women under Different Communal Laws in Vogue in India,* Bombay. The Advocate of Indian Press, 1933.

Mehta, Sushila, *Revolution and Status of Women in India,* Delhi, Metropolitan Book Co., 1982.

Menon, M. Indu, *Status of Muslim Women in India,* Delhi, Uppal Pub. House, 1981,

Meyer, Johann Jakob, *Sexual Life in Ancient India, A Study in the Comparative History of Indian Culture,* N.Y., E.D. Dutton & Co., 1930.

Mies, M., *Indian Women and Patriarchy, Conflicts and Dilemmas of Students and Working Women.* Concept Publishers, 1980.

Miller, Carroll H. *Foundations of Guidance.* New York, Harper and Brothers, 1961.

Miller, Frank W. *Guidance—Principles and Services*. Ohio, Charles E. Merrill Books, 1961.

Minault, Gail, *Secluded Scholars, Women's Education and Muslim Social Reform in Cobaial India.* Delhi, Oxford Univ. Press, 1998.

Misra, R.S., *Women Education and the Upanishadic System of Education,* Allahabad, Chugh Pub., 1993.

Misra, Rekha, *Women in Mughal India.* Delhi, Munshiram Manoharlal.

Mitra, CR and others, *Challenge and Response—Towards a New Education Policy and Beyond, 1986.*

Moddie, A.D., *The Brahamanical Culture and Modernity,* Lond., Asia Pub. House, 1968.

Moneil, Elton B. and Rubin Zick, *The Psychology of Being Human,* San Francisco, Canfield Press, 1977.

Montagu, Ashley, *The Natural Superiority of Women,* N.Y., The Macmillan Co., 1968.

Mujtaba, Sayid, Lari, Rukni Musawi (Translated by Goulding, F.J.), *Western Civilisation Through Muslim Eyes,* Qum, Iran, Ansariyan Publication.

Munson, Harold L. *Foundations of Developmental Guidance.* Boston, Allyan and Bacon, 1971.

Murphy, G., *An Introduction to Counselling in the School.* New York, Harper and Row, 1970.

Myers, G.E. *Principles and Techniques of Vocational Studies.* Government of India, Department of Labour, Exployment and Rehabilitat, 1972.

Myrdal, A. and Klien, V., *Woman's Two Roles,* London Routledge & K. Paul, 1968.

Nanda, B.R., *Indian Women,* Delhi, Vikas Pub. House, 1976.

Ohlsen, M.M. Group Counselling New York, Holt Rinchart and Winston, 1977.

Pal. B.K., *Problems and Concerns of Indian Women,* New Delhi, ABC Pub. House, 1989.

Pandey, Rekha, *Women from Subjection to Liberation,* New Delhi, Motilal Pub., 1989.

Pandit, S. K., *Women in Society.* Delhi, Rajat Pub., 1998.

Pasricha, Prem. *Guidance and Counselling in Indian Education.* New Delhi, NCERT, 1976.

Patterson, C.H. *Therories of Counselling and Psycho-therapy*. New York, Harper and Row, 1973.

————. *Counselling and Guidance in Schools, A First Course.* New York, Appleton Century Crafts, 1966.

Paul, Diana Y, *Women in Buddhism,* California, Asian Humanities Press, 1979.

Pepinsky, Harold B. and Pepinsky, Pauline Nichols. *Counselling Theory and Practice.* New York, The Ronald Press Company, 1954.

Peters, H.J. and Hanson, J.C. (ed.) *Vocational Guidance and Career Development.* New York, Macmillan, 1968.

Phandis, Urnifla, *Women of the World.* Delhi, Vikas Pub. House, 1978.

Pinkham, Mildreth Worth, *Women in the Sacred Scripts of Hinduism,* N.Y.AMS Press Inc., 1941.

Pinto, Diana V. *Counselling, Theory, Research and Practice.* Chicago, Rand McNally College Publishing Company, 1978.

Prakash, G., *After Colonialism, Imperial Histories and Post Colonial Displacements,* Princeton University Press, 1995.

Rajgopal, T.S., *Indian Ideal of Womanhood,* Calcutta Ramakrishna Mission, 1969.

Ramabal, Saraswati Pundita, *The High Caste Hindu Woman.* Philadelphia, Jas. B. Podgers Printing Co., 1888.

Rani, K., *Role Conflict in Working Wives*, New Delhi. Chetana Publications, 1976.

Rao, Narayan. *Counselling Psychology.* New Delhi, McGraw Hill Publishing Company Limited, 1981.

Rege, Y.M., *Whither Women, Bombay,* The Popular Book Depot, 1938.

Rehman, M.M. and Biswal. *Education, Work and Women, An Enquiry into Gender Bias.* New Delhi, Commonwealth Publishers, 1993.

Robinson, F.P. *Principles and Procedures in Student Counselling.* New York, Harper and Row, 1950.

Roby, Pamela, *Women in the Work Place,* Cambridge, 1981.

Roeber, E. C., Smith, G. E. and Erickson, E.E. *Organisation and Administration of Guidance Services.* New York, McGraw Hill, 1955.

Rohibaugh, Joanna Bunker, *Women, Psychology's Puzzle*, N.Y., Basic Books Inc., 1979.

Ross, Aileen D., *The Hindu Family in its Urban Setting*, Toronto, Univ. of Toronto Press, 1961.

Sachidananda and Sinha, Ramesh P., *Women's Right, Myth and Reality*, Jaipur, Printwell Pub., 1984.

Schwarz, P.A. and Krug, R.E. *Ability Testing in Developing Countries, A Handbook of Principles and Techniques.* New York, Praeger, 1972.

Sengupta, Padmint, *The Story of Women of India*, New Delhi, Indian Book Co., 1974.

Sharma, Anuradha, *Women and Work, Human Resource Management Perspective*, New Delhi, Gyan Pub., 1999.

Sharma, Usha and Sharma, B.M., *Committees and Commissions on Women Education*, New Delhi, Commonwealth Pub., 1995.

Shartle, Carrol, L. *Occupational Information.* New York, Prentice Hall, 1961.

Shertzer, Bruce Stone, Shelly, C. *Fundamentals of Guidance.* Boston, Houghton Miffin Co. 1976.

Shridevi, *A Century of Indian Womanhood*, Mysore, Rao and Raghavan, 1965.

Singh, Amarjit. *Is Intelligence Inherited?—A Critical Synthesis and Review of Research Findings.* New Delhi, NCERT, 1978.

Singh, Indu Prakash, *Women, Law and Social Change in India*, New Delhi, Radiant Pub., 1989.

Singh, Uttam Kumar and Nayak, AR, *Women Education*, New Delhi, Commonwealth Pub. in association with Dr. Zakir Husain Institute for Non-formal and Continuing Education, Discovery Pub. House, 1996.

Slocum, Walter L. *Occupational Careers, Sociological Perspective.* Aldine Publishing Co., 1968.

Smith, G.E. *Counselling in the Secondary Schools.* New York, MacMillan, 1955.

Smith, H M. and Eckerson, L.O. *Guidance Services in Elementary Schools.* Washington, Government Printing Press, 1966.

Smith, M.R. (ed.) *Guidance-Personnel Work-Future Tense.* New York, Teachers College Press. Columbia University, 1966.

Spearman, C.E. *The Nature of Intelligence and Principles of Congnition.* London, Macmillan, 1923.

Srinivasan. M.N., *The Changing Position of Indian Women*, Delhi, Oxford Univ. Press, 1970.

Stewart, N.R. and others. *Systematic Counselling*. N.J., Prentice Hall, 1978.

Strange, Ruth. *Counselling Techniques in College and Secondary School*. New York, Haarper and Brothers, 1937.

Subbamma, Malladi, *Women, Tradition and Culture*, Delhi, Sterling Pub.. 1985.

Suguna, B, *Working Women and Religion*, New Delhi, Discovery Publishing House, 1994.

Super, Donald E. Appraising Vocational Finesse. Harper and Brothers.

Super, Donald E. *Psychology of Careers*. New York, Harper Row, 1957.

Tandon, R.K., *Women, Nature, Education, Teaching and Rights*, Commonwealth Pub., 1996.

Thomas, F. Station. *Dynamics of Adjustment*. New York, MacMillan Co., 1953.

Thomas, P. *Epics, Myths and Legends of India*. Mumbai, D.B. Teraporevala, 1961.

Thomas, P. *Indian Women Through the Ages*, N.Y., Asia Pub. House, 1964.

Thomas, P. *Women and Marriage in India*, Lord, George Allen and Unwin, 1939.

Thorndike, R.L. and Hagen E. *Measurement and Evaluation in Psychology and Education*. New Delhi, Wiley Eastern Pvt. Ltd., 1969.

Tikoo, Prithvi Nath, *Indian Women*, Delhi, B.R. Publishing Corporation, 1985.

Tolber, E.L. *Counselling for Career Development*. Boston, Houghton Miffin, 1974.

Traxler, A.E. and North, R.D. *Techniques of Guidance*. New York, Harper and Row, 1957.

Trivedi, Harshad R. *Scheduled Caste Women Studies in Exploitation, with Reference to Superstition, Ignorance and Poverty*, Delhi, Concept Pub. Co., 1976.

Tyler, L.E. *The Work of the Counsellor*. New York, Appleton Century Crafts, 1969.

Upadhya, Bhagvrat Saran, *Women in Rigveda,* Delhi, S. Chand and Co., 1983.

Vashishta, B.K., *Encyclopardia of Women in India,* New Delhi, 1976. Parveen Encyclopaedia.

Vaughan, T.D. *Educational and Vocational Guidance Today.* London, Routledge and Kegan Paul, 1968.

Vernon, P.E. *Intelligence and Cultural Environment.* London, Methuen, 1969

Vitels, M.S., *Motivation and Morale in Industry.* New York, Morton 1953.

Vreede de Stuers., *Girl Students in Jaipur. A Study in Attitude towards Family Life, Marriage and Career,* N.Y., Assen, Van Gorcum and Co., 1970.

Vyas, Anju and Singh Sunita, *Women's Studies in India,* New Delhi. Sage Pub., 1993.

Warters, Jane. *Techniques of Counselling,* New York, McGraw Hill 1964

Watson, T., *Management Organization and Employment Strategy,* London, Routledge and Kegan Paul, 1986.

Weitz, Henry. *Behaviour Changes Through Guidance.* New York, McGraw Hill, 1964.

Whyte, F.W., Money and Motivation, New York, Harper and Row. Inc., 1955.

Williamson, E.G. *How to Counsel Students.* New York, McGraw Hill, 1939.

Wren, Gilbert C. *The Counsellor in a Changing world Washington,* American Personnel and guidance Association 1962.

Zeitlin, Irving, M. *Rethinking Sociology, A Critique of Contemporary Theory,* Appleton-Century Crafts, New York, 1973.

Zeran, Franklin R. and Riccio, Anthony C. *Organization and Administration of Guidance Services.* Chicago, Rand McNally and Co., 1962.

Index